Publisher's Preface

Human Kinetics is proud to publish the first edition of the *Dictionary of the Sport and Exercise Sciences*. We have recruited authors who are experts in their disciplines, have chosen qualified reviewers to critique the definitions submitted, have used our editorial staff to add or delete selected terms as well as refine and clarify definitions, and have enlisted our production staff to present the information in the most helpful format possible. We believe that this publication will be beneficial to the professionals and students of the many subdisciplines that make up the exercise and sport sciences.

We realize that in compiling a resource that is the first of its kind we have left room for improvement. We invite you to tell us your ideas—additional terms to include, definitions to clarify, or features to add to improve the dictionary's usefulness. Please send any suggestions you have to

Dictionary of the Sport and Exercise Sciences
ATTN: Editorial Director
Human Kinetics
P.O. Box 5076
Champaign, IL 61825-5076

DICTIONARY

OF THE

SPORT AND

EXERCISE

SCIENCES

Mark H. Anshel, PhD, Editor
Patty Freedson, PhD
Joseph Hamill, PhD
Kathleen Haywood, PhD
Michael Horvat, EdD
Sharon A. Plowman, PhD

MARLBOROUGH STUDY CENTRE

Human Kinetics Books
Champaign, Illinois

Library of Congress Cataloging-in-Publication Data

Dictionary of the sport and exercise sciences / by Mark H. Anshel,
    editor; Patty Freedson . . . [et al.].
        p. cm.
    ISBN 0-87322-305-5
    1. Sports sciences--Dictionaries.   2. Exercise--Physiological
aspects--Dictionaries.   I. Anshel, Mark H. (Mark Howard), 1948-
II. Freedson, Patty, 1953-
GV558.D53   1991
613.7'103--dc20   90-45252
                                                                CIP

ISBN: 0-87322-305-5 (case)
        0-87322-379-9 (paper)

Copyright © 1991 by Human Kinetics Publishers

Figure on p. 11 from R. Adams and J. McCubbin: *Games, Sports, and Exercises for the Physically Disabled*, 4th ed. Philadelphia: Lea & Febiger, 1990. Adapted by permission.

Figure on p. 88 from *Teaching Team Sports* (p. 12) by Joan A. Philipp and Jerry D. Wilkerson, 1990, Champaign, IL: Human Kinetics. Copyright 1990 by Joan A. Philipp and Jerry
D. Wilkerson. Reprinted by permission.

Figure on p. 132 from *A Textbook of Histology* (10th ed.; p. 206) by Don W. Fawcett, M.D.,
1975, Philadelphia: W.B. Saunders. Copyright 1975 by Don W. Fawcett, M.D. Reprinted
by permission.

Figure on p. 143 from *1951 Yearbook of Physical Medicine and Rehabilitation* (p. 10) by Deaver,
Buck, and McCarthy, 1952, Chicago: Year Book Medical Publishers. Copyright 1952 by Year
Book Medical Publishers. Reprinted by permission.

Acquisitions Editor: Rick Frey, PhD; **Developmental Editor:** Holly Gilly; **Assistant
Editors:** Dawn Levy, Robert King; **Copyeditor:** Wendy Nelson; **Proofreader:** Karin
Leszczynski; **Production Director:** Ernie Noa; **Typesetters:** Sandra Meier, Angela K.
Snyder, Yvonne Winsor; **Text Design:** Keith Blomberg; **Text Layout:** Tara Welsch; **Cover
Design:** Hunter Graphics; **Interior Art:** Janet Sinn, David Gregory; **Printer:** Versa Press

Printed in the United States of America   10 9 8 7 6 5 4 3 2

Human Kinetics Books
A Division of Human Kinetics
P.O. Box 5076, Champaign, IL 61825-5076
1-800-747-4457

Canada: Human Kinetics, Box 24040, Windsor, ON N8Y 4Y9
1-800-465-7301 (in Canada only)

Europe: Human Kinetics, P.O. Box IW14, Leeds LS16 6TR, England
0532-781708

Australia: Human Kinetics, Unit 5, 32 Raglan Avenue, Edwardstown 5039,
South Australia
(08) 371 3755

New Zealand: Human Kinetics, P.O. Box 105-231, Auckland 1
(09) 309-2259

Preface

The need for this dictionary reflects a number of very positive developments in the sport and exercise sciences. Our field is growing in maturity, sophistication, and the sheer number of participants. A select group of scholarly academic subdisciplines, derived mostly from physical education, have sparked scientific inquiry to better understand the factors that underlie human performance. And each of these subdisciplines has further expanded into other areas of science (e.g., psychology, biology, physics, psychophysiology, artificial intelligence) to delve deeper into complex phenomena in attempting to explain, predict, and describe behavior. This increase in knowledge, expertise, and research funding has fostered the expansion of graduate programs and has spurred more people into study and employment in the sport and exercise sciences. Dictionaries in psychology, biology, music, medicine, dance, and art, among others, have been published for many years. The sport and exercise sciences warrant similar recognition.

The need for clarifying, simplifying, understanding, and properly using our own nomenclature has become increasingly important for effective communication. The same terms are commonly used in the literature in different contexts, and with less consistency and precision than is desirable. A comprehensive reference source relative to the language of sport and exercise science is needed.

Dr. Mark Anshel recognized this need and began to write to authors and editors of other lexicons. Equipped with their suggestions, he approached Human Kinetics publisher Rainer Martens about producing a sport and exercise science dictionary, and they agreed on the general direction, purpose, and content of the project. It was determined that the dictionary would include terms from nine subdisciplines of the sport and exercise sciences: adapted physical education, biomechanics, exercise physiology (including the areas of body composition and cardiac rehabilitation), motor control, motor development, motor learning, sport pedagogy, sport psychology, and sport sociology. (Areas that have not been covered in this dictionary include dance, physical education, research design, sports medicine, statistics, and specific sports.) It was agreed that the purpose of the dictionary would be to provide readers with clear, comprehensive, reliable, and up-to-date definitions of terms used by sport scientists.

After those decisions were made, Dr. Anshel was given the green light to solicit a writing team. He faced some initial difficulty in recruiting skilled writers in the various sport and exercise sciences. Scientists who met our criteria for credibility (university faculty with a PhD, an established research record, and extensive familiarity and recognized mastery in the area of expertise) tend to be—and probably should be—more concerned with research, grant writing, and promotion and tenure activities than writing books. Moreover, lexicography is a task that few find pleasant or easy. But after 6 months of solicitation, a team of skilled writers, capable and motivated to get the job done, was formed. We, the writers, are Mark H. Anshel, Department of Human Movement Science, University of Wollongong, Wollongong, New South Wales, Australia (sport psychology and sport sociology); Patty Freedson, Department of Exercise Science, University of Massachusetts, Amherst, Massachusetts, USA, and Sharon A. Plowman, Department of Physical Education, Northern Illinois University, DeKalb, Illinois, USA (body composition, cardiac rehabilitation, exercise physiology); Joseph Hamill, Department of Exercise Science, University of Massachusetts, Amherst, Massachusetts, USA (biomechanics); Kathleen Haywood, Department of Physical Education, University of Missouri at St. Louis, St. Louis, Missouri, USA (motor control, motor development, motor learning); and Michael Horvat, Division of Health, Physical Education and Recreation, University of Georgia, Athens, Georgia, USA (adapted physical education and sport pedagogy).

The entire group of us then met with Dr. Martens and Dr. Julie Simon, vice president of Human Kinetics, to plan the dictionary's protocol. Armed with that understanding, each of us began to compile words and definitions from the subdisciplines for which we were responsible. When we were done we had some 3,000 defined terms derived from professional refereed research journals and textbooks. Now that the long and arduous process is complete, we hope that the availability of this publication will achieve several ends:

- Promote the understanding and correct use of terminology among students, educators, and scientists
- Identify areas of common ground among the sport and exercise sciences in light of overlapping research interests and shared use of scientific literature among investigators of human performance
- Improve scholarly writing and familiarize students with the meanings of sophisticated terms to clarify, and perhaps minimize, scientific jargon

If the dictionary realizes those expectations, it will have been well worth the effort to write it.

Mark H. Anshel, Editor
Patty Freedson
Joseph Hamill
Kathleen Haywood
Michael Horvat
Sharon A. Plowman

Acknowledgments

I wish to express my deepest gratitude and respect to my colleagues for their full commitment, energy, talent, and graciousness in successfully completing this extensive project.

I thank the following authors and editors of other lexicons for their advice and encouragement: Dr. James P. Chaplin (*Dictionary of Psychology*), Dr. Edwin B. Steen (*Dictionary of Biology*), and David B. Guralnik (Editor in Chief, *Webster's New World Dictionary*).

The definitions in this dictionary were subjected to the blind peer review of expert academic scholars who were asked to promote clarity and accuracy and to detect omitted terms and definitions. I applaud their excellence in a difficult task.

Further appreciation is extended to Dr. Rainer Martens, publisher, whose professional support and foresight were required throughout the planning of this project; and to Dr. Richard Frey, acquisitions editor, and Holly Gilly, developmental editor, for enthusiastic support and talent during writing and editing. The authors have learned and benefited from their professional interaction.

Mark H. Anshel
Editor

Rules for Use

Arrangement of Entries: All main entries, including single words, phrases, hyphenated compounds, acronyms, and proper names, are printed in bold and are listed using the letter-by-letter method of alphabetization. For example, note the correct order of the following entries: *allergen, allergy, all-or-nothing law, alpha system*.

Proper Names: Surnames (e.g., authors of a publication or theory) and company names (e.g., equipment manufacturer) are not included in terms unless they are scientifically associated in the professional literature (e.g., *DeLorme technique, Sargent's Jump and Reach Test*).

Variant Spellings: When a word can be spelled more than one way, the spelling used is either that most often found in the literature or what appeared in the author's reference.

Cross-References: Cross-referencing occurs in three instances. First, when terms have the same meaning but one term is more commonly used, the definition is given with the more common term. The second term is listed as a synonym, and the reader is directed to the more common term at the second term's entry. For example, for the terms *red blood cell* and *erythrocyte*, the definition is given only under *erythrocyte*, which says "Also called *red blood cell*." At the *red blood cell* entry, the reader is told to "See *erythrocyte*," with no definition given.

Second, the reader is directed to "See also" another entry in the case of supplemental information. For example, *aggression* lists the word's definition as well as cross-references to *defensive aggression, instrumental aggression*, and *goal aggression*.

Finally, for antonyms the reader is directed to "Compare" another term. For example, at *flexion* the reader is told to "Compare *extension*" after the definition is given. Similarly, at *extension* the instruction to "Compare *flexion*" appears.

Multiple Definitions: When a term is defined variously in the literature, the most common and preferred use of the term is defined first.

If a term is defined differently in several disciplines, the first definition is the most "generic" definition, followed by more discipline-specific definitions labeled with these abbreviations:

ad—adapted physical education
bc—body composition
bm—biomechanics
cr—cardiac rehabilitation
ep—exercise physiology
mc—motor control
md—motor development
ml—motor learning
pd—sport pedagogy
ss—sport sociology
sp—sport psychology

General Content: Every attempt was made to eliminate sexism, racism, and other prejudices from all definitions.

Because we wanted to define terms clearly and concisely in a style free of jargon and technical language, definitions were paraphrased from the original publications in which they appeared.

Figures have been included for some terms to illustrate or clarify their definitions.

Words such as *coach, athlete, performer,* and *competitor* are not included in definitions unless a term relates specifically to a sport environment. Definitions may reflect both the generic and competitive sport contexts in which terms are used.

A

AAHPERD Physical Best: Comprehensive fitness education and assessment program for youth published by the American Alliance for Health, Physical Education, Recreation and Dance in 1988. Fitness test components include cardiorespiratory fitness (1-mile walk/run), body composition (sum of triceps and calf skinfolds), flexibility (sit and reach), abdominal strength and endurance (maximum sit-ups in 1 minute), and upper body strength and endurance (pull-ups).

abduction: Sideward movement or withdrawal from the midline or sagittal plane. Compare *adduction*.

abduction

ability: General capacity to perform on a range of motor skills. Relatively permanent and enduring after childhood, and underlying the person's present state. Thought to be both genetically determined and influenced by learning experiences. Also called *motor ability*.

ability-orientation: Tendency of an individual to maximize opportunities to attribute high ability to oneself while minimizing attributions of low ability to oneself. For instance, a tendency to associate team success with one's own high ability and team failure with poor performance of teammates and/or superior performance of opponents.

absence seizure: See *petit mal seizure*.

absolute: Units of work, power, or energy that are not adjusted for body size, gender, or fitness differences; non–weight bearing activities are measured in absolute units; examples include kg/min, watts, L/min.

absolute angle: Angle of a body segment with respect to an absolute reference frame, with the origin at the proximal joint center (generally with respect to the right horizontal).

absolute error: Measurement that indicates amount of deviation from a criterion or target without regard to the direction of that deviation. Recorded on a single trial or calculated by averaging the absolute value of error scores on a series of trials.

Academic Learning Time–Physical Education (ALT–PE): Amount or unit of time a student is engaged in relevant physical activity in a manner that allows for success or achievement; appropriate success rate for doing the task correctly as it is defined in the lesson is approximately 80%.

academic penalties: Use of academic sanctions, such as giving failing grades, as a punishment for violations of school rules.

academic sport psychology: Scientific discipline concerned with the influence of psychological variables on physical performance and the effect of participation in physical activity on psychological variables.

acceleration: 1. The change in velocity divided by the change in time. 2. The time rate of change of velocity. 3. The first derivative of velocity and the second derivative of position. Acceleration is measured in meters per second squared (m • s^2) and is usually designated by the letter a. See also *angular acceleration, radial acceleration, tangential acceleration*.

$$a = \frac{\text{change in velocity}}{\text{change in time}}$$

$$= \frac{v_i - (v_i - 1)}{t_i - (t_i - 1)}$$

$$= \frac{dv}{dt}$$

where v_i = velocity at time i
t_i = time i
dv = instantaneous change in velocity
dt = instantaneous change in time

acceleration curve: 1. Plot of the rate of change in velocity over time. In the study of physical growth, the velocity of growth in height, weight, or some anthropometric measurement is often plotted to highlight landmarks or important periods of growth. **2.** [md] Representation of the second derivative of the function represented by the distance curve, the extent of change plotted over time.

accelerometer: Instrument that measures acceleration.

accessibility: Availability of instructional programs, sports, buildings, facilities, and so on to the disabled.

acclimatization: Physiological changes that occur in the process of adapting to a new environment, such as high altitude.

accommodating resistance exercise: See *isokinetic.*

accommodating resistance machine: See *isokinetic.*

accommodation: 1. In Piagetian theory, adaptation of schemas (thought structures) to new experiences. **2.** Action of the ciliary muscle to change the curvature of the eye's lens to view objects at varying distances. **3.** Adaptation to constant sensory stimulation by a raising of the absolute threshold level, that is, the minimal level of strength necessary for detection of a stimulus.

accountability: [ad] Process of meeting long- and short-term objectives on a student's individualized educational program within a designated time frame; the state of being answerable and responsible for the education of individuals with disabilities.

achievement: The level of learning a student attains, usually as a result of instructional outcomes and teacher behavior.

achievement motivation: Predisposition to approach or avoid competitive situations; usually characterized by the interaction between personality factors (e.g., motives to approach success and avoid failure) and situational factors (e.g., the subjective probability of success and the reciprocal incentive value of such success). See also *achievement need, fear of failure, fear of success.*

achievement need: Drive or desire to strive for self- or externally-evaluated goals.

achievement situation: Situation in which it is expected that the person's performance will be evaluated (e.g., a competitive sport event).

achondroplasia: Form of dwarfism resulting from an inherited factor that inhibits growth, characterized by disproportionately short height, limbs, hands, and feet; a flattened bridge of the nose, a bulging forehead, and normal intelligence.

acid: Chemical substance that gives up hydrogen ions (H^+) in a solution.

acid–base balance: Proper ratio of hydrogen ions to hydroxyl ions in a solution; usually expressed as pH, may be unbalanced in heavy exercise. See also *pH.*

acquired disability: Disability that occurs after birth through injury, trauma, or illness. Also called *adventitious disability.* Compare *congenital.*

actin: Thin protein constituent of the myofibril contractile structure; binds to myosin to form crossbridges to facilitate muscle contraction.

action potential: Quick change from the resting potential in electrical activity across a nerve or muscle cell membrane that generates an electrical current.

action-scaled assessment: Assessment of environmental dimensions according to (scaled to) one's body size, mass, anthropometric proportions, and functional capabilities, to determine whether an action is feasible, as opposed to assessment in extrinsic units, such as feet or meters. For example, stairs of a given step-height are judged to be "climbable" or "not climbable" given one's height and leg length; an adult might judge "climbable" a set of stairs that an infant judges "not climbable."

activation: 1. Used inerchangeably with *arousal.* Intensity of behavior (neural arousal), usually indicated on a continuum from deep sleep to extreme excitement.

Measured through central assessments (e.g., brain activity) or peripheral assessments (heart rate or muscle activity). **2.** Heightened psychological and physiological state of a person as indicated by feelings and emotions and by bodily responses such as respiratory rates and sweating.

active insufficiency: Inability of a multiarticulate muscle to create sufficient tension to cause full range of motion at all joints the muscle simultaneously crosses.

active recovery: Restoration of homeostasis following exercise that involves continued movement of the exercised musculature; facilitates lactate removal because of augmented blood supply secondary to vasodilation; end result is a faster return to pre-exercise conditions.

activity analysis: See *task analysis.*

activity fragmentation: Breaking down the skills of an activity, for practice, into units that are not meaningful and coordinated; making the focus of an activity something that is not a meaningful activity in itself.

activity time: [pd] Period during which most students are actively involved in physical activity related to the instructional goals of a program. Also called *motor-engaged time.*

acuity: Sharpness or clarity of vision, hearing, or tactile sensations.

acute: Having a rapid onset of short duration.

Adam's position: Position used to determine if scoliosis is structural or functional. The individual stretches forward, bending at the waist, with arms hanging downward.

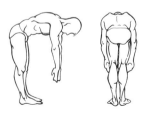

Adam's position

adaptation: 1. [ep] Persistent changes in structure or function particularly related to response to a training overload. **2.** [mc] The adjustment in cognitive development a child makes to environmental restrictions, and subsequent intellectualization of the adjustment through assimilation and accommodation.

adaptation level (AL) theory: The suggestion that a subjective point of neutrality develops midway between two stimuli. After presentation of the two stimuli, a person responds to those stimuli as being a certain number of units from this adaptation point.

adapted physical education: Education involving modifications or adjustments of traditional physical education activities to enable disabled children to participate safely according to their functional abilities.

adapted physical educator: Trained specialist responsible for evaluating, designing, and implementing physical education programs for disabled children.

adaptive achievement pattern: Pattern of achievement behavior characterized by cognitive, motivational, and emotional components. Cognitively, entails maintaining effective strategies or the development of new and sophisticated strategies for adverse situations. Motivationally, involves challenge-seeking and high persistence when confronted by obstacles. Emotionally, characterized by pride and satisfaction in terms of the degree of effort exerted in both successful and unsuccessful conditions. Compare *maladaptive achievement pattern.*

adaptive behavior: Functioning in broad areas such as personal independence, socialization, number and time concepts, and physical development. Includes mental retardation if deficits in adaptive behavior and significant subaverage intellectual functioning occur simultaneously during the development years.

adaptive learning: Adjustment or adaptation of the learner to environmental conditions presented, and adjustment or adaptation, by the teacher, of environmental conditions in order to effect changes in the learner's present level of functioning.

adaptive learning environment: Adjusted learning situation that facilitates learning or removes situational factors that interfere with the learning process.

adaptive teaching: Use of alternative instructional routes, based on the characteristics of the learner and the environment, to achieve a goal.

adduction: A pulling toward the midline of the body or the return movement from abduction. Compare *abduction*.

adenosine diphosphate (ADP)/ adenosine monophosphate (AMP)/ adenosine triphosphate (ATP): The three interconvertible compounds where the nucleotide adenosine is attached to one (AMP), two (ADP), or three (ATP) phosphate molecules. Molecular interactions and repulsive forces result in bonds of high potential energy formed with di- and triphosphate bonds. ATP stores energy in the body; hydrolysis of ATP yields 7.3 kcal of energy; ATP is synthesized by the phosphocreatine system, glycolysis, Krebs cycle, and electron transport/oxidative phosphorylation.

adherence: Maintenance of participation in an exercise or fitness program, whether individual or group based, structured or unstructured. Usually measured by the number of consecutive absences from exercise sessions, attendance at a specified proportion of sessions, or the proportional number of weeks that an exercise goal was met. Also called *exercise adherence*.

adipose tissue: Connective tissue in which body fat is stored, mainly in the form of triglyceride.

ADP: See *adenosine diphosphate*.

adrenal cortex: Outer portion of the adrenal glands, which are located on the superior pole of each kidney; secretes corticosteroids, including aldosterone and cortisol.

adrenaline: See *epinephrine*.

adrenal medulla: Central portion of the adrenal glands; secretes epinephrine and norepinephrine in response to sympathetic stimuli.

adrenergic fiber: Postganglionic neuron of the sympathetic system that secretes mainly norepinephrine.

adventitious disability: See *acquired disability*.

advocacy: [ad] Time and effort devoted to changing society's attitudes and aspirations regarding individuals with disabilities.

aerobic: In the presence of, requiring, or utilizing oxygen.

aerobic energy: Energy that results from the breakdown of carbohydrates, fats, and protein within the Krebs cycle and the electron transport system; oxygen is required in this type of energy transformation.

aerobic metabolism: Chemical changes in living cells by which energy in the form of ATP is created in the presence of oxygen; also known as the oxygen system.

aerobic power: See *maximal oxygen uptake*.

aerobic threshold: A 2-mM concentration of lactic acid in blood plasma; theorized to be the intensity of work where aerobic metabolism is the major contributor of energy for muscular work.

aerodynamic lift force: Lift force produced when an object moves through air.

aerodynamics: Branch of fluid dynamics that deals with the forces and effects of air on objects moving through air.

affect: A person's emotional response to a situation.

affective: Regarding an individual's attitudes, feelings, emotions, or temperament, including the degree of desire to feel motivated to learn and develop motor skills.

afference: Sensory neural commands ascending to the brain.

afferent neuron: Nerve cell that carries nerve impulses from the sensory receptors to the central nervous system (brain and spinal cord). Also called *sensory neuron*.

affiliation incentives: 1. Personality disposition reflecting a desire or need to join a group. **2.** Opportunities, involving making friends or maintaining already existing friendships, that are perceived as providing social reassurance that one is acceptable or worthwhile.

affordances: Actions or behaviors provided or permitted an actor by the places, objects, and events in an environment. For example, a small rock affords throwing, but a boulder does not.

afterload: Amount of resistance the ventricles must overcome during ventricular contraction; quantified using systolic blood pressure.

age-predicted maximum heart rate: Estimated attainable highest number of ventricular contractions, computed by subtracting one's age from 220; considered a fairly accurate estimate of a sample's true maximum heart rate and generally within 10 to 15 beats of an individual's actual maximum heart rate; frequently used to prescribe target heart-rate ranges.

aggression: Literal meanings include to walk toward or approach, to move against, or to move with intent to hurt or harm. See also *goal aggression, instrumental aggression, state aggression.*

aggression incentive: Opportunity for a competitor to subdue, intimidate, dominate, or injure others.

aggressive behavior: Overt verbal or physical act that leads to psychological or physical injury to another person or oneself. See also *assertive behavior.*

aging: 1. The normal process of growing old, without regard to chronological age, characterized by a loss of ability to adapt. **2.** Continuing molecular, cellular, and organismic differentiation.

aging-related maculopathy: Condition in which the macula of the retina is altered by some of the following: atrophy of neural elements, pigment disruption, drusen formation, abnormal blood vessel growth, and scarring.

agnosia: Inability to correctly identify familiar persons or objects. See also *auditory*

agnosia, finger agnosia, spatial agnosia, visual agnosia.

agonist: A muscle directly engaged in a muscular contraction and working in opposition to the action of another muscle. Compare *antagonist.*

air conduction loss: Complication in the outer- or middle-ear, including the tympanic membrane, ossicular chain, or eustachian tubes, that restricts the transmission of sound.

air resistance: See *drag force.*

alactacid phase: Former name for the rapid phase of excess postexercise oxygen consumption.

alertness: 1. Attentiveness, so as to be able to respond quickly. **2.** Condition of increased electrical activity in the cerebral cortex resulting from stimulation of the reticular formation.

algebraic error: See *constant error.*

algorithm of reflexes: A set of (central nervous system) triggers that can evoke a reflex pattern after a period of conditioning.

alkaline reserve: Concentration of one or more basic ions, usually in the form of bicarbonate (HCO_3-), available to buffer acids and maintain pH; especially important for athletes in predominantly anaerobic sports that produce high levels of lactic acid.

allergen: Substance that produces an allergic reaction.

allergy: Hypersensitivity to normally harmless substances when they are inhaled, ingested, injected, or absorbed.

all-or-nothing law: [bm] The prediction that a myofibril of a muscle will contract fully when its activation threshold has been reached; that is, that the myofibril either will contract fully or will not contract at all.

alpha system: Innervation of the extrafusal muscle fibers by alpha motoneurons.

AL theory: See *adaptation level theory.*

ALT–PE: See *Academic Learning Time–Physical Education.*

alveolar ventilation: The volume of air exchanged between the alveolus and capillary blood; equals tidal volume minus anatomical dead space volume times respiratory frequency. See also *anatomic dead space, tidal volume.*

ambient temperature and pressure saturated (ATPS): The volume of air at ambient temperature (273 K + actual surrounding temperature °C), actual barometric pressure saturated with water vapor. Gas volumes collected by open circuit spirometry and most pulmonary function measures as initially measured are at ATPS. ATPS volumes must be converted to BTPS or STPD reference conditions before they can be used to examine respiratory volumes or metabolic measurements.

amblyopia: Deviation or inability to focus or coordinate both eyes simultaneously on the same object. Also called *lazy eye.*

ambulatory: Related to walking; able to walk.

amelia: Absence of a limb or limbs present at birth.

amelioration: Improvement in a condition or disability.

amenorrhea: The absence of menses; prevalence is approximately 10% to 20% among athletes, particularly runners, and 5% in the general population.

ament: Obsolete term referring to a person with intellectual subnormality.

AMP (adenosine monophosphate): See *adenosine diphosphate.*

amphetamines: Group of pharmacologic compounds that exert powerful stimulating effects on central nervous system function similar to epinephrine; banned substances considered by some to be ergogenic aids for athletic performance.

anabolic steroid: Drug that functions similarly to the male sex hormone, testosterone, but is manufactured to emphasize protein-building characteristics used by athletes to enhance muscle mass, strength, and power; associated with liver disease, infertility, elevated total cholesterol, depressed levels of HDL cholesterol, edema, and other health problems; a banned substance.

anabolism: The process of building tissue; amino acids provide the major building blocks for the synthesis of cellular components and new tissue.

anaerobic: In the absence of, not requiring, or not utilizing oxygen.

anaerobic capacity: Maximal amount of energy that can be created by anaerobic glycolysis; measured by high-intensity tests of 20 to 60 s; represented in the Wingate test by the 30-s mean power value. See also *Wingate anaerobic power test.*

anaerobic fitness: Ability to perform high-intensity, all-out exercise.

anaerobic metabolism: Chemical changes in living cells by which energy in the form of ATP is created or utilized in the absence of oxygen; major energy production pathway for high-intensity, short-duration activities; subdivided into an alactic portion, where stored ATP-PC predominates to fuel activity lasting less than 30 s, and the lactic acid system, in which lactic acid is formed as a by-product and is the predominant energy system in activity lasting less than 3 min. See also *glycolysis.*

anaerobic power: Maximal rate (amount per unit time) at which energy can be produced by the ATP-PC system; measured by high-intensity tests of 1 to 10 seconds duration; represented in the Wingate anaerobic power test by the peak power (mechanical output) generated in a 5-s period. See also *Wingate anaerobic power test.*

anaerobic threshold: See *lactate threshold.*

analog signal: A recording of data in which the data has an amplitude that varies continuously for all time.

analog-to-digital converter: Device used in a computer that samples an analog signal and converts it to a digital signal. See also *analog signal, digital signal.*

anatomical position: Position of the human body standing with feet together, arms at the sides, and palms facing forward.

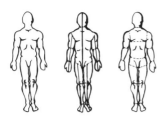

anatomical position

anatomical task analysis: Evaluation of functional ability level of specific muscle groups involved in a skill or movement pattern.

anatomic dead space: Areas of the respiratory tract that are not involved in gas exchange with the blood; includes the nose, mouth, trachea, bronchus, and bronchioles; size in milliters roughly equals one's weight in pounds.

androgyny: A condition of possessing both masculine and feminine characteristics. Positively related to measures of psychological well-being such as self-esteem (i.e., the feelings persons have about themselves).

androgyny index: See *biacromial/bicristal ratio*.

anecdotal records: [pd] Observational notes taken during a teaching session to evaluate performance and perceptions during the instructional period.

anemia: Deficient number of red blood cells in the blood; due to too-rapid loss, or reduced production rate, of red blood cells. Reduces oxygen transport capacity of the blood, which may impair exercise performance.

angina: Pain expressed as burning, discomfort, pressure, shortness of breath, or tightness in chest, jaw, arm, or shoulder areas; ischemia in heart; induced or increased severity with exertion when oxygen requirements to the heart are increased. Also called *angina pectoris*.

angina pectoris: See *angina*.

angioplasty: Procedure used to treat coronary artery occlusion in the cardiac catheterization laboratory; uses a catheter with an inflatable balloon at the tip; catheter is passed through the femoral or brachial arteries into the diseased coronary artery or arteries; after the tip of the catheter is in the diseased vessel, the balloon is inflated to compress the blockage into the vessel wall.

angle–angle plot: Diagram plotting the rotation occurring at one joint against the rotation at a second joint, usually for the purpose of comparing multijoint movements for invariance.

angle of attack: Angle of relative air flow to the surface of a projectile in flight.

angle of attitude: Angle of an axis of a projectile in flight relative to the horizontal.

angle of gait: Included angle formed by a line drawn from the midpoint of the calcaneus to the midpoint of the second toe of the same foot and the line of progression.

angle of incidence: Angle formed by the velocity vector of a projectile prior to impact to a line normal to the surface at the point of impact of the projectile and the surface.

angle of projection: Angle of the velocity vector of a projectile relative to the horizontal. Also called *angle of release, angle of takeoff*.

angle of pull: Angle between the line of force application of the muscle on its insertion and the primary axis of the bone into which it is inserted.

angle of reflection: Angle formed by the velocity vector of a projectile after impact to a line perpendicular to the surface at the point of impact of the projectile and the surface.

angle of release: See *angle of projection*.

angle of takeoff: See *angle of projection*.

angular acceleration: 1. The change in angular velocity divided by the change in time. 2. The time rate of change of angular velocity. 3. The first derivative of angular velocity and the second derivative of angular position. Measured in radians per second squared (rad $\cdot$ s^{-2}) and usually represented by the Greek letter alpha. See also *acceleration*.

$$\alpha = \frac{\text{change in angular velocity}}{\text{change in time}}$$

angular displacement: Smallest angle between the initial and final positions of a rotating body. Measured in radians. Also called *displacement*.

angular distance: Angle between the initial and final positions of a rotating body measured following the path taken by the rotating body; measured in radians.

$$\text{angular distance} = \text{angle}_i - (\text{angle}_i - 1)$$

angular impulse: 1. Product of the applied torque and the time over which the torque was applied. **2.** Area under a torque–time curve (the integral of torque as a function of time). Measured in newton-meters • seconds (N-m • s). Also called *impulse*.

angular kinematics: Description of angular motion in terms of angular displacement, angular velocity, and angular acceleration.

angular momentum: 1. The quantity of angular motion. **2.** The product of moment of inertia of a body about an axis and angular velocity of the body about that same axis. **3.** The moment of linear momentum. Measured in kilogram-meters squared per second (kg-m^2 • s^{-1}) and usually designated by the letter H. Also called *momentum*.

$$H = \text{moment of inertia} \times \text{angular velocity}$$

angular motion: 1. The motion occurring when one point on an object is fixed (an axis of rotation) and all other points on an object rotate about the axis. **2.** The motion occurring when points on an object do not move the same distance in the same time. **3.** The motion resulting from a force that is not applied through the center of gravity of the object. Also called *rotary motion*.

angular speed: A scalar describing the magnitude of angular velocity. Measured in radians per second (rad • s^{-1}).

angular velocity: 1. The vector describing the change in angular position divided by the change in time. **2.** The time rate of change of angular position. **3.** The derivative of angular position as a function of time. Measured in radians per second (rad • s^{-1}) and usually represented by the Greek letter omega. See also *angular speed, velocity*.

$$\omega = \frac{\text{change in angular position}}{\text{change in time}}$$

anisometric movement: Movement in which some resistance to the movement increases as the distance moved increases.

ankylosis: Abnormal immobility or fixation (fusion) of a joint, resulting from disease or surgery.

anomaly: Abnormal or irregular condition.

anorexia: Obsession with thinness, involving a lack of appetite and weight loss, often resulting in the loss of lean body tissue.

anoxia: Condition in which there is insufficient oxygen in the blood (to a greater degree than hypoxia) to sustain adequate functioning of the tissue. See also *hypoxia*.

antagonist: A muscle that has an opposite effect on movers or agonist muscle by opposing the action or contraction of the muscle. Also called *contralateral muscle*. Compare *agonist*.

anteroposterior (AP) axis: 1. A horizontal axis, in an absolute reference frame, in the anteroposterior direction (front to back of the body). **2.** A horizontal axis, in an absolute reference frame, through the joint center from the front to the back of the joint.

anteroposterior ground reaction force component: The shear, horizontal force component of the ground reaction force acting in the direction of movement.

anthropometer: Instrument for measuring the linear breadth or width of a body segment, such as the shoulders or hips. Also called *breadth caliper*. See also *blade anthropometer, bow caliper*.

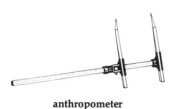

anthropometer

anthropometry: Branch of science concerned with comparative measurements of the human body, its parts, and its proportions, often to establish frequency of occurrence among cultures, races, sexes, age groups, cohorts, and so on.

anticipation time: Error score on a coincident timing task, in units of time, often carrying an indication of direction, usually negative numbers as early responses and positive numbers as late responses.

anticipation timing: Coordination of a movement response to an environmental event that must be predicted by the performer; for example, a baseball batter coordinating the swing to arrival of the pitch. See also *coincidence-anticipation*.

antigen: A substance that stimulates the production of antibodies or produces an allergic reaction. See also *allergen*.

antigravity muscles: Muscles that contribute to maintaining an upright posture.

anxiety: Subjective feeling of apprehension or perceived threat, sometimes accompanied by heightened physiological arousal. Similar but not identical to fear. See also *cognitive state anxiety, competitive trait anxiety, somatic state anxiety, state anxiety, trait anxiety.*

anxiety management training: Technique for developing control over stressful situations. For example, subject is trained to recognize early physical signs of tension build-up through imagery, then use deep muscle relaxation to decrease this tension.

anxiety–performance hypothesis: Prediction that in competitive situations, cognitive anxiety (i.e., thoughts of perceived threat) will be more consistently and

strongly related to sport performance than to somatic state anxiety.

anxiety-prone: Highly susceptible to anxiety and overarousal.

anxiety-stress spiral: Process whereby an initial increase in anxiety leads to a decrease in performance that, in turn, results in even greater anxiety. Can be alleviated by reducing the anxiety and tension.

aortic valve: The semilunar (referring to shape) valve separating the aorta from the left ventricle; prevents blood from flowing back into the ventricle and allows adequate pressure to build up for efficient pumping of blood into the systemic circulation. Also called *left semilunar valve*.

AP axis: See *anteroposterior axis*.

Apert's syndrome: Lack of development of the cranial area, from premature closure of bony sutures, often leading to microcephaly and mental retardation.

aphasia: Impairment or difficulty in comprehending or using spoken language.

apophysis: A portion of the shaft of a bone serving as the point of attachment for a predominant muscle and as a site that contributes to configurational aspects of bone growth (i.e., rather than growth of the bone in length).

appendicular skeleton: A division of the human skeleton comprising the shoulder girdle, upper limbs, pelvic girdle, and lower limbs.

application: A teaching strategy that communicates a concern for shifting the student focus from how to do the movement to how to use the movement.

applied behavior analysis: Use of principles in behavioral psychology to (a) develop strategies for analyzing behavior into small components, (b) provide instructional techniques for developing component behaviors, (c) strengthen and maintain desirable performances, and (d) generalize certain desirable behaviors to new environments and situations.

applied behavior management: Techniques used by one person to control (reinforce or extinguish) the behavior of another person.

applied sport psychology: 1. The practice of sport psychology with direct implications for understanding, describing, predicting, and/or controlling the psychological and behavioral factors underlying sport performance. 2. The use of psychological knowledge to enhance the development of performance and satisfaction in athletes and others associated with sports.

appositional growth: Growth by addition of new layers upon previously formed layers, prevalent when rigid materials such as bone are involved.

appraisal: 1. (primary) Subjective judgments about the nature and meaning of a situation. It is divided into three categories: irrelevant, benign-positive, and stressful. 2. (secondary) Self-judgments about one's ability to cope successfully with a situation. In addition, the person evaluates what might and can be done about the stressful situation while taking into account which coping strategies are available, the probability of the stretegy's success, and the ability to apply the strategy effectively.

apraxia: Impairment or difficulty in selecting, initiating, or completing purposeful movement.

aptitude: Capacity that affects one's ability to learn specific subject matter; low-aptitude students may require highly structured settings, many responses, and useful feedback, whereas high-aptitude students may benefit from individual teaching strategies that allow them to proceed more rapidly.

aquaphobia: Fear of water.

aqueous humor: Fluid occupying the space between the lens and cornea of the eye.

arbiter: Person who enforces rules of participation in sport competition and administers sanctions (penalties) in cases of rule violations. Also called *referee, umpire*.

Archimedes' principle: Principle, first stated by the ancient Greek scholar Archimedes, that a submerged or partially submerged object will experience an upward buoyant force equal to the weight of the volume of fluid displaced by the object.

archival research: Research based on recorded information, such as information about a sport contest.

arm manipulandum: Apparatus consisting of a tray parallel to the floor, on which a subject's arm rests in a pronated (palm down) position, allowing flexion and extension of the elbow. In some models, an attached torque motor allows the experimenter to add time constraints to aiming movements, and a potentiometer provides a record of kinematic characteristics of the movement.

arm preference: A person's choice to use one or the other arm to perform a given task; it may or may not be the person's dominant arm.

arm trajectory: Path taken by the arm in reaching or aiming movements.

arousal: See *autonomic arousal, electrocortical arousal, physiological arousal, psychological arousal*.

arrhythmia: See *dysrhythmia*.

arterial blood: Oxygenated blood, bright red in color; delivered to the various muscles and other organs of the body.

arterial PO$_2$: The partial pressure of oxygen in the arterial blood; equals around 100 mm Hg at rest.

arteriosclerosis: Hardening and thickening of the arteries causing a loss of elasticity in the blood vessels.

arteriovenous oxygen difference (AVO$_2$D): The difference in the oxygen content of arterial and mixed venous blood; at rest, AVO$_2$D is approximately 4 to 5 ml of O$_2$ per 100 ml of blood; during vigorous exercise, AVO$_2$D may reach 15 mg of O$_2$ per 100 ml of blood; the difference equals the amount of O$_2$ extracted by the muscle.

artery: Any of the tubular branching muscular and elastic-walled vessels that carry oxygenated blood systemically away from the heart.

arthritis: Disease that causes inflammation, swelling, and pain in the joints, affects movement, and may result in reduced range of motion, deformities, and contractures.

arthrodesis: Surgical fixation procedures to fuse a joint surface.

arthrogryposis: Congenital birth defect in which muscles or parts of muscles are missing. A variety of physical deformities may occur.

arthrology: Study of the articulations (joints) of the human body.

articulation: Junction of two contiguous bones in the human body in which the bones are joined in a functional relationship. Also called *joint*.

asocial: Displaying a lack of awareness of typical or normative peer-group behavior.

assertive behavior: Heightened physical behavior, acceptable yet forceful or active, without intent to harm or injure another person (or violate the constitutively agreed-upon rule of a sport being played). Differs from aggression with respect to the intent and outcomes of behavior. See also *proactive assertive behavior*.

assimilation: Cognitive process wherein children attempt to relate new experiences to their present interpretation of their world based on their past experience.

assistive device: Appliance that aids, facilitates, or compensates for ambulation, stability, correction of deformities, immobilization, or amplification to enhance functional ability.

associative coping style: Mental technique used for coping with psychological or physical stress, in which a person attends to internal stimuli such as thoughts, feelings, and bodily sensations while ignoring or reducing the input of external stimuli. For instance, a weight lifter tends to focus on the specific muscle groups involved in a lift prior to and during performance execution while ignoring input from other competitors and the audience. Compare *dissociative coping style*.

associative stage: The second phase in Fitts' model of learning a motor skill, in which the learner refines performance of a motor skill and is better able to detect and correct errors. Closed skills are solidified, and open skills are diversified. Performance of closed skills becomes more consistent, and the performer better adapts open skills to the changing environment. See also *autonomous stage, cognitive stage*.

associative strategy: 1. Technique that focuses attention on internal cues and information from the body or emotions during performance. **2.** Strategy that allows individuals to continually monitor their internal states. Also called *body-monitoring cognitive strategy*. Compare *dissociative strategy*.

A-state: See *state anxiety*.

asthenis: Loss of strength or weakness; lack of energy.

asthma: Condition caused by bronchoconstriction of the pulmonary pathways from allergies, physical activity, or other irritants; characterized by wheezing, coughing, and dyspnea.

astigmatism: Visual impairment caused by an irregularity in curvature of the cornea that impedes focusing light rays directly on the retina.

Astrand-Ryhming nomogram: Scale used to estimate aerobic capacity from a one-stage submaximal cycle ergometer test where work load and heart rate corresponding to the work load are used to derive the estimated $\dot{V}O_2max$.

asymmetrical contingency: In sport, a

assistive device

situation in which spectators' demands influence the sport organization's and athletes' responses, but sports and athletes do not influence spectators.

asymmetrical tonic neck reflex: An infant's extending the arm and leg on one side of its body in unconscious reaction to turning its head to that side while lying supine. Also called *tonic neck reflex*. Compare *symmetrical tonic neck reflex*.

asymmetry: 1. Lack of balance in shape, size, or relative position among parts on opposite sides of a dividing line. **2.** Differences in movement of the opposite hands or limbs, as when one finger has shorter mean time-intervals between taps in repetitive tapping of the right and left index fingers. **3.** Differences among positions when positions of body parts on one side of the body are compared to positions of corresponding parts or movements on the other side.

asymptomatic: Lacking clinical or physical symptoms of disease, although disease itself may be present.

asymptote: Theoretical limit approached, but never reached, by a graphed curve representing some performance function.

ataxia: Lack of muscular coordination characterized by poor balance and awkward motor movements; specific type of cerebral palsy resulting from damage to the cerebellum.

atherosclerosis: Arterial disease characterized by a narrowing of the vessels as a result of plaque buildup in the intimal (or inner) layer; underlying lesion for coronary artery disease that causes heart attacks and strokes. See also *plaque*.

athetosis: Type of cerebral palsy caused by damage to the basal ganglia. Characterized by uncoordinated movements under voluntary muscle control; slow, unpredictable, purposeless movements; and constant fluctuations in muscle tone.

athlete: 1. One who competes in structured, organized sport. **2.** Vigorous, powerful person who has acquired strength and skill through special training and exercise.

athlete-by-situation interaction model

of motivation: The theory that motivated behavior results from the continuous interaction of the athlete's personality, needs, and motives with the athletic environment, including the program's emphasis on competition, skill development, or affiliation.

athlete's heart: Hypertrophy or enlargement of the heart, particularly of the left ventricle, resulting from chronic exercise; does not appear to be associated with any known pathology.

atlantotaxial instability: Congenital condition involving a misalignment or displacement of the C1 to C2 vertebrae. Enlargement of space between these vertebrae allows excessive movement during flexion or hyperextension of the neck, exposing the spinal cord to potential danger.

atonia: A lack of muscle control or tonus that is associated with cerebral palsy or Down syndrome.

ATP (adenosine triphosphate): See *adenosine diphosphate*.

ATPS: See *ambient temperature and pressure saturated*.

A-trait: See *trait anxiety*.

atresia: 1. Congenital absence of a body part. **2.** Condition in which the external auditory canal is not completely developed.

atrioventricular (A-V) heart block: Conduction defect that occurs in the transmission of the action potential through the A-V junction; in first-degree A-V block, the transmission is slightly delayed and the P-R interval exceeds 0.20 s; there are two forms of second-degree A-V block (Mobitz I and Mobitz II), but in each the atrial stimulus does not get transmitted and a ventricular depolarization (QRS) is dropped; in third-degree or complete A-V block, the atrial impulses (P waves) and ventricular depolarizations (QRS) are completely dissociated.

atrioventricular (A-V) node: Area of the heart between the atria and ventricles that delays the electrical impulse sent from the sinoatrial (S-A) node approximately 0.10 s to allow the atria to contract and force blood into the ventricles; transmits an impulse to the A-V bundle (bundle of His).

atrioventricular (A-V) valves: See *mitral valve, tricuspid valve*.

atrium: Upper chamber of the heart that receives blood from the superior and inferior vena cava and from the pulmonary vein.

atrophy: Gradual shrinking or wasting away of muscle tissue from disease or disuse. Also called *muscle atrophy*.

attention: 1. Preferential response to relevant stimuli, to the exclusion of others. **2.** Setting of the sensory and central nervous systems for maximal stimulation.

attentional focus: Focus on relevant information while performing.

attentional focus model

attentional mechanism: Neural process in the brain in which external cues are perceived and processed.

attentional narrowing: Process of reduced peripheral cue utilization, often due to increased arousal or anxiety.

attentional style: Predisposition to attend to the environment in a certain personalized manner; depicted as internal, external, broad, or narrow.

attention deficit disorder: Increased activity or motion that prohibits an individual from sitting or standing for a sufficient duration to concentrate on a task.

attenuation of force: Reduction in an applied force.

attitude: 1. Evaluative internal state that creates a readiness or predisposition to respond with certain positive or negative behaviors that are directed in relation to the attitude object; learned or organized through experience. **2.** Idea charged with emotions that predisposes certain actions in response to a particular set of social situations. **3.** General and enduring positive or negative feeling about some person, object, or issue. See also *student attitude, teacher attitude*.

attribution model: Description of the ways individuals explain their decisions or performance outcomes or perceive causes of events in achievement-related situations such as competitive sport. Such attributions are thought to serve psychological and social functions and to be motivated by learned or social needs to enhance self-esteem, gain social approval, and so on. See also *causal elements*.

attribution theory: A cognitive explanation of motivation in which the perceived causes of an event, the manner in which these causal inferences are reached, and the consequences of these causal beliefs play an important role in explaining behavior. Posits that individuals continually make causal judgments when analyzing various sources of information available to them. See also *attribution model, causal dimensions, Kukla's attribution theory*.

attribution training: Program designed to increase persistence and effort after failure by teaching persons to attribute failure to a lack of effort or the need to improve skill.

Atwater general factors: The net energy available to the body from food nutrients and alcohol; approximately 4, 9, 4, and 7 kcal per gram of carbohydrates, fats, proteins, and alcohol, respectively.

atypical body alignment: Body posture that is mechanically or physiologically deviant from proper body structure, resulting from structural or functional problems or imbalances.

audible goal locator: Motor-driven sounding devices that help visually impaired individuals determine directions and positions in the environment.

audience effect: Tendency of observers to affect motor performance either favorably or unfavorably depending on various environmental, psychological, and social factors related to the performer, the situation, and characteristics of the observers.

audiogram: Graph of minimal level of

sound that can be heard at various frequencies for each ear.

audiologist: Specialist who evaluates speech, language, and hearing processes that cause hearing and communication disorders.

auditory acuity: Sensitivity in detecting the presence of a sound at any given pitch.

auditory agnosia: Inability to correctly identify familiar persons or objects by sound.

auditory discrimination: Ability to distinguish two sounds on a characteristic such as pitch, loudness, or speech sound.

auditory figure–ground perception: Ability to hear the auditory stimuli of interest amidst irrelevant background noises and sounds. See also *figure–ground perception.*

auditory localization: Ability to indicate the location from which a sound originates. Also called *sound localization.*

auditory memory: Retention, and sometimes reproduction, of a sequence or pattern of either speech or nonspeech sounds.

auditory–tactile integration: The matching of an auditory event with its corresponding tactile stimulation; that is, the matching of a sound with the event that also caused tactile stimulation.

auditory–visual integration: The matching of an auditory event with its corresponding visual object, source, or event; that is, matching of a sound with sight of the object or event from which the sound comes.

augmented feedback: Verbal or nonverbal information available to a performer from a source not normally associated with a task, regarding performance of that task.

augmenter: Person who tends to exaggerate the strength of incoming stimuli. Augmenters may have a relatively low pain tolerance and be easily distracted by environmental stimuli. Compare *reducer.*

aura: Warning sensation, derived from auditory, olfactory, or tactual input, that may precede a convulsive seizure.

autism: Psychological disorder characterized by absorption in self-centered subjec-

tive mental activity, especially when accompanied by a marked withdrawal from reality.

autocratic leadership style: Decision making based on group leader's personal authority rather than group discussion or consensus. For instance, coaches who dictate team strategy, rather than seek discussion and agreement about strategy, are using an autocratic style. Compare *consultive style.*

autogenic training: Mental training program in which an individual attends to internal feedback, based on verbal cues and visual images, to reach a state of relaxation.

autohypnosis: Self-hypnosis in which a person achieves a hypnotic state without the assistance of another person; can be (a) self-induced or (b) induced by posthypnotic suggestion following heterohypnosis (i.e., after being hypnotized by a specialist).

autonomic arousal: Physiological measure of arousal under the immediate control of the autonomic nervous system; may be integrated by the somatic nervous system and endocrine mechanisms. Usually determined by palmar sweating, electrical properties of the skin, circulatory changes, respiration, and muscular contraction (electromyography).

autonomic nervous system: The part of the nervous system that regulates involuntary functions of the heart, viscera, glands, and smooth muscle; composed of the sympathetic and parasympathetic nervous systems, which typically counterbalance each other.

autonomous stage: Third phase of Fitts' motor-skill learning model, in which performance is habitual, little attention to production of the skill is required, and although performance variability is minimal, any errors in skill execution can be corrected by the performer. See also *associative stage, cognitive stage.*

A-V: Atrioventricular.

aversive event: Stimulus or situation that suppresses, weakens, or increases a behavior resulting in the termination of the stimulus.

AVO₂D: See *arteriovenous oxygen difference*.

avoidance reaction: [md] Withdrawal of the hand and arm upon contact with an object; evident in the first weeks after birth. Later in the first year, there is an attempt to avoid the object rather than a withdrawal.

avoidance training: Teaching an individual to perform a behavior that defers or averts the presentation of an aversive stimulus.

awkwardness: Nonspecific clumsiness characterized by problems or faults in some movements but not in others.

axial skeleton: The division of the human skeleton comprising the skull, vertebral column, and thorax.

axis of rotation: The point, either within or external to the object, about which the object revolves.

axon: Conducting portion of a nerve fiber; in a motor neuron, the part that extends from the spinal cord to the muscle fiber and delivers the electrical current (action potential).

B

Babinski reflex: Reactive fanning out and extension of the toes in response to a stroking of the plantar surface (sole) of the foot from heel to toes.

Babkin reflex: Head flexion, eye closure, and mouth opening in an unconscious reaction to pressure applied to both palms of an infant. Also called *palmar-mandibular reflex*.

Bachman ladder: Apparatus for testing balance ability, consisting of a freestanding ladder with staggered rungs for the right and left feet, which the subject must climb to the greatest height possible, without skipping rungs, before balance is lost and the task is restarted.

backward chaining: Developing a behavior by learning individual components of that behavior in reverse order. A sequence of responses is developed in a backward manner, with the terminal response being developed first, then the next-to-last response, and so on. Forward chains are referred to as "shaping." Also called *chaining*. See also *shaping*.

balance: 1. Ability to maintain or control upright body position. **2.** Ability to maintain body equilibrium or steadiness.

Balke test: Treadmill protocol used to determine maximal oxygen consumption; incremental, continuous constant-speed test, starting at a 0% grade and a speed of 3.3 mph for 1 min; the second-stage grade is increased to 2%; every subsequent minute the grade is increased 1%.

ballistic movement: Rapid movement initiated by strong muscular contraction, carried on by momentum, and terminated by (a) interference with an external object, (b) reaching the limit of motion, and/or (c) contraction of antagonist muscles.

ballistic skills: Motor tasks in which force is applied to an object, with or without an implement; a subdivision of fundamental manipulative skills, including throwing, striking, volleying, and kicking.

bang-bang control: Type of controller signal that is all-or-nothing; this type of signal may be involved in movements made with added, viscous loads, with an optimum time.

barometric pressure: Pressure of the atmosphere expressed in terms of the height of a column of mercury; at sea level, approximately 760 mm; important variable for converting ventilation volumes to standard conditions. See also *body temperature and pressure saturated (BTPS), standard temperature and pressure dry (STPD)*.

baroreceptors: Sensory organs that respond to changes in pressure. In the cardiovascular system, found in the aortic arch and carotid sinus; when stretched by an increase in pressure, a reflex slowing the heart rate, as well as a compensatory dilation of the peripheral vasculature, occurs.

barrel chest: Abnormally rounded chest.

basal ganglia: Premature portion of the brain beneath the cortex that modifies and alters instructions from the motor cortex to the muscles to initiate voluntary movement.

basal metabolic rate (BMR): The minimum level of energy required to sustain the body's vital functions in the waking state; measured by determining oxygen consumption via open or closed circuit spirometry.

base: Chemical substance that gives up hydroxyl ions (OH^-) in solution.

baseline: Frequency or rate at which a behavior is performed prior to a treatment or intervention program. A set of critical observations or data used for comparisons or as a control.

base of support: The area of body part(s) in contact with a resistive surface that provides a reaction force to the applied force of the body.

Basic Motor Ability Test–Revised: Norm-referenced test for children 4 to 12 years old that assesses gross and fine motor skills. The test includes 11 items covering a range of skills including flexibility, agility, balance, fine motor coordinations, and locomotor and manipulative skills. Test–retest reliability is .93.

Bassin anticipation timer: Apparatus to measure coincidence-anticipation accuracy; requires subject to respond, usually by pressing a button, at the moment the subject anticipates the arrival of a moving light at a target point (simulated by sequentially triggered lights).

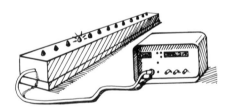

Bassin anticipation timer

Bayes theorem: [cr] Implies that the predictive value of an exercise test depends on the prevalence of disease in the population being tested; implies that the population with coronary heart disease or risk factors for coronary heart disease is more likely to be correctly identified compared to individuals with no disease or risk factors; postgraded exercise test (GXT) odds of coronary heart disease equal pretest odds of the disease (based on the prevalence of disease in population being tested) times the likelihood ratio of the test results (i.e., odds of a test being true); pretest odds of disease range from 1:19 for asymptomatic individuals to 9:1 for individuals with angina; likelihood ratio is 7 if GXT is positive and 3 if GXT is negative. See also *graded exercise stress test*.

Bayley Scales of Infant Development: Norm-referenced test for children between 2 and 30 months of age, consisting of three scales. The mental scale measures object manipulation and response to visual and auditory stimuli; consists of 163 test items. The motor scale measures fine and gross motor coordination; consists of 81 items. A behavior scale assesses various factors such as attention and social behavior through interview. A modified version for handicapped children is available. Split-half reliabilities range from .68 to .93.

Becker's muscular dystrophy: Form of muscular dystrophy caused by a recessive X-linked chromosome afflicting males. Similar to Duchenne muscular dystrophy although it is less severe, progresses more slowly with a later onset, and is less debilitating.

behavior: Observable or measurable action or response.

behavioral activating system: Arousal system that is responsive to conditioned stimuli and appears to become activated during approach and avoidance situations; measured by heart rate.

behavioral analysis: An approach to skill instruction intended to shape or modify skilled behaviors and to maintain or control those behaviors at desired levels.

behavioral approach: Systematically applied techniques used to change behavior(s); based on direct observation and measurement of the person's actions.

behavioral coaching: In sport, a strategy that requires the coach (team leader) to break down a sport skill into component parts and offer specific instruction, modeling, and positive feedback before and after the athlete's performance directed at each segment of the skill. The objective is to improve the quality of coaching instruction and feedback to the competitor.

behavioral contract: Sophisticated behavior management technique; a written agreement between the teacher and student(s) specifying the target behaviors and responsibilities of each person within a designated time period. The student has a role in defining the expected behaviors and appropriate rewards. Also called *contingency contract*.

behavioral inhibitory system: Anxiety-response system that becomes active during the passive avoidance of fear-inducing situations. Most appropriately measured by electrodermal activity.

behavioral intention: Cognitive antecedent of an act implying a decision to behave in one way as opposed to others—for example, reflecting upon past successes or failures before voluntarily approaching or avoiding certain competitive (achievement) situations.

behavioral objective: Established condition or criterion for mastering specific, observable skills that currently are not possessed by the learner.

behavioral repertoire: Behaviors an individual is capable of performing during a particular time period.

behavior control: Exertion of power or influence over others through alteration of environmental variables to achieve a specific goal; may be positive or aversive. Also called *control*.

behavior disorders: Overt traits manifested by learners, related to deviant conduct, personality, immaturity, or delinquent behaviors.

behavioristic leadership style: In sport, a consistent application of principles of behavioral psychology to improve and maintain athletic behavior; implies that the competitor's behaviors are a function of (or are modified by) their consequences.

behavior management: See *behavior modification*.

behavior modification: 1. Systematic approach designed to initiate, develop, maintain, or enhance a desirable response.

2. Program to weaken, decrease, or eliminate a response by changing or altering the antecedent or environmental events prior to a response, or the consequences immediately following a response. Also called *behavior management*.

behavior proclamation: Behavioral contract that is a formal statement of contingencies applying to individuals or groups; the teacher (or leader) determines the target behaviors and reinforcements to be implemented.

behavior training: Implementation of strategies to reduce anxiety or cope with problem situations.

benign-positive appraisal: Type of primary appraisal that occurs when the outcome of an encounter is perceived as positive and preserves or improves well-being or promises to do so.

Bernoulli's principle: Principle that fluid pressure is inversely proportional to the velocity of the fluid.

beta blockers: Group of drugs that block beta receptors in the body; prevent normal activity of the sympathetic nervous system, thus slowing heart function; used in the treatment of coronary heart disease, hypertension, arrhythmias, thyroid gland disease, migraine headaches, and certain anxiety states; based on their spectrum of activity, they are classified as either selective or nonselective.

beta endorphins: See *endorphins*.

beta oxidation: Transformation of a fatty acid molecule to acetyl-CoA in mitochondria for further degradation in the Krebs cycle.

BIA: See *bioelectrical impedance analysis*.

biacromial/bicristal ratio: 1. Ratio formed by dividing biacromial breadth by bicristal (biiliac) breadth and multiplying the quotient by 100; indicates the proportionality of trunk build. **2.** Ratio of shoulder width to hip width. Also called *androgyny index, biacromial/biiliac ratio*.

biacromial/biiliac ratio: See *biacromial/bicristal ratio*.

biacromial breadth: Anthropometric measure of skeletal breadth across the shoulders, taken at the outside edges of the right and left acromial processes of the scapulae.

biarticulate muscle: Muscle that crosses two articulations.

bicarbonate-carbonic acid system:

$$CO_2 + H_2O \rightleftharpoons H_2OCO_3 \rightleftharpoons H^+ + HCO_3^-$$

Carbon dioxide combines with water to form carbonic acid, which ionizes and dissociates into hydrogen ions (that need to be buffered) and bicarbonate; 60% to 80% of the carbon dioxide produced in the body is transported in the form of bicarbonate; bicarbonate is primarily formed in red blood cells but is transported in the plasma. See also *buffer, carbaminohemoglobin*.

bicondylar breadth: Anthropometric measure of skeletal breadth across the knee, taken across the distal condyles of the femur.

bicristal breadth: Anthropometric measure of skeletal breadth across the hips, taken at the outside edges of the iliac crests. Also called *biiliac breadth*.

bicuspid valve: See *mitral valve*.

biepicondylar breadth: Anthropometric measure of skeletal breadth across the elbow, taken across the epicondyles of the humerus.

bigeminy: Irregular heart rhythm in which each normal sinus beat is followed by a premature beat that originates in either the atria or the ventricles.

biiliac breadth: See *bicristal breadth*.

bilateral: Pertaining to or affecting two sides or symmetry of the body.

bilateral integration: Smooth coordination or interaction of both sides of the body to execute a physical or motor skill.

bilateral transfer: The benefit to performance of a task with one hand or foot that arises from prior learning of the same task with the other hand or foot.

bimanual: Pertains to two hands acting

or moving at the same time, although not necessarily in symmetrical movement.

binocular: Utilization of both eyes to see an object, with fusion of the two images into one.

bioelectrical impedance analysis (BIA): Method used to determine body composition. A known amount of electrical current is transmitted through the body, and resistance (or impedance) to the current is measured; because fat is a poor conductor, resistance is related to the amount of fat; impedance is also dependent on the length (height) and cross-sectional area (weight) of the conductor; stature and body weight are included to predict percent body fat.

biofeedback: Visual and/or auditory input from equipment that measures one or more physiological responses; used for learning relaxation; individuals in biofeedback programs eventually should be able to initiate similar bodily (relaxation) responses without interacting with equipment.

biofeedback

biological age: 1. Indicator of biological maturation. 2. Age from conception rather than birth. 3. [ep] Age expressed relative to various performance capacities and physiological functions in comparison to other individuals of similar chronological age.

biological hypothesis: An explanation of performance superiority based on biological differences or physical characteristics. Proposes that in sport, for example, positional segregation is a function of significant differences in body measures between blacks and whites; used to explain the under- or overrepresentation of blacks in various sport positions.

biomechanics: Field of study applying the principles of mechanics to the study of animate movement.

bipedal: Having or using two feet.

bipolar lead system: In electrocardiography, the limb leads in which the difference in electrical voltage is recorded between a negative and a positive electrode; Lead I: right arm is negative and left arm is positive; Lead II: right arm is negative and left leg is positive; Lead III: left arm is negative and left leg is positive.

bit: Binary unit; equivalent to the result of a choice between two alternatives. In information processing, as the number of alternatives doubles, the number of bits increases by units of 1 (e.g., 2 alternatives = 1 bit, 4 alternatives = 2 bits, 8 alternatives = 3 bits, etc.).

black-box approach: Study of human skill performance by association of stimuli and responses, without regard to the intervening structures but inferring intervening processes. For example, from this perspective one might present various stimuli to a performer and merely record the subsequent responses without concern for the intervening perceptual, cognitive, or motoric structures through which information passed. Inferences might be made, however, regarding perceptual, cognitive, or motoric processes involved in processing the information.

blade anthropometer: Instrument with straight arms used to measure the linear breadth or width of a body segment, in which a fixed arm is positioned and a movable arm is slid into place.

blindism: Purposeless, repetitive mannerism commonly seen in the blind, such as rubbing the eyes.

blindness: Lack of sight or inability to distinguish a bright light from 3 ft. See also *legal blindness*.

block rotation: Simultaneous forward

movement (lateral rotation) of the upper trunk and pelvis in ballistic skills.

blood doping: Removal of blood, followed by reinfusion of the red blood cells several weeks later, in an effort to increase the hemoglobin concentration and thus the oxygen-carrying capacity of the blood; has been used by athletes to enhance endurance performance; a banned procedure.

blood flow: The quantity of blood flowing through a vessel or group of vessels in a given period of time; during exercise, increases to skeletal muscle and decreases to visceral organs; highly regulated by the diameter of the arterioles.

blood gas: See *arterial PO₂, mixed venous PCO₂, mixed venous PO₂*.

blood lipids: Fats circulating in the blood plasma; includes chylomicrons, HDL, LDL, VLDL, and triglycerides.

blood plasma: Fluid portion of the blood; decreases with exercise as fluid diffuses out of the vascular system; amount of decrease is directly proportional to the relative work load; returns to baseline levels shortly after cessation of exercise.

blood pressure: The force exerted by the blood upon the walls of the blood vessels, especially the arteries; varies with blood volume and sympathetic tone, compliance of the vascular wall, and individual's age and health. Systolic pressure results from heart contraction (approximately 120 mm Hg); diastolic pressure results from the heart's relaxation (approximately 75 to 80 mm Hg); systolic blood pressure rises with exercise (up to approximately 200 mm Hg); diastolic pressure remains fairly close to baseline levels.

blood volume: The volume of blood circulating through the body; includes blood cells and plasma (approximately 5 L for an individual of average size).

BMI: See *body mass index*.

BMR: See *basal metabolic rate*.

body alignment: Body posture. See also *atypical body alignment*.

body awareness: 1. Recognition, identification, and differentiation of the location, movement, and interrelationships of body parts and joints. **2.** A performer's spatial orientation and perceived location of the body in the environment.

body composition: In physical growth, the partitioning of body mass into lean body mass and fat; used to study age-related and differential sex characteristics of growth and maturation.

body concept: See *body schema*.

body density: Mass of the body tissue per unit volume (g/cc); typically expressed as body weight (kg)/body volume (L); may be used to estimate percent body fat by either the Siri or the Brozek formula. See also *body volume, Brozek equation, Siri formula*.

body dimensions: Lengths, breadths, and circumferences of various body parts or segments. Often such measurements are used to monitor physical growth and maturation.

body image: One's concept of how one's body appears to others and how it performs.

body mass index (BMI): Ratio of body weight (kg) to height (m²); provides a gross estimate of appropriateness of weight for height; used to assess growth and nutritional status.

body-monitoring cognitive strategy: See *associative strategy*.

body part identification: The component of body awareness wherein parts of the body can be named or located in response to a label.

body percept: See *body schema*.

body-righting reaction: See *body-righting reflex*.

body-righting reflex: One example of a derotative righting reaction in which an infant's head and upper trunk rotate in reaction to forced rotation of her or his legs and pelvis, in order to keep the head and body aligned. Also called *body righting reaction, derotative righting.* See also *neck-righting reflex.*

body-scaled: Adapted to the overall physical size of an individual or a body component; for instance, object sizes, distances, or tasks scaled to individuals' body sizes when group members vary in body size.

body schema: One's concept of one's own physical dimensions as based on sensory-motor input; allows for coordinated movement of the body and body parts in space. Also called *body concept, body percept.*

body sway: Small, oscillatory movements of the body around a base center during balanced standing, sometimes studied for a time period following a disturbance in balance. Also called *postural sway.*

body temperature and pressure saturated (BTPS): The volume of air expressed at body temperature (usually 273 °K + 37 °C or 310 °K), a barometric pressure (Pb) at sea level of 760 mm and saturated with water vapor with a partial pressure of 47 mm at 37 °C (PH$_2$O); actual measured ambient volumes are converted to these standard conditions to remove the influence of varying pressure, temperature, and humidity on air volumes, using the following equation:

$$\text{volBTPS} = \text{volATPS (Pb} - \text{PH}_2\text{O/Pb} - 47 \text{ mm Hg)(310 °K/273 °K} + \text{T °C)}$$

body volume: Body mass divided by body density; based on Archimedes' principle that the volume of a body is proportional to the weight of water displaced by the body; thus, body volume may be assessed hydrostatically by measuring either the weight of water displaced by the body (direct) or the change in weight of the body submerged (indirect); expressed in liters or kilograms, because 1 L = 1 kg at 25 °C; used to calculate body density for the estimation

of percent body fat. See also *hydrostatic weighing.*

body weight: The gravitational force that the earth exerts on a body at or near its surface; the product of body mass (in kilograms) and acceleration due to gravity (9.81 ms^{-2}); measured in newtons (N).

Bohr effect: The right and downward shift of the oxygen–hemoglobin dissociation curve caused by an increase in blood acidity, temperature, concentration of carbon dioxide, or 2,3-DPG; facilitates the unloading of oxygen at the tissue level and occurs with exercise; reduced hemoglobin–oxygen affinity.

bomb calorimeter: Device used to measure the total energy value of various food nutrients by combusting the food and measuring the heat liberated.

bone-on-bone force: Summation of all contact forces acting on the articulating surfaces forming a joint; the sum of the reaction forces at a joint.

borderline hypertension: High blood pressure that can be treated with dietary intervention, exercise, or other nonpharmacological treatment such as weight loss; persistent systolic blood pressure of 140 to 150 mm and/or diastolic blood pressure between 85 to 90 mm. See also *hypertension.*

borderline mentally handicapped: Individuals who possess IQs of 70 to 85 and manifest learning problems but do not meet the legal definition of mentally retarded.

boundary layer: Region of relative motion between adjacent layers of a fluid flowing over an object that is moving through that fluid.

bow caliper: Instrument with C-shaped, curved arms that measures the linear breadth or width of a body segment.

bradycardia: A slowed heart rate that is clinically defined as a resting heart rate below 60 bpm; causes include endurance training, administration of drugs that stimulate the vagus nerve, beta blockers, or disease.

braille: System of letters, numbers, and other language symbols formed with raised (tactile) dots; used by blind individuals for reading and writing.

a	b	c	d	e	f	g	h	i	j
1	2	3	4	5	6	7	8	9	0

k	l	m	n	o	p	q	r	s	t

u	v	x	y	z	w	capital sign	numeral sign

braille

breadth caliper: See *anthropometer.*

breathing: See *pulmonary ventilation.*

breathing exercises: Activities that emphasize proper breath control and increase the strength and endurance of ventilatory muscles for individuals with pulmonary deficiencies. Also called *diaphragmatic breathing.*

brittle bones: See *osteogenesis imperfecta.*

broad attentional style: See *attentional style.*

bronchodilation: Expansion of the pulmonary pathways during activity to meet the need for increased oxygen.

bronchospasm: Spasmodic contraction of smooth muscles of the bronchial tubes that constricts the pulmonary pathways and reduces the flow of oxygen to and from the lungs.

Brozek equation: Formula used to estimate percent body fat when body density (Db) is known:

$$\text{percent body fat} = (4.570/Db - 4.142) \cdot 100$$

Bruce test: An exercise testing protocol used on a treadmill for diagnostic purposes; involves increasing the grade and speed incrementally every 3 min until the subject reaches maximal oxygen consumption or is symptom limited; the following describes the protocol:

Stage	Speed (mph)	Grade (%)	MET	VO$_2$ (ml/kg/min)
I	1.7	10	4.0	14.0
II	2.5	12	6.6	23.1
III	3.4	14	10.0	35.0
IV	4.2	16	14.2	49.7
V	5.0	18	16.1	56.4

Bruininks-Oseretsky Test of Motor Proficiency: Norm-referenced test battery, for children 4.5 to 14.5 years of age, testing motor proficiency and fine and gross motor skills. It can distinguish normal and gross motor dysfunction populations. The long form has eight subtests and 46 test items; a short form has 14 items. Test–retest reliability is .87 for the long form, .86 for the short form.

BTPS: See *body temperature and pressure saturated.*

buffer: Substance that reduces changes in pH that would otherwise occur with the addition of excess acid or base; the buffering of hydrogen ions from carbonic and lactic acid is particularly important during exercise.

bulimia: Eating disorder characterized by frequent abnormal and constant craving for food, manifested as binge eating with intervals of dieting, self-starvation, or purging (vomiting).

bundle branch block: Conduction defect that occurs below bundle of His in left or right bundle branches; because action potential must travel from unblocked branch through system via myocardial cells to other branch, the QRS complex is abnormally wide and possibly notched; ECG analysis allows for differentiation of left or right block.

buoyancy: Ability of an object to float in a fluid.

buoyant force: Force acting through the center of buoyancy of a body and equal and opposite to the weight of the volume of fluid displaced by the body.

burnout: 1. The result of constant or repeated emotional pressure or physical overtraining associated with an intense involvement with people over long periods of time. **2.** Psychological condition in which stress becomes excessive and chronic. Leads to less energy, motivation, productivity, tolerance, and patience, while feelings of helplessness (losing control) and inaccurate decision-making intensify. **3.** [ep] See *overtraining*.

$$\boxed{C}$$

CABG: See *coronary artery bypass graft*.

cadence: In locomotion, the number of steps completed per unit of time.

calcaneus: The heel bone.

calcium channel blockers: Group of drugs that either block calcium entry into cells or prevent the mobilization of calcium from intracellular stores; inhibit the excitation–contraction coupling that eventually causes dilation of smooth muscle tissue; used in the treatment of coronary heart disease, arrhythmias, mild hypertension.

caloric expenditure: Energy cost of a particular activity performed over time; usually measured via indirect open circuit spirometry and calculated as oxygen consumption ($\dot{V}O_2$ L/min) times the caloric equivalent corresponding to the respiratory exchange ratio (approximately 5 kcal/L $\dot{V}O_2$). See also *energy expenditure, respiratory exchange ratio*.

caloric intake: Amount of potential energy stored in the food ingested.

caloric output: Energy spent in performing a given amount of work.

calorie: Measure of energy equal to the amount of heat energy required to raise 1 g of water 1 °Celsius (°C). See also *kilocalorie*.

calorimeter: Apparatus for measuring the quantity of heat energy produced or evolved from a substance or a metabolic process.

calorimetry: Measurement of heat energy liberated or absorbed in metabolic or combustive processes; direct method measures heat production in an airtight insulated calorimeter; indirect method estimates energy cost based on oxygen consumption and carbon dioxide production. See also *closed circuit spirometry, open circuit spirometry*.

capacitance vessels: The large veins of the systemic circulation, with the ability to accept as much blood as is necessary. During exercise, venous return increases, and the capacitance vessels receive a larger amount of the total blood volume per unit time than during resting conditions.

capacity interference: Prediction that performance decreases when two tasks with high attentional value are performed simultaneously.

capillary density: Number of capillaries per square-millimeter area of muscle tissue. Increase in the capillary density is seen with aerobic training, primarily in slow-twitch muscle fibers; causes decrease in distance a gas must diffuse, directly increasing the rate of diffusion.

carbaminohemoglobin: Combination of hemoglobin and an amino compound (NH) with carbon dioxide; results in a weak acid that alters the blood chemistry pH; a means by which carbon dioxide is transported back to the lungs for elimination; accounts for 20% of CO_2 transport.

carbohydrate loading: Process of nutritional modification that results in a supercompensation of glycogen stores in muscle fibers; following muscle glycogen depletion via a low-carbohydrate diet and exercise, a diet rich in carbohydrates is given; can increase muscle glycogen storage approximately 3 to 4 times the normal levels; has been shown to aid performance that is longer than 60 min at an intensity above 70% of $\dot{V}O_2$max.

carbon dioxide produced: Volume of carbon dioxide expired per unit time; carbon dioxide is exhaled as a consequence of substrate metabolism and lactate buffering; increases with exercise and is measured by determining the volume of expired air and the concentration of carbon dioxide in the expired air.

carbon dioxide rebreathing: A noninvasive, indirect method for determining cardiac output; primarily used during exercise to derive estimates of the partial pressure of arterial and mixed venous CO_2; partial pressures are converted to content using the CO_2 dissociation curve, and the following equation is used to estimate cardiac output (Q):

$$Q = VCO_2/(\text{mixed venous } CO_2 \text{ content} - \text{arterial } CO_2 \text{ content})$$

Also called *indirect Fick technique.*

carbonic anhydrase: Zinc-containing enzyme found only in erythrocytes; catalyzes the reaction between carbon dioxide and water to form carbonic acid at a rate 5,000 times greater than in a noncatalyzed reaction; important in regulation of the rate at which CO_2 is transported back to the lungs from the tissues.

cardiac catheterization: Procedure involving insertion of a fine catheter through an arm, neck, or leg artery into the heart; further manipulation of the catheter tip within the heart permits measurement of pressures and withdrawal of blood for measurement of oxygen saturation; also, injection of radio-opaque contrast medium in conjunction with cine film recording allows clinician to evaluate adequacy of coronary blood flow; useful diagnostic tool for assessment of coronary artery disease.

cardiac conduction system: Specialized nervous tissue over which the heart's action potential is propagated; normal conduction is initiated at the sinoatrial node, passes through the atrial internodal pathways to the atrioventricular node, to the bundle of His, the right and left bundle branches, and finally along the Purkinje fibers. See also *action potential, electrocardiogram.*

cardiac cycle: One complete round of atrial and ventricular systole and diastole; each cycle normally is initiated with depolarization at the sinoatrial node and concludes with ventricular repolarization; on the electrocardiogram a cycle may be measured from any landmark on one beat to the same landmark on the next beat; typically R-R'. See also *depolarization, diastole, electrocardiogram, heart rate, repolarization.*

cardiac hypertrophy: Increase in size of heart cells; may occur as a training adaptation to volume overload in endurance athletes, resulting in an increase in left ventricular chamber size, or to a pressure overload in resistance athletes, resulting in an increase in left ventricular wall thickness; variety of pathological conditions, including heart valve disease and hypertension, can also cause ventricular hypertrophy.

cardiac index: Cardiac output per square meter of body surface area; approximate values for a normal, healthy 70-kg individual are 3.0 L/min/m^2 at rest and 15 L/min/m^2 during maximum exercise.

cardiac muscle: Specialized striated muscle with centrally located nuclei; fibers are arranged in a latticework and transverse boundaries intersecting configuration and are separated by low-resistance membranes called "intercalated discs"; cardiac cells are autorhythmic—when one becomes excited, the action potential spreads to all. Also called *myocardium*.

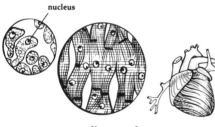

nucleus

cardiac muscle

cardiac output (Q): Quantity of blood pumped from the left and right ventricles per unit of time. Q is product of heart rate and heart stroke volume; at rest, Q is around 5 L/min; increases to 25 L/min at maximum levels of exercise for the average person; endurance athletes may have maximum cardiac output levels of 35 to 40 L/min.

cardiac rehabilitation: Multidimensional program of post myocardial infarction or post coronary artery bypass surgery designed to restore the individual to optimal functioning and prevent further complications or occurrences.

Phase I: Patient remains in hospital; patient and family are educated about the potential benefits of the rehabilitation program; patient is constantly assessed by the coronary care nurse and cardiac rehabilitation personnel; after assessment, the patient exercises in supine, sitting, and upright positions; depending on severity of disease, exercise program may be either active or passive; patients recovering from myocardial infarction are encouraged to perform passive exercise; sessions last 10 to 15 min (as many as 3 to 4 times per day) and are supervised by a cardiac nurse, an exercise specialist, a physical therapist, or a rehabilitation nurse; aims of this phase are to (a) decrease problems such as muscle atrophy and low blood pressure due to prolonged bed rest, (b) provide the patient a sense of reassurance, and (c) reduce the length of hospital stay.

Phase II: Begins immediately after the patient is discharged from the hospital; aims of this phase include (a) improved capacity for physical work, (b) upgrading of clinical status, and (c) enhanced psychosocial well being. Hospital-based program administered on an outpatient basis, usually three times per week, under the direct supervision of nurses and exercise specialists.

Phase III: Usually conducted at home or in a YMCA or school gymnasium; supervised by nurses and/or exercise specialists; exercise is performed for up to 30 to 45 min; efforts are toward increasing exercise tolerance.

Phase IV: Continuation of phase III; long-term recovery and maintenance of exercise programs, such as walking and jogging, to optimize cardiovascular functional capacity.

cardiac somatic coupling hypothesis: Hypothesis that reduced heart rate, as measured while the subject attends to environmental input, may result from reduced tension in the muscles during this attentive state. Compare *intake-rejection hypothesis*.

cardinal axis: Any of three axes of the body that pass through the body's center of gravity and divide the body into equal moments about the center of gravity (top–bottom, right–left, dorsal–ventral).

cardiovascular fitness: A level of aerobic fitness brought on by continuous involvement in rhythmic exercise of duration and intensity sufficient to tax the cardiovascular system chronically to the point of physiological adaptation; the ability to deliver and use oxygen under the demands of intensive, prolonged exercise or work.

card sorting box: Apparatus consisting of compartments into which subjects must sort a deck of cards, as quickly as possible, based on a designated criterion.

Cartesian coordinate system: An x, y, z reference system, either 2-dimensional (2 axes) or 3-dimensional (3 axes), in which a point is located as a distance from each of the axes. Points are referenced in (x, y, z) order.

catabolism: Any degradation process where nutrients are broken down in the body resulting in a release of energy.

cataract: Abnormality of the eye in which the normally transparent lens becomes opaque or cloudy.

catch trial: Experimental trial within a series, in which an anticipated stimulus is not presented, thereby eliminating the need to respond. Often used to determine the point after which it is too late for a subject to inhibit the response.

catch-up growth: Increase in growth rate with restoration of favorable environmental conditions after a period of influence by one or more negative factors. Extent of growth restoration depends on the length, timing, and severity of the negative condition.

catecholamine: Any of a group of substances of specific chemical composition that act as hormones and/or neurotransmitters (epinephrine, norepinephrine, dopamine); elicit strong physiological responses via the autonomic nervous system and hormonal secretion from the adrenal medulla; with exercise, increase in concentration in the blood, resulting in increases in heart rate and blood flow to the working musculature to enhance oxygen delivery.

catharsis hypothesis: Proposal that observing others' aggressive behavior, as vicarious experiences, can reduce a person's pent-up emotions, resulting in, for instance, a lower probability of acting aggressively. *Catharsis* literally means to cleanse or purify.

catheter: Tube inserted into the bladder through the urethea to empty the bladder or kidneys.

causal dimensions: The three dimensions in terms of which, according to attribution theory, the causes of performance outcome are explained: locus of causality, stability, and controllability. They may be measured on the Causal Dimension Scale.

causal elements: Factors cited as explanations of performance outcome; typically features of performer, task, or some external factor, such as ability, effort, task difficulty, and luck. Also called *perception of causality*.

causality: The assignment of an explanation to a situation in which it is assumed that the introduction of one factor (the independent variable) results in a change in a second factor (the dependent variable).

causal schema: Relatively permanent structure of a person's beliefs about relationships between observed events (effects) and perceived causes of events.

CBAS: Acronym for the Coaching Behavior Assessment System used for coding and systematically analyzing behaviors of sport coaches in natural field settings.

centering: Process of focusing one's attention on relevant stimuli.

center of buoyancy: Theoretical point at which the buoyant force acts on an object immersed in a fluid.

center of gravity: 1. Theoretical point on which the total effect of gravity acts or appears to act. 2. Point about which the sum of the torques of the body segments equals zero.

center of mass: Theoretical point at which

all of a body's mass is considered to be concentrated.

center of percussion: A point on an object where, if the object is struck at that point when pivoting about another point, no pressure is produced at the pivot point.

center of pressure: Point at which the resultant of a contact force acts on an object instantaneously.

center of rotation: Point about which an object revolves. See also *axis of rotation*.

central deafness: Hearing impairment resulting in an abnormality in the auditory nerve or central nervous system, although the hearing mechanism is intact.

central demanding stimulus: Input located at a person's center field of vision. Also called *foveal demanding stimulus*.

central efferent monitoring: Concept that outgoing efferent signals to the muscles that direct movement are checked against a neural copy of the commands for that movement within the central nervous system, and that sensory feedback, therefore, plays no necessary role in monitoring and controlling the movement.

central group member: Group member who, in contrast to a peripheral group member, has a strong desire for group success, favors highly challenging group goals, and plays a group role of primary importance for achieving those goals (e.g., a talented athlete who gets considerable playing time during a contest).

centrality: Degree of closeness of a group member to the center of the group's interaction network, as measured by the manner in which the person interacts with other group members, most notably, the frequency and range of these interactions. Also a function of the degree to which the person must coordinate her or his tasks with other members.

centrality theory: In sport, the contention that leadership or success in sport is related to occupying a player role that involves a high degree of interaction with other team members. Thus, a catcher in baseball and a center in basketball would be predicted to demonstrate more leadership skills than players at other positions, due to their highly interactive roles during contests.

central pattern generator: See *pattern generator*.

central vision: Vision of objects projected around or on the retinal fovea via eye movements, yielding the sharpest sight and color vision.

centrifugal force: Pseudo-force equal to and acting in the direction opposite to the direction of centripetal force (that is, acting away from the axis of rotation). Compare *centripetal force*.

centripetal acceleration: See *radial acceleration*.

centripetal force: Force acting toward the center of rotation, responsible for keeping the object following a curved path. Compare *centrifugal force*.

$$F_{centripetal} = \frac{m \cdot v^2}{r}$$

where m = mass of rotating object
r = distance from axis of rotation to center of gravity of rotating object
v = linear velocity of the rotating object

cephalocaudal development: Sequential direction of growth and behavioral development that proceeds from head to feet.

cerebellum: Portion of the brain above the brain stem just below the cerebral hemispheres; coordinates the action of voluntary muscles that relate primarily to balance, postural adjustment, and locomotion.

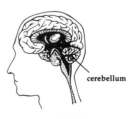

cerebellum

cerebral palsy: Motor impairment caused by damage to the developing brain, usually prenatally or during the birth process; symptoms vary depending on the location and extent of brain damage.

cerebrospinal fluid: Clear water liquid that bathes and protects the four ventricles of the brain; serves as a buffer from sudden pressure changes and impact, and provides the brain system with nutrition.

cervical: Pertaining to the neck region, as in cervical vertebrae or cervical nerves.

chaining: 1. [mc] Central feature of a motor control theory that holds that sensory feedback from early components of a movement acts as a stimulus to trigger the succeeding components until the movement is completed. Also called *peripheral hypothesis, S-R chaining, stimulus-response chaining.* 2. [ad] See *backward chaining.*

chemical maturity: Achievement of adult values in the composition of the fat-free body; generally assumed to be 73.8% water, 6.8% mineral, and 18.8% protein; contraindicates the use of adult equations to estimate percent fat in children.

chemoreceptors: Sensory nerve endings, located in the aortic arch and in the carotid sinuses, that respond to changing arterial blood chemistry; when arterial PO_2 decreases (as with a change in altitude) or arterial PCO_2 decreases (as in hyperventilation), the chemoreceptors are stimulated, and ventilation increases.

child-designed instruction: Games, activities, or teaching sequences used in the instructional process that are based on creative and imaginative input from learners.

choice reaction time: Reaction time measurement requiring the earliest possible response to more than one stimulus, usually with a different response matched to each of the possible stimuli. See also *reaction time, simple reaction time.*

choking: 1. Inability to perform up to previously exhibited standards. 2. Performance decrements under pressure circumstances.

cholesterol: A derived fat; an essential substance both synthesized in the body by the liver and ingested in the diet from animal sources; high levels and especially a high ratio of total cholesterol to HDL are associated with an increased incidence of atherosclerosis and risk for coronary heart disease; regular exercise may be associated with lower levels of blood cholesterol. See also *chylomicron, high density lipoprotein, low density lipoprotein, very low density lipoprotein.*

chorea minor: Acute disease affecting the central nervous system, causing tics, motor awkwardness, tremors, and wandering movements primarily in the hands. Also called *St. Vitus's dance, Sydenham's chorea.*

choreoathetosis: Form of cerebral palsy characterized by variations in muscle tone and involuntary movements of the arms and legs.

choroid: Middle layer of the eyeball, between the sclera and the retina.

chromosome: Strand of DNA apparent in the cell nucleus containing the cell's genes and hereditary makeup. See also *Down syndrome.*

chronic: Disabling, sometimes permanent, condition that has a gradual onset over a long duration.

chronological age: An individual's calendar age, from birth to a specified date.

chronologically age-appropriate skills: Physical and motor skills that children normally participate in and are expected to attain during the developmental process.

chronotropic response: Altered rate or timing of heart rate in response to drug therapy or autonomic nervous system stimulation or inhibition.

chylomicron: Microscopic particle formed when a beta-lipoprotein encloses a globule of phospholipid, cholesterol, or triglyceride; 80% to 90% of fat absorbed from the gut is transported to the venous blood via the thoracic lymphatic duct as chylomicrons; most chylomicrons are removed from the blood into adipose tissue or the liver. See also *cholesterol, high density lipoprotein, low density lipoprotein, very low density lipoprotein.*

cinematography: Motion picture technology; used to record and store information concerning continuous human movement.

circuit training: Exercise program consisting of a series of stations; exercise at each station is performed for a specified time or number of repetitions; components may include resistance exercises using weight machines or free weights, calisthenics, and aerobic activities such as running or cycling.

circular aggression effect: The generation of further aggression by acts of aggression, continuing until the circle is broken by positive or negative reinforcement.

circumduction: Sequence of movements of a segment occurring in the sagittal, frontal, and oblique planes so that the movement as a whole describes a cone, as in arm or trunk circling.

citric acid cycle: See *Krebs cycle.*

class frequency planning: Factor in organizational planning that equates number of instructional sessions with volume of information to be learned.

classical conditioning: Type of learning in which a neutral or conditioned stimulus is paired with an unconditioned stimulus to evoke a response; after repeated trials, the conditioned stimulus alone is enough to elicit a response.

classification assessment: Evaluation used to classify children by homogeneous ability or skill levels.

class movement patterns: Safe and on-task work by class members in order to accomplish specific objectives.

class rewards: Reinforcement a group or class can earn for appropriate behavior. Also called *group contingencies.*

classroom climate: Positive or negative interactions during an instructional program, indicating teacher's or students' degree of satisfaction; a measure of effective teaching, obtained from direct observations of student behavior.

classroom management: Establishment and maintenance of order in the classroom environment.

classroom organization: Structures or behavior settings affecting classroom events and processes and used in achieving classroom order.

cleft palate: Congenital birth defect characterized by an opening in the roof of the mouth (palate) extending through the upper lip.

climate: [ss] Psychosocial environment (atmosphere) of a group or team; quality and quantity of interaction among group members. Also called *group climate, social climate.*

climbing reflex: Involuntary, alternate upward arm movements by an infant held vertically; a seldom-observed response controversially claimed by some to constitute a reflex.

clinical sport psychologist: Professional with a graduate degree in clinical psychology; typically a member of a nationally recognized psychological or psychiatric organization. Deals with traditional clinical issues, including assessing psychopathology, providing individual and group psychotherapy, providing crisis intervention, treating neurotic, psychotic, and personality disorders, and dealing with drug dependency, psychosomatic problems, and eating disorders. May address similar concerns with sport participants, including use of performance-enhancing techniques.

clique: Small social unit within a larger group, comprised of individuals who frequently interact socially and feel a close affiliation to the exclusion of other group members.

clonus: Rapid succession of alternate contractions and relaxation of muscles.

closed circuit spirometry: Indirect method for measuring energy expenditure; oxygen consumption is measured by a subject's inhaling a known volume of 100% oxygen contained within a spirometer; exhaled CO_2 is absorbed using a CO_2 absorber; amount of oxygen consumed equals the difference between initial and final oxygen volume in the spirometer; expressed as volume/minutes; generally used to determine resting oxygen consumption. See also *open circuit spirometry*.

closed environment: A setting for motor skill performance that is spatially consistent from one performance to another and where initiation of movement is self-paced.

closed kinetic chain: Body configuration where movement begins at the segment most free to move and ends at the segment that is fixed. (For example, during a vertical jump, the trunk is the segment most free to move, and the feet are fixed.)

closed-loop control: Mode of motor control wherein movement parameters are sent from a (functional) control center to initiate, maintain, and complete the movement; completion of the movement depends upon sensory feedback and its comparison to a representation of the intended movement, which may already be stored in memory.

closed skill: Self-paced motor task performed in an environment that is stable, unchanging, or predictable.

clumsiness: Difficulty in learning motor skills, and inefficient, asynchronous performance of movements appropriate for one's age and the circumstances.

clustering: 1. Grouping of students by their similarities according to selected variables such as skill or size. **2.** Learner strategy of organizing items to be learned by grouping them according to shared characteristics.

coach–athlete compatibility: Compatibility of a coach's behavior with an athlete's wishes and expectations, and vice versa.

Coaching Behavior Assessment System: See *CBAS*.

coaction: Independent performance of the same type of activity by two or more individuals who may or may not be observing each other's actions or working alongside each other, and may or may not be competing against each other. See also *competitive coaction, noncompetitive coaction effect, rivalry*.

coactive audience: A group passively observing a performer while independently performing the same task.

cochlea: Fluid-filled structure in the inner ear containing thousands of hair cells that are set in motion when sound is transmitted from the movement of the oval window to the inner ear. Movement of the hair cells discharges electrical impulses to the central nervous system for interpretation.

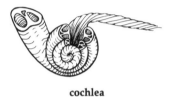

cochlea

cocontraction: Simultaneous agonistic and antagonistic muscle actions.

coding: Transformation of information without loss of meaning, usually involving a change in the form of that information; in human performance, the transfer is within the central nervous system, as from one processing stage to another, or storage into memory. See also *encoding*.

coefficient of drag: Index of the "streamlinedness" of an object dependent upon its shape and orientation relative to fluid flow; the lower the coefficient, the more streamlined the projectile.

coefficient of friction: Index of ease with which one surface slides over another; computed as the ratio of the magnitude of friction force to the magnitude of normal force.

coefficient of restitution: Index of elasticity of an object reflecting the ability of the object to return to its original shape once deformed; measured by the ratio of the impulse of rebound to the impulse of impact.

cognition: Act or process of knowing; thoughts and feelings, such as expectations, imagery, self-verbalization, and attributions.

cognitive–affective stress management training: Approach (model) for coping with stress involving cognitive and relaxation skills.

cognitive appraisal: 1. Unique manner in which an individual interprets a situation, often differing from person to person. 2. A person's assessment of a stressful situation in comparing the situational demands with his or her ability (resources) to meet those demands; if resources exceed demands, stress response is minimal; if perceived demands exceed perceived resources, stress response is higher. Appraisal of the consequences of the event may influence the stress response. If the consequences are highly related to success or self-esteem, stress will be maximal.

cognitive attribution model: Explains causal attributions as a function of trying to obtain cognitive mastery and processing information about performance outcomes according to whether causes are perceived as (a) within oneself or in the environment (locus of causality) and (b) as changing or unchanging over time (stability). See also *attribution model*. Compare *functional attribution model*.

cognitive–behavioral interventions: In sport, interactive use of strategies based on thoughts (e.g., imagery or self-monitoring) and overt actions (e.g., an established protocol for precontest psyching up or warming up) used by a sport competitor to improve athletic performance.

cognitive coping: Use of mental techniques to overcome psychological and physical stress; in a competitive sport context, enacted prior to or during performance. See also *associative coping style, dissociative coping style*.

cognitive dissonance theory: Prediction that conflict within a person's thoughts, opinions, attitudes, and behaviors (i.e., dissonance) results in the need to reduce this conflict and strive for a state of consistency; thus, persons seek to achieve consistency of thought and behavior and avoid inconsistency. When inconsistency (dissonance) is encountered, it may be dealt with through rationalization, attitude change, and selective perception.

cognitive evaluation theory: Proposes that two factors, one's perception of one's own competence and one's perception of one's control over one's actions and environment, underlie intrinsic (internal) motivation. The theory includes a controlling aspect and an information aspect. Ostensibly, perceiving one's behavior as controlled by external forces, and obtaining information that indicates failure, decreases intrinsic motivation (controllability and information aspects, respectively); whereas perceiving one's actions as self-controlled, and receiving information that promotes a sense of competence and self-determination, increases intrinsic motivation. Thus, intrinsic motivation predicts that a person will choose to engage in an activity based on the enjoyment it provides and his or her need to feel competent; extrinsic rewards probably tend to shift the point of control from internal (e.g., fun) to external (e.g., a trophy, money, or recognition).

cognitive events: Experiences that partially explain anxiety and, more generally, personality. These include the ways a person searches for and selects environmental cues relevant to thought and action, integrates new information with old, and makes decisions that result in observable behavior.

cognitive mediational model: Approach to coping with anxiety; assumes that emotional arousal is mediated by cognition rather than elicited directly by environmental cues, and that, to reduce anxiety and other maladaptive emotional responses, a person should modify the thoughts that elicit and reinforce these emotions.

cognitive modeling: Technique of demonstrating skills in which a model verbalizes task-related information during skill execution.

cognitive model of achievement motivation: Contention that behavior is a function of various goals, including demonstrating ability, obtaining social approval, and enjoying a challenging task.

cognitive processing: In movement training, understanding, remembering, and integrating information about motor skill development.

cognitive restructuring: Intervention used to identify and change irrational self-statements to reduce anxiety. Goal is to help subject (a) recognize that beliefs, often invoked unconsciously, promote emotional arousal, (b) identify underlying ideas and recognize their irrational and self-defeating nature, (c) actively attack irrational ideas and replace them with thoughts that prevent or reduce anxiety, and (d) practice and rehearse the new modes of thinking and to use them in real-life situations.

cognitive set: Predisposition to approach a problem or react to a situation in a certain way or using a specific strategy.

cognitive stage: First step in Fitts' model of motor learning, in which the performer comes to understand the task and formulates an execution plan; characterized by variability in performance, large errors, and frequent mental or physical errors. See also *associative stage, autonomous stage.*

cognitive state anxiety: Perception of threat exhibited by feelings and emotions as opposed to physiological responses; usually caused by negative expectations (e.g., worry) about success or negative self-evaluation; may be of a trait or state nature; characterized by negative self-talk and unpleasant visual imagery; best reduced by cognitive techniques such as positive self-talk and thought-stopping. Compare *somatic state anxiety.* See also *state anxiety, trait anxiety.*

cognitive strategy: Mental technique designed to alter the way a person consciously takes in, thinks about, or responds to (i.e., processes) information.

cognitive style: Learner's preferred manner of processing information, including perception, cognition, and problem solving. Also called *perceptual style.*

cohesion: 1. Development and maintenance of a group; forces acting on members to remain in the group. 2. Adhesive property that binds group members together. 3. Resistance of a group to disruptive forces; measured as (a) individual-to-individual relationships (friendship and influence or power), (b) individual-to-group relationships (sense of belonging, value of membership, enjoyment), and (c) the group-as-a-unit (teamwork and closeness). Also called *group cohesion.* See also *pendular model of cohesion, social cohesion, sociometric cohesion, task cohesion.*

cohort: Group of individuals with a common characteristic. In motor development, the characteristic is often time of birth, although there is no definitive time span for inclusion.

coincidence-anticipation: Skill of watching a moving stimulus and accurately timing a response to coincide with the arrival of a stimulus at a designated target. An example is batting a pitched ball. Also called *coincident timing, transit reaction.*

coincident timing: See *coincidence-anticipation.*

colinear forces: System of forces whose lines of action lie along a common line.

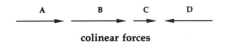

colinear forces

collaborative learning: See *cooperative learning.*

collaborative relationships: See *cooperative learning.*

collective efficacy: A group's effectiveness, resulting from its confident expectation that it will successfully reach its intended goal. See also *self-efficacy*.

combinations: Movement variations that combine task components to vary the difficulty of the task.

command style: In education, a teaching style characterized by the teacher making all decisions about the skill while the learner follows directions for performance.

communication: Imparting or interchange of thoughts, opinions, or information by speech, writing, or signs; transmission and exchange of information conveying meaning between two or more people.

compatibility: [ml] Harmonious relationship between a signal or stimulus and the response. Compatibility exists, for example, if when a row of lights and a row of buttons are presented, the response requested is to press the button located under a light rather than one to the right or left. Also called *stimulus–response compatibility*.

compensation: Development of a special talent or ability to offset a limitation, disability, or lack of functioning.

compensatory eye movement: Movement of the eyes to maintain fixation on an object, due to the head lagging behind the eyes because of differences in inertia and therefore speed of eye and head movement.

compensatory movement: Reactionary attempt to regain equilibrium or a normal body position.

compensatory tracking: Task in which a subject is to maintain a constant speed, pressure, or light in varying conditions.

competence: Ability or capacity to deal effectively with one's surroundings or in performing a task.

competence motivation: 1. Theory that individuals have inherent needs to perform mastery activities for intrinsic rewards such as joy, fun, or happiness. 2. Extent of one's self-perception as being competent at a skill in relation to task demands. Related to persistence and interest in mastering a skill.

competence motivation theory: Attempts to describe, explain, and predict the inherent desire to participate, strive for, and demonstrate personal competence in particular achievement areas. To satisfy the need for competence, a person attempts to master selected skills and aspects of his or her environment. Competence motivation is improved or maintained if positive emotions result from successful performance.

competency: In education, a specific skill or training needed by teachers, such as skill required to provide physical education programming for the disabled; or a goal or criterion that should be achieved.

competency-based curriculum: A content framework or approach to teaching that holds a group or learner to a task until mastery is achieved within a designated criterion, time, or level of accuracy.

competing hypothesis: Assertion that the more widespread sport participation in urban and relatively large communities than in smaller communities results from greater availability of physical facilities, organized activities, leadership, and opportunities to participate—and that this is a cause of the disproportionately higher representation in sport of elite players from larger communities.

competition: 1. Achievement situation in which participants expect their performance to be evaluated. 2. Social interaction in which individuals or groups jointly struggle toward a goal that can be attained by only one of the groups or individuals.

competitive ability: After childhood, a relatively permanent capacity to perform in evaluation-based achievement situations.

competitive coaction: Interaction of group members with rivalrous intentions, promoted by awards or instructions to compete in anticipation of comparison of scores; for example, members of a golf team are competitive coactors because each competes against one representative from the opposing team. Competitors may or may not observe each other during performance. Similar to coaction, except entails higher degree of competition and the inclusion or intention of rivalry. See also *rivalry*. Compare *noncompetitive coaction effect*.

competitive goal: Achievement objective based upon the performance of another individual. See also *rivalry*.

competitiveness: 1. Desire to strive for success and win in interpersonal competition. 2. General achievement orientation directed toward specific sport activities. 3. Disposition to strive for satisfaction when making comparisons with some standard of excellence in the presence of evaluative others.

competitive social situation: Situation in which competitors' goals are linked so closely that there is a negative correlation between their goal attainments. For instance, an athlete may be able to reach a goal only at the cost of teammates' failing to attain their goals.

competitive state anxiety: In sport, extent to which an individual perceives a specific competitive sport situation as threatening at the time of competition.

competitive stress: Negative emotional reaction when self-esteem is threatened. Thought to occur when an imbalance is perceived between the performance demands of competition and the performer's own ability to successfully meet those demands. Particularly likely to occur when consequences of failure are appraised by the performer as important.

competitive trait anxiety: Predisposition to perceive situations in sport or other competition as threatening. Thought to be stable and enduring, similar to any other personality trait.

compliance: Persistence at an activity or program over time or until meeting a particular goal; a function of process motivation. See also *adherence*.

component steps: Levels within intratask sequences of skill development, classified by body areas, such as legs or trunk.

composition of vectors: Attainment of a single vector describing the resultant action of two or more vectors from the addition of those vectors.

compression force: Result of a system of equal and opposite forces acting toward the surface of a structure, causing stress and strain within the structure.

concentration: Cognitive activity of retaining a mental and physical focus on a performance task.

concentric action: Muscle action in which the muscle shortens, causing the attachments to move closer together.

concentric contraction: Any movement involving a shortening of muscle fibers while developing tension (e.g., biceps muscle during an arm flexion movement); an isotonic, dynamic, or positive contraction.

concept: In learning theory, a group of responses or ideas that share common characteristics.

conceptual tempo: Measure of cognitive style wherein a learner is categorized as reflective or impulsive.

concrete operations stage: Piaget's third stage of cognitive development, characterized by (a) use of rules based on tangible instances rather than abstractions, (b) awareness of alternate solutions, (c) examination of parts of knowledge of the whole, (d) mental representation of objects, events, or actions, and (e) ability to order a set of variables according to a specified characteristic. The stage spans approximately 7 to 11 years of age. See also *formal operations stage, preoperations stage, sensorimotor stage*.

concurrent feedback: Information obtained by the performer during skill execution; used to regulate moment-to-moment performance of participants, especially during execution of continuous and tracking skills; differs from terminal feedback, which occurs following performance.

concurrent forces: System of forces meeting at a common point.

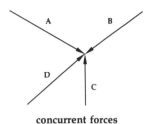

concurrent forces

conditioned stimulus: Previously neutral stimulus that, through repeated associations with an unconditioned stimulus, generates power to evoke a response.

conduction: Mechanism of energy transfer in which heat is transmitted from a warmer object to a cooler object via direct physical contact between the two; the passage of action potentials by nerve or muscle tissue.

conferencing: In education, any form of one-to-one discussion between the teacher and student used to develop or understand a specific task.

confidence: Positive self-evaluations in relation to the demands of a general, situation-related movement situation. For example, one can be confident in athletics but not in academics. See also *movement confidence*.

congenital: Present at birth, as with a trait, condition, or disease; due either to heredity or to an influence arising during gestation. Compare *acquired disability*.

congestive heart failure: Deficiency of cardiac function characterized by dilation of at least one chamber accompanied by increased diastolic volume, increased venous blood volume, slow circulation time, and reduced stroke volume; heart unable to maintain adequate circulation; left ventricular failure can be caused by myocardial infarction, valve disease, or hypertension and in turn causes congestion or accumulation of fluid in lungs or breathlessness; right ventricular failure is usually caused by lung disease, and congestion or fluid accumulation occurs in lower limbs and liver; condition is progressive and can be fatal. Also called *heart failure*.

conjunctiva: Delicate membrane that covers and lines the exposed surface of the eyeball.

consequence: Any stimulus, negative or positive, resulting from a behavior.

conservation: Properties (e.g., weight, volume) of a substance (e.g., water) remaining unchanged when other properties of the substance are changed (e.g., the water is poured into a narrower, taller container). The ability to comprehend conservation is achieved during a certain stage of childhood development.

conservation of momentum: A law, derived from Newton's first law of motion, stating that a system of bodies will continue to move in a straight line unless acted on by an external force.

consolidation: A characteristic of developmental stages indicating that the behaviors of a stage gradually emerge and mix with behaviors of the previous stage, with the later behaviors being reworked and performance being improved.

consolidation theory: Notion that during rest, information obtained from prerest trials is combined and strengthened (i.e., consolidated), at least for high-drive subjects, resulting in improved postrest performance resulting from a condition called "reminiscence."

constant error: Measurement indicating amount of deviation from a criterion or target and the direction of that deviation, such as early/late or short/long. Recorded on a single trial or calculated by averaging error scores on a series of trials while accounting for the sign (direction) of the deviation. Also called *algebraic error*.

constant velocity: An object's velocity

when there is no change in the object's direction or speed. See also *velocity*.

constitutive rules: In sport, the official rules of a sport, defining the goal of competition, acceptable means for attaining that goal, the area and duration of play, appropriate equipment, and other issues assuming that all participants agree to play by these rules.

constraint: 1. Morphological, mechanical, or environmental restriction or limitation on performance of a movement. **2.** Process of linking muscle collectives such that there is automatic compensation to preserve the relationship of individual muscles in the collective.

consultive style: Sharing of problems between the group leader and one or more members. The leader may solicit from the group suggestions for solving the problem prior to making a decision. Compare *autocratic leadership style*.

contact force: Force derived from contact with another object; may affect the first object's movement.

content analysis: In education, the division of a task or skill into manageable teaching units.

contest: Individually focused activity emphasizing self-discovery through competition governed by informal or formal rules, and having no consequences beyond those affecting the individual and emerging in the contest activity. Also called *match*.

contextual interference: Detrimental influence on performance arising from the situation (context) in which a skill is practiced.

context variables: In education, the unique aspects of the student, school, facilities, and class size that may affect student achievement.

context variation: Varying the settings or environments of movements or actions.

contiguity: The principle of contiguity states that reinforcement promotes a desirable outcome if it closely follows a response.

contingency: Relationship between a response or behavior to be changed and the events or consequences that follow that behavior. The principle of contingency states that reinforcement should occur only following a desired response.

contingency contract: See *behavioral contract*.

contingency management: Behavior management technique that alters the relationship between a behavior and its consequence.

contingency observation: Removal of a student from active participation in an activity in order to self-correct a behavior by observing the behavior being performed correctly. Also called *peer isolation*.

contingency theory: The suggestion that leader effectiveness is situation-specific, and that leadership styles (e.g., autocratic and task-oriented or democratic and interpersonally oriented) may be effective in some situations but not in others. Also called *Fiedler's contingency theory*.

continuous reinforcement: Schedule of reinforcement in which a response is reinforced every time it is performed.

continuous skill: Motor task with an arbitrary beginning point and an arbitrary end point, often but not necessarily cyclic. Compare *discrete skill*.

contractility: A muscle's characteristic contraction reaction to a stimulus.

contracture: Shortening, tightening, or abnormal contraction of a muscle or joint capsule that restricts mobility and range of motion in the joint.

contralateral: On the opposite side of the body.

contralateral muscle: See *antagonist*.

control: 1. In movement control, reflex and voluntary mechanisms and underlying processes that guide movement. **2.** Assignment of values to the variables in the function that constrains movement variables to a behavioral unit. **3.** In experimental methodology, the arrangement of conditions in an experiment such that the independent variable(s) is the sole influence on the dependent variable. **4.** [pd] See *behavior control*.

control hypothesis: Explanation for positional segregation, positing that certain minorities are excluded from elite sports and from positions that have the greatest opportunities for influencing the outcome of the contest (e.g., golf, tennis, quarterback in American football).

controllability: 1. Dimension of attribution theory regarding the ways persons explain the causes of their behaviors that may or may not be under their control. Effort is the only controllable attribution; ability, task difficulty, and luck are not controllable. 2. A basis of our judgments and responses to others when we praise others for high effort, especially after they succeed, and criticize others if their failure is due to a lack of effort.

controlling aspect: See *cognitive evaluation theory*.

control process: 1. Function that facilitates transfer of information within the nervous system; many of these functions are involved in memory; some are under an individual's direct control, and others are automatic. 2. Memory strategy that can help an individual remember more effectively.

control variable: Factor that, when changed, does not alter the pattern of coordination in a skill. An example is changing the speed in a walk. Also called *nonessential variable*.

convection: Transfer of energy (usually heat) between the body and air or water as a result of circulation of air or water molecules next to the skin.

convergent inquiry: Teaching procedure that allows students to discover answers to a series of imposed questions with a wide range of acceptable answers; requires problem solving and reasoning skills. Compare *divergent inquiry*.

convergent question: Type of question used to require analysis and integration of previously encountered material; learner must use problem solving and reasoning to formulate an answer or solution. Compare *divergent question*.

convulsive disorder: See *seizure*.

cool-down: Light-intensity exercise done at the end of an exercise session to enhance the rate of recovery; also performed to reduce the likelihood of venous pooling and feeling of lightheadedness.

cooperation: The ability to interact and work with a group to obtain a common goal.

cooperative learning: Students interacting and working together to meet the demands of a game or sport. Also called *collaborative learning, collaborative relationships, cooperative play*.

cooperative play: See *cooperative learning*.

cooperative social situation: Situation in which the goals of different competitors on the same team are linked so closely that a positive correlation exists between their mutual attainment, and hence it is mutually beneficial for all of those athletes to reach their goals.

coordination: 1. Harmonious movement of independent body parts. 2. In regard to motor control, the relationship among movement variables (the potentially free variables) that constrains them into a behavioral unit. See also *general motor ability, skill, timing*.

coordination variable: Factor that, when changed, necessitates a new pattern of coordination. For example, a sprinter encountering a hurdle must change from a running step to a leap or hurdle step. Also called *essential variable*.

coordinative structure: Class of movements with common active muscle groups (sometimes spanning many joints) constrained to function as a single unit. The collective is part of a hierarchy of organized movement execution that reduces the number of parameters that must be controlled. Also called *muscle collective, muscle linkage, synergy*.

COPE Model: Based on four cognitive-behavioral techniques, conducted in sequence, commonly used by elite athletes to overcome (cope with) potentially noxious stimuli during performance: (a) control emotions, (b) organize input into meaningful versus nonmeaningful categories, (c) plan the next response, and (d) execute the response.

coping skills model: General approach to helping subjects deal with anxiety and other unpleasant thoughts, partly through using relaxation techniques to reduce anxiety. Typically accomplished with the aid of a clinician. See also *cognitive-affective stress management training, stress inoculation training.*

coplanar forces: System of forces whose lines of action lie in the same plane.

coriolis force: Radial force, always directed toward the joint center, produced when a segment is rotating about a joint center that is itself rotating.

cornea: The transparent covering of the eye, responsible for refraction of light rays.

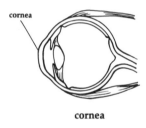

cornea

corollary discharge: Hypothesized set of neural signals within the central nervous system, sent from the motor system to the sensory system, that prepares the latter for consequences of the planned movement.

coronal plane: See *mediolateral plane.*

coronary artery bypass graft (CABG): Surgical technique incorporating the use of a leg vein graft to bypass the diseased portion of the coronary vessel; serves to increase blood flow and relieve symptoms of angina pectoris, and may prevent the development of myocardial infarction; either single or multiple bypass grafts can be used to treat coronary artery disease.

coronary blood flow: The fraction of total blood flow that passes through the coro-

nary blood vessels surrounding the heart. Can be reduced by either a lowered cardiac output or narrowing of the coronary artery lumen; in mild cases, causes myocardial ischemia and angina pectoris; severe obstruction can cause myocardial infarction.

coronary heart disease risk factors: Characteristics that have been shown to increase probability of developing coronary heart disease; primary or major risk factors include elevated blood lipids (cholesterol, LDL cholesterol) or a ratio of total cholesterol to high density lipoprotein greater than five, hypertension, cigarette smoking, abnormal resting electrocardiogram, family history of heart disease, and diabetes mellitus; secondary or implicated factors include obesity, physical inactivity, and psychological stress.

corporal punishment: The infliction of punishment on an individual's body, as by striking, in an effort to decrease or eliminate inappropriate behavior.

corrective therapy: Therapy utilizing physical activity to rehabilitate mechanical alignment or postural deficiencies, and rehabilitation of physical impairments.

cortisol: An adrenocortical hormone; stimulates gluconeogenesis and is therefore classified as a glucocorticoid; promotes fat utilization by mobilizing adipose stores; facilitates vascular response to catecholamines and inhibits inflammatory reactions; release of cortisol is stimulated by stress (e.g., exercise or emotion) or by decreased blood glucose levels; acute bouts of long, intense exercise cause an increase in cortisol release, which may remain elevated for about 2 hours post exercise.

counseling sport psychologist: Person trained and certified or licensed as a counseling psychologist, and who engages in the clinical practice of counseling sport participants (e.g., coaches or athletes).

counseling sport psychology: Interaction between a sport participant (coach or athlete) and a trained counseling psychologist for the purposes of (a) information gathering that requires listening skills, (b) helping the client (sport participant) solve problems by looking at alternative approaches and solutions to issues, and (c) giving information or advice. Ultimate objectives of counseling may include improving sport performance, increasing the satisfaction of being a sport participant, enhancing communication or relationships with others, improving a mental component of competition, reducing stress, dealing with a psychopathological disorder (e.g., depression, low self-esteem, suicide), and coping with success or failure.

counterconditioning model: Cognitive approach to coping with anxiety, involving reducing the connection between anxiety-provoking stimuli and anxiety-based responses. To suppress anxiety responses, the treatment goal is to replace sympathetic activity with behaviors that invoke parasympathetic innervation.

coupled movements: Cyclic movements that are matched in interval. For example, entrained (synchronized) oscillators.

coupling: Mode of cooperation among self-sustaining oscillators wherein they become matched in interval. Hence, coupled oscillators provide a model for human interlimb coordination.

covariation principle: Prediction that the subject will attribute behavioral outcomes to external causes (task difficulty or luck) when the subject's performance is similar to that of the others to whom the subject is comparing himself or herself.

covariant: Private event, such as a thought, fantasy, or image, that is not observable to anyone other than the individual experiencing the event; can be altered by application of consequences following the event.

convergent question: Type of question used to require analysis and integration of previously encountered material; learner must use problem solving and reasoning to formulate an answer or solution.

covert modeling: Mental technique that involves learning new behaviors or altering existing ones by imagining scenes of others or oneself interacting with the environment.

coxa plana: Degeneration or deterioration of the head of the femur and resultant inflammation of the hip joint.

CP: See *creatine phosphate*.

craniotenosis: Immature closure of the sutures in the skull.

crawling: Locomotion with the body in a prone position, trunk on the ground. The feet or knees exert a pushing motion, and the arms engage in pulling; often confused with creeping.

crawling reflex: Movements of an infant's arms and legs in a crawling-like pattern while in a prone position, as an involuntary reaction to pressure applied to the sole of one foot or both feet alternately.

creatine kinase: Enzyme governing the reaction between adenosine diphosphate (ADP) and creatine phosphate in the formation of adenosine triphosphate (ATP) in the immediate energy system; used as a blood marker to assess the extent of skeletal muscle damage following eccentric exercise.

creatine phosphate (CP): High-energy phosphate compound stored in skeletal muscle; CP has greater bond energy than ATP, so it is used to phosphorylate ADP to form ATP to provide immediate energy; very important in supplying energy for high intensity activities that last less than 30 s.

credulous argument: Hypothesis that based on personality profiles accurate predictions can be made about sport performance.

credulous sport personology: The view that trait psychology is capable of accurately predicting success in athletics. Compare *skeptical sport personology*.

creeping: Locomotion on hands and knees with the trunk off the ground. Although first attempts can be characterized by movement of one limb at a time, or homolateral movement of the arm and leg (i.e., arm and leg on the same side of the trunk), the developmentally advanced pattern is contralateral (i.e., opposite arm and leg). Often confused with crawling.

cretinism: Absence or loss of functioning of the thyroid gland, resulting in developmental and learning disorders. Also called *hypothyroidism*.

criterion: In education, a performance measure used to evaluate the effectiveness of the instructional program or progress of a student.

criterion-referenced test: Evaluation of children's performance based on a behaviorally established standard or level of mastery to meet an educational goal when available norms are not applicable or available; standards are generally based on biomechanical or developmental criteria.

critical learning period: See *sensitive period*.

critical period: See *sensitive period*.

cross-disciplinary team: See *multidisciplinary team*.

cross dominance: See *mixed dominance*.

crossed extension reflex: Reflex that facilitates extension of a flexed leg when the opposite leg is flexed, allowing the child to creep and eventually walk.

crossed eyes: See *strabismus*.

crossing midline: Component of body awareness wherein (a) a task is completed by a body part crossing the body's midline, or (b) movements on each side of the midline are sequenced.

cross-lateral integration: Ability to use and coordinate both sides of the body.

cross-modal concepts: Form of intersensory integration in which information presented in two different sensory modalities (tactile and visual, for instance), is interrelated based on a concept or principle. For example, someone seeing a smooth ball and feeling the same ball without seeing it integrates the concept of smoothness across the tactile and visual senses.

cross-modal equivalence: Form of intersensory integration in which a stimulus or set of stimulus features are recognized as the same when presented in different sensory modalities. Thus, observing evenly spaced quarter notes is perceived similarly as hearing evenly spaced tones.

cross preference: The selection of one eye, hand, or foot over the other for a particular task when the selected eye, hand, and foot are on different sides of the body (for example, left eye, right hand, left foot).

cross-sectional design: Experimental technique used to imply development by studying groups of varying ages at one time rather than following a single group for a period of time to obtain repeated observations.

cross-talk: In electromyography, the interference on the electrical signal recorded from one muscle caused by the electrical signal of a nearby muscle when recording muscle electromyograms.

cross-training: Chronic exercise program incorporating activities that may synergistically support overall physical fitness; fitness probably results from some central physiological adaptations without peripheral overtraining; example: swimming, biking, and running done for triathlon training.

crural index: Ratio of thigh length to leg length.

cue: Stimulus used by a performer to make a discrimination.

cue-reduction feedback: Input that presents a limited number of task-related cues.

cue utilization theory: Contention that attentional narrowing during motor performance, usually accompanied by heightened arousal or anxiety, reduces the availability of important visual and auditory information (i.e., cues) to the performer. Underarousal broadens attentional focus, which allows the influx of irrelevant or redundant cues. Either of these conditions tends to inhibit optimal performance.

curvilinear motion: Linear motion along a curved path.

cutaneous perception: The component

of kinesthesis that provides information about stimulation of the skin and underlying tissues.

cyanosis: Bluish color of the skin and mucous membrane resulting from insufficient oxygen.

cybernetic: Pertaining to control processes or mechanisms and related communication systems, and often to responses dependent on adaptability derived from response-produced (internal) feedback.

cycle constancy: Recurrence of a specific motor task within a consistent time frame, allowing the learner to predict when stimuli will be presented and consequences will be delivered.

cystic fibrosis: Genetic, life-threatening disease that involves malfunction of the exocrine glands, pareneatic insufficiency, and progressive lung dysfunction from the production of sputum and colonization of bacteria in the bronchial tubes.

dangling: In education, time breaks in the momentum of a lesson that slow down or disrupt the flow of the lesson and attention of the learners.

data smoothing: Removal of "noise" or the extraneous portion of the signal from the raw data signal; may be accomplished using mathematical procedures such as digital filters, splines, or polynomial fits.

deaf: Nonfunctional or lack of measurable hearing (more than 90 dB) to understand speech.

deafferentation: Procedure of surgically removing or interrrupting sensory pathways to prevent nerve impulses from reaching higher brain centers.

deamination: Removal of amino groups from an amino acid; during protein metabolism the NH_3 groups are cleaved off so that glucose may be formed from the carbon skeleton; can occur by transamination and oxidative deamination.

deceleration: Decrease in an object's velocity per unit time.

decibel: Unit of measurement of the intensity (loudness or softness) of sound.

decision mechanism: Component of an information processing system wherein a plan of response is selected.

decoding: Learner's process of using skills and knowledge to understand sensory information and initiate a movement.

defensive aggression: Active resistance to perceived threats. Behavior that results in alleviation of aversive treatment and may reduce the occurrence of further aversive treatment.

defensive proactive assertive behavior: Acceptable yet forceful behavior that attempts to deprive another of a valued resource or expected gain, such as football player tackling the advancing ball carrier by using legal body contact.

degrees of freedom: 1. [mc] The number of free variables. In movement control, these free variables (muscles, joints) must be regulated to produce intentional or purposeful movement. **2.** [mc] The number of planes in which motion at a joint is possible. **3.** [bm] An axis through the geometric center of a joint about which movement is permitted. **4.** [bm] The number of independent coordinates necessary to specify the position of an object. **5.** In statistical analysis, the number of observations less the number of restrictions on these observations.

dehydration: Excessive or abnormal depletion of body fluids; when fluid loss is greater than 1% of body weight, decrements in plasma volume, cardiac output, work capacity, muscular strength, and exercise performance may result; fluid loss in excess of 2 to 3 L causes a reduction in sweating and thus an increase in core temperature, enhancing the risk of heat stress; exercise in the heat exacerbates the risk of dehydration if adequate fluid replacement is not maintained as sweating increases.

deinstitutionalization: Social movement of returning handicapped individuals from a large hospital to community-based residences and work settings. Compare *institutionalization.*

delayed feedback: Lagged delivery of information about performance normally received during or after a movement.

delayed knowledge of results: Lagged delivery of terminal feedback [knowledge of results (KR)] given a learner after a movement.

delayed onset muscle soreness (DOMS): Muscle discomfort experienced 24 to 72 hours post exercise; eccentric exercise has been found to result in intense DOMS; may be a consequence of skeletal muscle damage, but the precise mechanism causing DOMS has yet to be elucidated.

delay interval: Period of time between two events; for example, between a motor response and the presentation of knowledge of results, or vice versa.

delay of gratification: 1. Provision of reinforcement or rewards on an intermittent basis or at the end of a unit rather than on an immediate basis. **2.** Time interval between the response and the actual delivery of the reward or reinforcement.

delay of reinforcement: Amount of time or interval between a response and a reinforcer.

delegative leadership style: Occurs when group leader allows group members to make decisions. Leader's role is only to implement decisions made by group members.

deletion: Loss of genetic material from a chromosome.

delinquency deterrence hypothesis: The hypothesis that participation in athletic competition deters wrongful behaviors of juveniles.

DeLorme technique: See *progressive resistance exercise.*

delta efficiency: Calculation for work efficiency from a baseline measure, subtracting the energy used for zero work (e.g., limb movement during zero-resistance cycling) from the equation so that delta efficiency equals the change in work divided by the change in the energy expenditure expressed in work-equivalent units.

dementia: Deterioration of psychological, emotional, or cognitive functioning resulting from organic brain disorders.

democratic leader: One who encourages member interaction without prior permission and allows members to make decisions and plans that effect the group.

democratic leadership: In sport, leadership style encouraging coach–athlete inter-action and frequent decision-making by team members, usually pertaining to group goals, practice methods, and game tactics and strategies.

demyelinating disease: Progressive spasticity and paralysis that occurs as the myelin sheath surrounding the brain and spinal cord degenerates. See also *multiple sclerosis.*

dendrite: Branching process of proto-plasm that conducts impulses toward the body of a nerve cell.

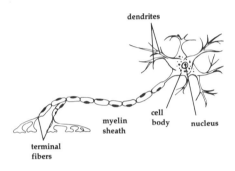

dendrites

cell
body

myelin
sheath

nucleus

terminal
fibers

dendrite

density: Mass per unit volume; measured in kilograms per meters cubed (kg $\cdot$ m^{-3}).

$$\text{density} = \frac{\text{mass}}{\text{volume}}$$

dental eruption: Initial appearance of the teeth. Age of dental eruption is often used as an indicator of a child's physiological maturation.

Denver Developmental Screening Test: Norm-referenced test for children from birth to 6 years of age that screens chil-dren for developmental delays. Four areas are assessed: personal-social, fine-motor adaptive, language, and gross motor. In-cludes 105 items, but typically only 20 need to be administered to each child; a short form of 12 items is available.

dependent variable: Condition in an ex-periment that is observed for change while independent variables are manipulated by the experimenter.

depolarization: Literally means the pro-cess that neutralizes polarity; at rest any body cell has a larger number of negatively than positively charged ions inside the cell and more positively than negatively charged ions outside the cell; state is main-tained when a nerve cell is not transmitting impulses, and therefore the resting mem-brane potential (RMP) is approximately -60 millivolts (mv); excitation of the cell mem-brane causes an influx of Na$^+$ and efflux of K$^+$; causes a rapid ionic shift of sodium ions from the outside to the inside of a muscle or nerve fiber; this shift changes the interior polarity from negative to positive and is the first stage of an action potential. See also *repolarization, restoration of ionic balance.*

deprivation: Withholding or restricting access to or availability of a reinforcer.

depth perception: One's judgment of the distance from oneself to an object or place in space.

derotative righting: See *body-righting re-flex, neck-righting reflex.*

desire for group failure: Person's expec-tations for his or her group to fail at a chal-lenging task, and the ensuing comfort expe-rienced when these expectations are met.

desire for group success: Person's ex-pectations for his or her group to success-fully accomplish a challenging group task, and the ensuing pride and satisfaction expe-rienced when those expectations are met.

desists: Behavior-management strategy used to weaken, decrease, or eliminate an inappropriate behavior by reprimanding a student for an inappropriate response. The reprimand should be clear, firm, well-timed, unemotional, and directed at the original behavior. Also called *verbal desists.*

deterministic perspective: Sport per-sonality viewpoint that behavior is deter-mined for, rather than by, an individual.

detraining: Reversal of adaptations to

chronic exercise once an exercise program has been terminated; effects of detraining occur more rapidly than training gains, with significant reductions in oxygen transport, enzyme activity, and overall work capacity being seen within two weeks of cessation of training. Also called *reversibility principle.*

development: Process of continuous change to a state of specialized functional capacity and adaptation to maintain that state. Often confused with growth and maturation.

developmental age: An individual's approximate age in terms of development and maturation, regardless of chronological age.

developmental analysis: Analysis of lesson content divided into extension, refinement, and application.

developmental approach: Selection and matching of instruction to the ability levels of children as measured by developmental milestones.

developmental delay: 1. Failure of a developing organism to exhibit a skill or behavior within the chronological age span during which most members of the species exhibit that behavior. **2.** Initial exhibition of a skill or behavior at an older age than onset in the majority of a species. Also called *developmental lag.*

developmental disorders: Disabilities resulting in malformation during the developmental process that restrict the physical or mental capabilities of children.

developmental lag: See *developmental delay.*

developmental period: Period of time used to measure structural growth from birth to approximately 18 to 20 years.

developmental sequence: Progression of qualitative changes in behavior or movements that eventually lead to mature behavior or mechanically efficient movement. This progression is assumed to be consistent across normal individuals and the changes intransitive (fixed in order). Also called *intratask development.*

Developmental Test of Visual Perception: Norm-referenced assessment of visual perception, hand–eye coordination, and motor skills dependent on vision for children 3 through 9 years of age. The battery has five subtests with a test–retest reliability of .80 to .98.

deviant behavior: Behavior judged by others to be outside an acceptable realm or norm.

diabetes: Metabolic disorder in which the body's ability to produce and use insulin for sugar metabolism is impaired; the individual is unable to utilize sugar properly to sustain muscular functioning.

diagnostic integrity: Direct relationship between assessment and instructional methodology, and programming to remediate suspected difficulties or functional deficits. Also called *prescriptive integrity.*

diameter: Bone width. In anthropometry, bone diameters are obtained to quantify frame size. Selected diameter measurements include biacromion, chest, biiliac, bitrochanter, knee, ankle, elbow, and wrist.

diaphragmatic breathing: See *breathing exercises.*

diastole: Resting phase of cardiac cycle during which cardiac muscle relaxation, chamber filling, and coronary circulation occur. See also *cardiac cycle, systole.*

difference limen: See *just noticeable difference.*

difference threshold: See *just noticeable difference.*

differential attractiveness of positions hypothesis: An explanation of positional segregation in sport, based on claim that minorities (a) tend to select positions that provide the greatest opportunities for individual rewards or achievement, or (b) consciously avoid positions that are highly competitive and offer the least likelihood of successful attainment.

differential reinforcement: Procedure of reinforcing an appropriate response in the presence of one stimulus while extinguishing an inappropriate response in the presence of another stimulus.

differentiation: 1. [bm] Mathematical process whereby a derivative of a function is computed; the process of calculating the slope of a line tangent to a function. 2. [mc] Development of a mass of homogeneous cells into specialized tissues.

diffusion: Passive exchange of fluids, gases, or solids across a barrier as a result of a concentration gradient or thermal agitation. In the lungs, the process by which the exchange of gasses between the lungs and blood occurs.

digital filter: Frequency-selective data-smoothing technique that attempts to selectively reject or attenuate the ''noise'' in a raw data signal.

digital signal: Recording of data in which the data is defined at discrete intervals in time and qualified.

digitization: Process of representing an analog signal in digital form. In cinematography the process of applying x–y coordinate values to key points on a frame of film or video data.

digitizer: Apparatus used to convert analog, or continuous, information to digital, or numeric, information. When used with film, a single frame is displayed on the apparatus, and the points indicated by the operator are digitized.

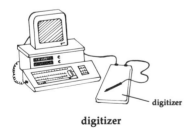

digitizer

digitizer

diplegia: Bilateral paralysis of the legs with possible involvement of the upper extremities.

diplopia: Double vision, or perception of two images at the same time while focusing on one object.

direct calorimetry: See *calorimetry*.

direct instruction: Teacher-centered instructional process. The teacher exclusively makes decisions about instructional goals, material to be learned, pace of the lesson, and level of correct response. Compare *indirect instruction*.

directional awareness: Understanding of concepts about movement direction, including such concepts as laterality and directionality.

directionality: 1. Ability to identify or project dimensions to the space external to the body. 2. Grasp of spatial concepts about the movements or locations of objects in the environment.

direct measure: In sport, a measurement of team cohesion based on the responses of team participants to questions about their perceptions of group member behaviors, interactions, and relationships that affect team climate.

direct service: Instructional opportunities or primary services provided for children under the Education of the Handicapped Act (EHA). Physical education is a direct service under the EHA, and physical, occupational, or vocational therapy are classified as related services.

disability: Impairment of physical, mental, or emotional functioning that may or may not limit the person's ability to perform certain tasks.

discipline: In education, the maintenance of behavior that is consistent with the educational goals of the specific learning situation and environment.

discounting principle: The value of intrinsic motivation is decreased when an extrinsic reward is perceived as more important than the intrinsic value of participating. See also *overjustification hypothesis*.

discourse: [pd] Communication system used during the instructional process and in the classroom.

discovery learning: Method of instruction in which the learner is encouraged to explore a wide variety of responses, but challenges and problems are gradually funneled by the instructor so that the learner eventually discovers a particular response. Also called *guided discovery learning*.

discrete skill: Motor task with a clearly defined beginning point and a clearly defined end point. Compare *continuous skill*.

discrimination: Ability to decipher variations in sensory stimuli.

discrimination weights: Set of equally sized and identical containers varying in weight, often in 5-gram intervals, which a subject must discriminate between based on weight.

discriminative motor skills model: Predicts a specific or discriminative relaxation response with biofeedback training.

discriminative stimulus: Antecedent event signaling that a response will be reinforced, thus increasing the probality that a similar response will reoccur.

displacement: See *angular displacement, linear displacement*.

dissipative structure: Natural system (physical, social, biological, or chemical) subject to friction (a nonequilibrium system) that requires energy input to remain stable. Dissipative structures are used as models for movements such as the step cycle. Examples of dissipative structures are pendula and percussion instruments.

dissociation: A characteristic of learning-disabled children; the inability to perceive things as a whole; can be social, visual, or auditory.

dissociative coping style: Mental technique, related to coping with psychological or physical stress, whereby attention is focused on external (environmental) stimuli. The person "dissociates" from, or attempts to ignore, internal sensations and feelings that may interfere with performance effectiveness. For example, runners might focus their attention on pleasant scenery rather than on the heavy breathing, sweating, and other less pleasant manifestations of physical effort. Compare *associative coping style*.

dissociative strategy: 1. Mental technique in which attention is focused on non-performance factors to distract performer from internal sensations such as discomfort or fatigue. **2.** Cognitive technique that allows for the distraction of feelings from the distress associated with hard physical work. Also called *distraction cognitive strategy*. Compare *associative strategy*.

distal: Point of a segment, bone, or muscle that is far from the axial skeleton. Compare *proximal*.

distal goal: Long-term goal.

distance curve: Plot of the extent to which some measurement increases over time. Regarding physical growth, often plots height, weight, circumference, limb length, etc., against advancing age.

distensibility: Property by which a muscle, when stretched or lengthened by an external force, will return to its original length unless stretched beyond its physiological limit.

distractibility: Extent to which environmental objects, noises, or situations interfere with an individual's ability to maintain concentration and on-task behavior.

distraction: Mental state immediately preceding arousal that can enhance or, in certain situations, impair performance, depending on the task's mental and physical demands.

distraction cognitive strategy: See *dissociative strategy*.

distress: Psychological or physiological processes harmful or unpleasant to the person. Activity associated with, or category of, stress. See also *eustress*.

distributed practice: Practice schedule with rest intervals interspersed between practice sessions. The amount of rest is relatively large, often equaling or exceeding the amount of practice. Also called *spaced practice*.

distributive justice: The distribution of rewards (e.g., salary or recognition) to recipients in accordance with their relative contributions. Unfair or inequitable distributions often result in behaviors intended to redress this injustice. See also *procedural justice, retributive justice.*

divergent inquiry: In education, the technique to encourage learning in which the teacher outlines a specific problem while learners are challenged to creatively solve the challenge with a variety of answers. Compare *convergent inquiry.*

divergent question: Type of question used to encourage problem solving or reasoning to answer a problem based on previously unencountered material. Compare *convergent question.*

doll-eye reflex: Infant's involuntary eye response of looking up when its head is flexed or of looking down when its head is extended.

dominant response: Actions that have the highest probability of occurrence based on the level of previous skill mastery. Correct, well-learned responses are dominant after task mastery, but wrong or inappropriate responses are dominant during the skill-learning period. According to social facilitation hypothesis based on drive theory, presence of an audience elicits the dominant response. Compare *nondominant response.*

DOMS: See *delayed onset muscle soreness.*

dopamine: Catecholamine neurotransmitter secreted by the central nervous system; the immediate precursor of norepinephrine; a deficiency of dopamine may result in movement disorders such as Parkinson's disease.

dorsal: Pertains to the back, such as the back of the thoracic region or of the hand.

dorsiflexion: Foot movement, articulating at the ankle, upward and toward the anterior surface of the leg. Compare *plantar flexion.*

double hemiplegia: Paralysis of four extremities, with the hand and leg on one side

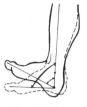

dorsiflexion

being more affected than those on opposite side.

double-knee lock: Pattern of walking or running where the knee changes from extension (at foot strike) to flexion (near midstance) to extension again (near toe-off).

double product: See *rate pressure product.*

double support phase: The portion of a cyclic locomotor skill when both legs support body weight, not necessarily evenly, as exhibited when both feet contact the ground.

Douglas bag: Type of bag used to collect expired air; used in open circuit spirometry when a computer data acquisition system is not available for measuring respiratory gas exchange.

Down syndrome: Chromosome abnormality resulting in moderate to severe mental retardation and characteristic appearance of short trunk and extremities, poor muscle tone, hyperflexibility, and congenital heart defects. Also called *trisomy 21.*

drag force: Resistive component of the fluid force acting in the same direction as the relative fluid flow past the object, resulting in a reduction in the object's velocity. Also called *air resistance.* See also *hydrodynamic drag.*

drive: Physiological condition that moves one to satisfy basic needs such as hunger or sleep.

drive theory: 1. Theory predicting a linear relationship between drive (physiological arousal) and learning. 2. Belief that performance is directly related to level of drive or activation; ostensibly, if the dominant response is the correct one, then higher drive corresponds to improved performance.

dropping out from sport: 1. Voluntary withdrawal from competitive sport that the participant had earlier voluntarily approached and shown some commitment to. 2. A dropout is a person who competed in a sport the previous year and voluntarily quit participation even though still eligible to compete; may be operationally defined in a specific situation or research study with respect to comparing persons who persist at the competitive activity and those who cease to participate.

dual-task procedure: Experimental method used to study attention demands by recording any interference in the performance of one task while a second task is performed simultaneously.

Duchenne muscular dystrophy: Pseudohypertropic, degenerative disease; the most prevalent type of muscular dystrophy, occurring primarily in males aged 4 to 7 years and affecting calf muscles and lower extremeties. Advanced cases include weakness and pronounced lordosis as the spine, pelvis, and shoulder girdle become involved.

Ductus arterious: Failure of the artery to close between the aorta and the pulmonary artery, resulting in an abnormal mixing of oxygenated and unoxygenated blood in the infant.

due process: [ad] A series of legal steps designed to protect the constitutional rights of handicapped individuals and their parents to ensure a proper educational experience.

duration: 1. Length of time a behavior persists. 2. Length of participation in a given activity.

duration of training: Daily time allotment of a training program; training must last at least 15 min per session at an optimal intensity before significant aerobic training changes occur.

duration recording: Assessment of the length of time involved in instruction, activity, waiting, and management during an instructional program or class.

dwarfism: Congenital disturbance of growth and maturation resulting in a person's being undersized. See also *achondroplasia*.

dyad: Group composed of two individuals.

dynamic analysis: Force–mass–acceleration analysis of movement in which the acceleration of the system is nonzero.

dynamic balance: Equilibrium maintained either on a moving surface or while moving the body through space.

dynamic equilibrium: The state of a system moving with zero acceleration.

dynamics: 1. Cross-disciplinary study of mechanics concerning systems in motion, including (a) an applied branch wherein concepts of change and rate of change are studied in natural phenomena, (b) a mathematical branch that uses differential equations, topology, and geometry, and (c) an experimental branch that deals in part with oscillators; latter often serves as a model for movement control in the sport sciences. 2. The field of kinematics and kinetics.

dynamic visual acuity: Sharpness of the sight when viewing moving objects or displays.

dynamogeny: The principle that energy from movement is proportional to the idea of the movement. The physical presence of another performer is a stimulus that arouses the competitive instinct. The presence of the leading performer in a race (the pacemaker), for example, can release nervous energy that, in an unpaced condition, would not be released. This effect might be compounded if a subject receives visual and auditory input from the pacemaker, possibly resulting in greater speed to the actor that inspires more effort.

dynamometer: Instrument used to measure the force or torque of a selected muscular contraction; typically operates on the principle of compression of a spring-loaded device.

dysfunction: Loss of functional ability, such as losing sensations in the lower extremities after a spinal injury.

dysfunctional aggressive behavior: In sport, an aggressive act that interferes with successful performance, such as committing a foul or intentionally contacting an opponent at the expense of meeting a goal.

dyskinesia: Condition characterized by motor restlessness, abnormal facial movements, and involuntary jerky, writhing movements.

dyslexia: Disturbance in reading ability caused by biological (particularly neurological) problems.

dysmelia: Absence of arms or legs.

dyspnea: Difficult, uncomfortable, or labored breathing; conscious awareness of breathlessness possibly due to exercise stress.

dyspraxic: Individual who has difficulty with motor planning or sequencing activities.

dysrhythmia: 1. Irregular rhythm of the cardiac cycle; may be of either atrial or ventricular origin. Also called *arrhythmia*. 2. [ad] Inability to maintain movement in conjunction with a specific rhythm or beat.

dystonia: Progressive movement disorder beginning with one foot's turning inward while walking; movements become pronounced and unusual as disease progresses; linked to a neurochemical imbalance in the basal ganglia in the brain.

early learning: 1. Beginning of the skill acquisition process. 2. Acquisition of a skill prior to physical or mental readiness and sooner than average for chronological age.

ear oximetry: Measurement of the oxygen saturation of arterialized blood; device is worn on the ear lobe, and the amount of light absorption is used as an indirect index of arterial oxygen saturation; during an exercise test, used to assess functional status in individuals who suffer from pulmonary disease where normal gas exchange and oxygen saturation is impaired.

eccentric action: Muscle action producing tension as muscle lengthens resisting segmental motion.

eccentric contraction: Muscle action producing lengthening of muscle fibers while developing tension, as in biceps during arm extension movement; a negative contraction.

ECG: See *electrocardiogram.*

echocardiography: Noninvasive diagnostic technique employed by cardiologists to evaluate heart valves and cardiac wall motion; ultrasound waves are directed through the chest wall overlying the heart, and the reflected waves are recorded on an oscilloscope or graphic recorder; the mobility and position of the external and internal structures (ventricular and atrial walls, pericardium, great vessels, and valves) can be obtained from the reflected echo waves and graphically recorded; reflected waves have varying acoustic densities and therefore produce distinct wave forms; helps in distinguishing healthy and diseased areas.

echolalia: Repetition of words, sounds, or sequences spoken by another individual.

ecological inventory: Checklist of behaviors or responses that a learner should master to achieve self-sufficiency in the natural environment.

ecological validity: Quality of a research setting indicative of its similarity to an actual performance setting.

economic opportunity set in sport: The higher a family's social class, the greater its members' capacities to acquire and possess material goods and services, so upper-class individuals have a greater number of material goods and services specific to sport than do lower-class persons; may partly explain the overrepresentation of the upper class and underrepresentation of the lower class in sport. See also *social-psychological opportunity set.*

ectomorph: Body type or classification of physical appearance characterized by tall height, slender frame, light bones, thin muscles, narrow shoulders, and long limbs.

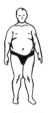  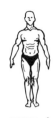

endomorph   ectomorph   mesomorph

basic body builds

ectopic beat: See *ectopic focus.*

ectopic focus: Abnormal origin point of the heart beat; normally, the sinoatrial (S-A) node initiates the action potential that produces the heart beat; occasionally, a portion of the myocardium, other than the S-A node, can initiate depolarization; happens either when the S-A node fails or different myocardial cells with physiological properties of the S-A node fire prematurely; abnormal points of generation of cardiac impulses may lie in the atria, at the junction of the atria and ventricles, or in the ventricular wall; heart beats arising from ectopic foci are dysrhythmias. Also called *ectopic beat.*

educable mentally retarded: Term used to designate a mild form of mental retardation suggesting that the person is capable of learning. See also *mildly mentally retarded.*

educational sport psychologist: Person with a certified graduate degree in sport psychology who provides information and training through lectures, presentations, or written documentation based on an educational rather than a clinical approach. Assessment instruments are used for educational purposes to enhance the growth and development of already healthy individuals. This person should have membership in a professional association that promotes the communication of scientific inquiry and practice in applied sport psychology.

EEG: See *electroencephalogram.*

effectiveness in teaching: Quality of instruction determined by systematic observation and documentation of the science of teaching to establish criteria to evaluate teacher behavior and the instructional process, and the degree to which testing accomplishes the goal of student learning.

effective target width: End-point variability of a set of aiming responses.

effector: Muscle or gland that responds to efferent (motor) neural commands.

effector mechanism: Component of an information processing system wherein the plan of response is translated into efference.

effect size: 1. Effects on student achievement based on the number and variability of students assigned to the teaching unit. **2.** Statistical term in which a standardized contrast is made between the means divided by the standard deviations.

efference: Motor neural commands descending from the brain to the periphery.

efferent copy: Hypothesized duplicate ("carbon copy") set of neural commands for movement that is sent to a comparison center where it can be used to check the response-produced feedback returning to the center.

efferent neuron: Nerve that conveys impulses outward from the central nervous system to the muscle receptors. Also called *motoneuron, motor neuron.*

efficacy: See *self-efficacy.*

efficacy expectations: See *self-efficacy.*

efficiency: Relating to human movement, the ratio of work accomplished to energy expenditure; in general, during exercise, efficiency of the human body is approximately 20% to 30%. See also *delta efficiency, theoretical efficiency.*

egocentric attributional bias: See *self-serving attributional bias.*

ego-enhancing strategy: Technique to promote attributing all success to internal causes (i.e., ability and effort). See also *attribution theory.*

ego-orientation/involvement: Extent to which sports are valued as personally important to the participant. Often related to sex differences in that sport success, in general, may be more important, and thus have greater implications for their self-concept, for males than for females.

ego-protecting strategy: Technique for attributing all failures to external causes. See also *attribution theory.*

EIB: See *exercise induced bronchospasm.*

ejection fraction: Percentage of the end diastolic volume that is pumped from the ventricle with each beat; generally 55% to 75% of the end diastolic volume; remains fairly constant or increases slightly as one goes from rest to exercise; absolute amount of blood ejected per beat increases, but since the absolute end diastolic volume increases, the proportion of blood ejected from the ventricle does not change significantly; in heart failure, decreases to below 50% of the end diastolic volume.

elaboration: In education, the formation of strategies to enhance learning, such as forming mental images or relating new information to previously learned material.

elastic energy: Potential energy developed when an object is stretched beyond its natural length. See also *potential energy.*

elasticity: Property of muscle in which a muscle will recoil when stretched by its antagonist.

electrocardiogram (ECG): Graphic illustration of the electrical current generated by excitation of the heart muscle; each normal cardiac cycle is represented by P, QRS, and T waves; used to evaluate cardiac electrical activity during resting and exercise conditions; for diagnostic purposes, twelve leads are evaluated that provide electrical activity of the heart from several different views.

P wave shows depolarization of the atria,
QRS wave shows depolarization of the ventricles,
T wave shows repolarization of the ventricles.

electrocortical arousal: Measurement of

electrical activity in the brain cortex that elicits an electroencephalogram (EEG).

electrode: Probe that measures a voltage field.

electroencephalogram (EEG): Recording of electrical brain wave patterns, used to determine dysfunctions or disruptions in the brain.

electrogoniometer: Instrument that provides an electrical signal that is converted to represent the relative angular movement at a joint.

electromechanical delay: Time period between the onset of electrical activity in a muscle and the first measurable tension.

electromyogram: Tracing that represents the activity of the electrically excitable membranes of the muscle.

electromyography (EMG): Measurement of the electrical activity of the excitable membranes of a muscle or group of muscles.

electron transport system (ETS): Final common pathway of aerobic metabolism; consists of a series of membrane-bound iron-proteins in the mitochondria that transfer electrons from coenzyme carriers (FAD and NAD) to oxygen, which is the final electron acceptor; water is formed as a by-product; the electrochemical energy released is harnessed or coupled to the formation of ATP from ADP and Pi; approximately 90% of the ATP formed aerobically happens this way; constitutes the respiratory chain. See also *oxidative phosphorylation*.

eliciting stimulus: Antecedent event that generally will evoke a response or behavior.

embedded referent: In temporal analysis of skill, specification of one action in relation to another; for example, concluding that knee extension follows plantar flexion.

embryo: The human organism from conception until approximately the end of the second prenatal month.

EMG: See *electromyography*.

emit: Execute a response spontaneously.

emotion: Reaction to a stimulus event, ei-

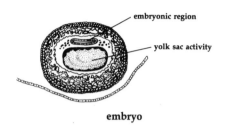

embryonic region

yolk sac activity

embryo

ther actual or imagined, involving change in the performer's viscera and musculature; experienced subjectively in characteristic ways; expressed through facial changes and behavioral tendencies; may mediate and energize subsequent behaviors.

empirical: Use of observations of, or experience with, a particular event to collect research data.

enabling objectives: Description of child performance that will contribute directly to the achievement of terminal goals.

encephalitis: Inflammatory condition of the brain caused by an acute viral infection and high body temperatures.

encoding: Transformation of perceptual input into a form in which it can be stored in the central nervous system (memory).

encoding specificity principle: Principle that the more similar a practice situation and test situation, the better the retention exhibited in a test. For motor skills, the relationship is most applicable to practice and performance testing of closed skills.

encopresis: Inability to control one's bowels.

end diastolic volume: Volume of blood in the ventricles just prior to ventricular contraction; at the end of the filling phase of diastole; absolute volume is related to the force of contraction of the ventricles during systole.

endergonic reaction: Nonspontaneous reaction that stores or absorbs energy from the environment.

endogenous: Occurring from internal as opposed to external, or environmental, factors. Compare *exogenous*.

endomorph: Body type or classification of physical appearance characterized by short height, heavy bones, soft muscles, medium shoulder width, wide hips, and stocky limbs.

endorphins: Naturally occurring substances manufactured in the brain that regulate emotion and pain perception. Have been invoked to explain euphoric sensations experienced during vigorous exercise, such as "runner's high," imperviousness to pain, "flow," and peak performance in sport. Also called *beta endorphins*.

end systolic volume: The volume of blood remaining in the ventricles after the active contraction phase (systole) of the cardiac cycle.

endurance: Ability to perform physical work for extended periods of time; cardiovascular endurance is influenced by an individual's $\dot{V}O_2max$ and the percentage of $\dot{V}O_2max$ at which steady-rate exercise can be maintained; muscular endurance is influenced by circulation and oxygen availability.

endurance fitness: Capability to perform prolonged aerobic exercise.

energy: Capacity to do work; measured in joules. See also *kinetic energy, potential energy, strain energy*.

energy balance: Equilibrium between energy intake (caloric consumption of food) and energy output (caloric expenditure predominantly in basal and work metabolism); there is no net gain or loss of body weight or body fat.

energy expenditure: The amount of energy liberated over a period of time; calculated using the product of oxygen consumption and caloric equivalent corresponding to the respiratory exchange ratio ($\dot{V}O_2$ L/min • caloric equivalent); expressed in work-equivalent units (1 kcal = 426.7 kg).

enthalpy: A system's energy change, taking pressure and volume changes into account.

entrainment: Mutual synchronization of two limit cycle oscillators in interval, permitting one to lead or lag the other. The synchronized oscillators provide a model for human interlimb coordination for the dynamical perspective.

entropy: Random, disordered form of energy; not available to do work. See also *second law of thermodynamics*.

environment: **1.** Factors external to the body when making a movement response that affect performance such as speed and direction of movement, position in space, and postural awareness. **2.** [pd] Summation of all the variables that affect the learner's performance, including previous behavior, sensory stimulation, feedback, and reinforcement.

environmental focus: Selectively attending to externally-derived input.

epicritic sensibility: Specific form of kinesthetic sensitivity wherein characteristics as opposed to affective qualities are perceived.

epilepsy: Disturbance in the electrochemical activity in the brain; characterized by, or triggers, seizures and/or convulsions.

epinephrine: Hormone secreted by the adrenal medulla in response to sympathetic nervous system (SNS) stimulation and causing the same effects as direct SNS stimulation; exercise stimulates its release and causes an increase in the rate and force of cardiac contraction (cardiac output), constriction of renal and cutaneous arterioles, dilation of skeletal and cardiac muscle arterioles, mobilization of fat from adipose cells, glycogenolysis, accelerated rate and depth of breathing, and bronchodilation; a catecholamine. Also called *adrenaline*.

epiphyseal growth plate: Area at the ends of long bones, between the epiphysis and shaft, where new bone cells are deposited, and allowing for growth in bone length. Also called *growth plate*.

equal educational opportunity: [ad] Education provided to handicapped children that enables them to attain benefits equal to, or educational goals consistent with, those of the nonhandicapped.

equally effective education: [ad] Education that is not identical to nonhandicapped education but provides the opportunity to achieve program goals and objectives in the least restrictive environment.

equifinality: The characteristic of a system wherein it always returns to its resting state, irrespective of its initial condition.

equilibration process: Alternation between periods of stability and instability as an individual moves through developmental stages. Instability is brought about by imbalance between the individual's mental structure and the environment, and the stability is brought about by consolidation, or mixing, of developmental stages for improved performance.

equilibrium: 1. The balanced or stabilized state of a system that is not being accelerated. **2.** System in which the sum of the external forces and torques is zero. **3.** Ability to maintain or control an upright body position.

equilibrium point hypothesis: Suggestion that active movement is controlled by shifts (associated with setting the stretch reflex threshold) in the equilibrium state of the motor system. Hence, muscle behaves like a nonlinear spring, and movement speed is altered by the nervous system specifying the equilibrium point shifts.

equilibrium reaction: Involuntary curving of the spine upward to maintain balance, undertaken by an infant when the supporting surface is tilted. Also called *tilting reaction*.

ergogenic aid: Any substance or technique apart from actual physical or mental training that improves athletic performance by either delaying fatigue or increasing work capacity; examples include carbohydrate loading, steroids, and blood doping; many such techniques are banned in competitive events.

ergometry: Technique of measuring work output by means of an apparatus that may be calibrated and produces measurable units of work (e.g., bicycle ergometer, arm-crank ergometer).

ergonomics: 1. The science of fitting the workplace to the worker. **2.** Biomechanical approach to workplace design.

error: 1. Deviation from a target or ideal, varying in amount or nature. **2.** An inappropriate choice. See also *absolute error, constant error, variable error*.

error control: Rate and elimination of inaccurate or inappropriate responses as related to skill acquisition.

error-free learning: A characteristic of programmed learning indicating that the skill acquisition is structured so that the learner experiences continual success, without error.

error-full learning: Trial-and-error process of motor skill acquisition in which a learner makes a variety of responses in early learning, including errors, but gradually learns the appropriate response for a situation.

error score: Quantitative measurement indicating deviation of a performance from a target or ideal.

erythrocyte: Blood cell containing hemoglobin and responsible for oxygen transport; carbon dioxide and carbon monoxide are also transported by erythrocytes. Also callled *red blood cell*.

escape training: Teaching a learner to emit behavior to terminate the circumstances or extract himself or herself from unpleasant or aversive situations.

essential variable: See *coordination variable*.

etiology: The study of the origin or cause of a disability, condition, or disease, including genetic, physiological, environmental, or psychological factors.

ETS: See *electron transport system*.

eustress: Nonspecific body response to a

demand of a pleasant nature to which the person must adapt, e.g., excitement, love, or happiness. See also *distress*.

evaluation apprehension: Arousing or anxiety-provoking effect of an audience or coactors on the performer who feels threatened from being evaluated by one or more of the observers. Positive or negative outcomes from this evaluation are anticipated.

evaluation potential: Perception or anticipation that one or more members of an audience will evaluate performance, likely leading to some positive or negative outcome.

evaporation: Conversion of liquid into vapor and its escape as vapor; the cooling of the body as a result of sweating is actually a result of the evaporation of perspiration from the body rather than of the actual sweating.

event recording: Cumulative documentation of the frequency with which a specific measurable behavior or response occurs within a designated time frame or interval.

eversion: Movement of a body part outward, such as a lateral movement of the sole of the foot. Compare *inversion*.

eversion

evoked potential: Electrical discharge recorded in one part of the nervous system (usually the cerebral cortex) as a result of a specific stimulus to another part of the nervous system.

excellence incentives: Opportunities for a competitor to demonstrate task mastery for its own sake or to perform the task better than anyone else.

exceptional: A term used to designate a person who deviates, above or below, from the norm, and who requires special programming to meet individual needs.

excess postexercise oxygen consumption: Oxygen consumption during recovery that is above normal resting values; comprised of a rapid phase (formerly called the "alactacid" phase) and a slow phase (formerly called the "lactacid" phase); replenishes depleted muscle stores of ATP and creatine phosphate, restores oxygen in muscle myoglobin, replenishes dissolved oxygen in the blood and tissues, and reconverts lactate to glycogen; reflects increased temperature, work of the respiratory musculature and heart, and elevated levels of epinephrine, norepinephrine, and thyroxine; historically called *oxygen debt*. Also called *recovery oxygen consumption*.

excitation contraction coupling: Process that initiates muscle contraction; neural stimulation of a muscle fiber causes an action potential to spread across and through the entire fiber, initiating the release of calcium and subsequent crossbridge formation between the actin and myosin filaments, followed by muscle contraction; the neural excitation is functionally and physically coupled to muscular contraction.

exemplary modeling: Correct execution of a skilled performance by a model.

exercise adherence: See *adherence*.

exercise induced bronchospasm (EIB): Constriction of the air passages in the lungs due to spasmodic contractions of the bronchiole smooth muscle brought on by the functional and physical stresses of exercise; the precise origin of the exercise induced constriction is not well understood.

exercise prescription: An individual program of exercise based on an individual's level of fitness and health status; should consider exercise intensity (e.g., percentage of maximum heart rate or rating of perceived exertion), frequency per week (e.g., three times/week), duration (e.g., 30 min/session), and mode (e.g., jogging).

exercise psychology: 1. Study of the psychological factors underlying participation and adherence in physical activity programs; partially explains or predicts differences between the exercise participant and nonparticipant. **2.** Application of psychological factors to the promotion, explanation, maintenance, and enhancement of behaviors related to physical work capacity. Related to, but not synonymous with, health and ergonomic (work) concerns.

exercise thallium scan: Technique of injecting a small amount of radioactive 201 thallium intravenously and visualizing its progress in the blood stream using a gamma camera; thallium will not perfuse into the ischemic or necrotic areas of myocardial tissue; therefore, this technique can be employed to assess the amount of viable tissue in patients with myocardial infarction; usually done in conjunction with graded exercise stress testing.

exergonic reaction: Spontaneous chemical reaction in the body resulting in liberation of energy; no energy input is required beyond activation energy.

exogenous: Occurring from an external cause, such as cultural deprivation, rather than an internal cause. Compare *endogenous*.

expectancy: Probability that a certain reinforcer will occur as a function of a specific behavior in a particular situation.

expiratory reserve volume: Additional volume of air beyond the normal expired tidal volume that can be forcibly expired from the lung; with exercise, the tidal volume increases, and part of the increase is as a result of utilizing part of the expiratory reserve volume; ranges from 1.0 to 1.5 L for an average male under resting conditions and may be reduced by 50% with exercise.

extending tasks: Expansion of task content by adding various dimensions, components, solutions, or skill components.

extension: Movement at a joint that causes an increase in the relative angle between the two segments. Compare *flexion*.

external attentional style: See *attentional style*.

external control: Perception that external factors such as task difficulty and luck determine performance outcomes. See also *attribution theory*.

external evaluation: Independent evaluation of a person or project to determine whether predetermined goals or objectives were attained.

external feedback: 1. Information received as the result of a response or act from an outside source. **2.** Feedback obtained through an external sense receptor, usually the eye or ear.

external force: Force outside of a defined system.

external imagery: Mental strategy in which one views one's own performance from the perspective of an external observer. Also called *third-person imagery*, *visual imagery*. Compare *internal imagery*.

external respiration: See *pulmonary ventilation*.

external rotation: Movement of a body part occurring when the posterior surface of the part is rotated away from the midline of the body. Compare *internal rotation*.

externals: Persons who tend to attribute their outcomes to outside forces such as luck, chance, or other people, and tend to feel less responsible for, and hence less motivated by, performance outcomes. For example, consistent failure will not demotivate externals to the same extent as it would internals. However, externals are also less motivated by success, presumably because they do not feel responsible for the success outcome and/or do not predict it will reoccur. Compare *internals*.

exteroreceptor: Sensory receptor that responds to stimuli outside the body, as in vision or audition.

extinction: Behavior management technique designed to weaken, decrease, or eliminate an inappropriate behavior by removing or discontinuing reinforcers that follow that behavior.

extrasystole: See *premature contractions*.

extrinsic: Coming from the outside, such as providing external motivation to complete a task by praising a student. Compare *intrinsic*.

extrinsic feedback: Information received as the result of a response or act from an outside source, typically not inherent in the task. Compare *intrinsic feedback*.

extrinsic mastery: A person's motivation to exhibit skilled performance due to the anticipation of an external reward. For example, a sport coach may advise his or her athletes that they will be rewarded only after properly demonstrating a certain strategy. Compare *intrinsic mastery*.

extrinsic motivation: Use of external rewards such as trophies or money to motivate behavior, using the assumption that performance can be controlled by external forces (e.g., money, trophies, and recognition), and if these forces were not present, the person would stop participating or would participate on a reduced level. Compare *intrinsic motivation*.

extropunitive behavior: Aggressive behavior against another person. Compare *intropunitive behavior*.

extroversion: Tendency to be outwardly expressive, active, and involved socially. Compare *introversion*.

eye dominance: Consistent preference to sight or to visually fixate objects with one eye instead of the other.

eye–hand coordination: Ability to perform hand movements precisely, based on visual information. Also called *hand–eye coordination*.

eye preference: Choice to sight or visually fixate with one eye instead of the other; preferred eye may or may not be the dominant eye.

F

facioscapulohumeral muscular dystrophy: Type of muscular dystrophy affecting males and females throughout life that is progressive and debilitating, although characterized by periods of remission and normal life span. Primarily involves muscles of the face and upper extremities.

fading: Behavior management strategy that involves the gradual removal of a stimulus, to develop certain behaviors or skills.

Techniques such as verbal instructions or physical guidance (prompts) are commonly used.

falling from glory theory: Assumption that athletes who reach optimal personal achievement early in their careers will have relatively more emotional pain and trauma in retirement because no other activity ensures them the social and personal esteem that sport did. The result is a poor adjustment to retirement.

false negative exercise test: Graded exercise stress test that is interpreted as normal but the individual actually has coronary heart disease; thus, the ability of a graded exercise stress test to diagnose coronary heart disease is not 100% accurate.

false positive exercise test: Graded exercise stress test that indicates myocardial ischemia (e.g., significant S-T segment depression) but, as further evaluation shows, the individual does not have significant coronary heart disease.

farsightedness: See *hyperopia*

fartlek training: From Swedish, meaning "speed play"; a method of interval training that does not use set times and distances but uses the natural terrain to dictate exercise intensity; can train both anaerobic and aerobic energy systems.

fast-twitch glycolytic fiber (FG): Large skeletal muscle fiber innervated by alpha-I motor neuron and characterized by a fast contraction time and low oxidative (aerobic) and high glycolytic (anaerobic) metabolic capacity; recruited primarily for high intensity contractions such as utilized in short distance sprint or power lifting. Also called *Type IIB fiber.*

fast-twitch oxidative glycolytic fiber (FOG): Large skeletal muscle fiber innervated by alpha-I motor neuron and characterized by fast contraction time and medium oxidative (aerobic) and high glycolytic (anaerobic) metabolic capacity; recruited primarily for high-intensity contractions such as middle-distance running events. Also called *Type IIA fiber.*

fat-free body weight: The weight of body tissue excluding extractable fat; equals body mass minus fat mass (essential plus storage fat).

fear of failure: 1. Component of achievement motivation theory that explains a person's predisposition to approach or avoid a competitive situation. It is the conscious motive to avoid experiencing the perception of failure and governs decisions about whether to engage in activities. **2.** Anticipation of a failure (negative) outcome, leading to heightened anxiety prior to engaging in the feared task, resulting in self-inflicted poorer performance.

fear of success (success phobia): 1. Component of achievement motivation theory that explains predisposition to approach or avoid a competitive situation; motive of an otherwise high achievement-oriented person who may suffer a self-inflicted decrement in performance and motivation during competition for psychological or social reason. **2.** Learned disposition resulting from social rejection and, for females, apprehension about perceived loss of femininity due to achieving; function of anticipated negative consequences of succeeding, such as higher expectations for future performance. **3.** Anticipation of negative consequences to success in achievement-oriented situations. Also called *motive to avoid success, success phobia.*

feature detection: Identification of a specified characteristic of a stimulus (such as size, orientation, shape, movement) permitting classification based on that characteristic.

feedback: 1. Any kind of information received as result of a particular response or act. **2.** Afferent neural information produced by sensory receptors as a result of movement (sensory feedback). **3.** The means by which input and output are linked to regulate a system.

feedforward: Information sent prior to execution of a movement, to eliminate delays inherent in feedback systems; derived from either an exteroceptive sensory modality or within the central nervous system, usually vision or audition. See also *central efferent monitoring, corollary discharge, efferent copy*.

feel-better phenomenon: See *psychological well-being*.

female apologetic: Female athlete who espouses more traditional or conventional sex-role attitudes about women's role in society, in effect who apologizes for engaging in a nontraditional (i.e., historically male-dominated) physical activity.

ferritin: Storage form of iron in the tissues (especially in the liver); formed when iron carried in the blood is taken up in the tissues and combined with apoferritin, a globular protein to form a crystalline protein; used as a clinical measure to investigate the origin of anemia.

fetus: The developing human organism from the end of the eighth week after conception to birth.

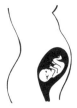

fourth month

fetus

FG: See *fast-twitch glycolytic fiber*.

fiber area: Measure of the proportion of space taken up by a particular fiber type or types.

fiber type composition: The makeup of a muscle that allows for classification into three types of muscle fiber (Type I, Type IIa, Type IIb); classification based on the enzymatic and protein composition, mechanical characteristics, contraction rate, and metabolic capabilities.

fibrillation: Rapid and irregular ectopic arrhythmia of either the atria or ventricles; in atrial fibrillation numerous small, weak depolarization waves spread throughout the atria, no discernible P waves are evident, QRS-T configuration is normal; ventricular fibrillation is characterized by strong and then weak highly irregular depolarization currents such that no pattern of atrial or ventricular waves can be recognized; if normal heart rhythm is not restored, ventricular fibrillation is fatal, as there is no effective pumping of blood from the heart.

Fick equation: Formula describing relationship between cardiac output, oxygen consumption, and arteriovenous oxygen difference:

$$\text{cardiac output (ml/min)} = \{[VO_2\,(\text{ml/min})]/\text{a-vO}_2 \text{ difference (ml/100 ml blood)}\} \times 100.$$

Fiedler's contingency theory: See *contingency theory*.

field dependence: Characteristic wherein the performer of a task tends to be influenced by irrelevant factors in the perceptual field.

field independence: Characteristic wherein a person can ignore irrelevant factors in the perceptual field in performing a task.

field of vision: Expanse of space measured in degrees that is visible with both eyes while looking straight ahead; 180° is considered normal.

figural aftereffect: Distorted perception of a visual display due to maintenance of stability in figure–ground relationships. After an inspection display is fixated, the effect occurs when gaze is shifted to a test display. For example, judgment of a distance in the test display might be distorted.

figure–ground perception: Ability to see an object of interest as distinct from the background.

filter mechanism: See *perceptual filter*.

fine motor skill: Type of skill performed by the small musculature, particularly of the hands and fingers.

finger agnosia: Inability to correctly identify familiar persons or objects by touch. Also called *tactile agnosia*.

finger dexterity: Ability to manipulate tiny objects, primarily with the fingers, or to control the fingers to tap or type in a skillful, smooth manner.

finger spelling: Communication method that spells out words by utilizing various motions of the hands and fingers.

finger tapping: Experimental task requiring a subject to tap a response key with one or more fingers repetitively.

first-class lever: Simple machine in which a fulcrum or axis of rotation is placed between the motive force and the resistive force.

first law of thermodynamics: Energy can be neither created nor destroyed, but only be transformed from one form to another; e.g., chemical energy in food converted to mechanical energy for muscle contraction.

first-order control system: Relationship between activation of a control device and movement of an indicator (such as on a display screen), where controller force is mapped to indicator velocity. Also called *velocity control system.* See also *zero-order control system.*

first-order traits: From Cattell's Personality Factor Questionnaire (16PF), the 16 fundamental structures of personality. Also called *primary factors, source traits.* Compare *surface traits.*

first-person imagery: See *internal imagery.*

fitness: One's capacity to perform work (exercise) of a specific intensity and duration; may be aerobic, anaerobic, or muscular. See also *anaerobic fitness, cardiovascular fitness, endurance fitness, strength fitness.*

Fitts' law: Fitts' law relates movement distance and movement precision.

$$MT = a + b \log 2 (2A/W)$$

where MT = movement time
A = movement amplitude
W = target width
a and b = constants

fixed-interval schedule: Schedule of administering reinforcement in which the first occurrence of the target behavior is reinforced after a designated time interval elapses. See also *reinforcement schedule.*

fixed-rate schedule: Schedule of administering reinforcement in which a behavior is reinforced after an unvarying number of responses. See also *reinforcement schedule.*

flaccid: Characterized by extreme weakness or a lack of muscle tone. See also *paralysis.*

flexibility: The range of motion about a joint.

flexion: Movement at a joint that causes a decrease in the relative angle between the two segments. Compare *extension.*

flight period: The period of time when a body has no contact with the ground; that is, when the body is a projectile.

flooding: Exposure to anxiety-provoking stimuli while preventing the occurrence of avoidance responses. Subject's prolonged exposure (i.e., flooding) to the anxiety-arousing stimuli (e.g., receiving unpleasant information feedback) in the absence of unpleasant experiences or feelings (e.g., competing in tense situations) will purportedly extinguish the anxiety. These experiences may be real or imagined, experienced together or separately.

floor effect: Existence of some minimal performance level, such as zero time or zero error, beyond which performance cannot improve. This is a function of the performance measure but can mistakenly imply that learning has stopped.

flow: 1. [pd] Movement concept; allows the performer to initiate and complete actions such as swinging a bat (free flow) or stopping or restraining actions such as running within a boundary (bound flow). Also called *pacing.* 2. [sp] See *state of flow.*

fluid mechanics: Branch of mechanics that involves the effects of fluids, primarily air and water, on moving objects.

flutter: Rapid but regular ectopic dysrhythmia predominantly of the atria; no discernible P waves are present, but F (flutter) waves with a characteristic sawtooth shape are; QRS-T configuration is normal and typically related to the flutter waves in a 2:1, 3:1, or 4:1 type pattern; atrial flutter indicates an abnormal heart.

focal seizure: See *jacksonian seizure*.

focused attention: Direction of the sensory and central nervous systems such that processing of a certain stimulus or set of relevant cues is facilitated. Width of the attentional band is variable, and focused attention implies a narrowing of the band.

focused awareness: During peak performance, optimal concentration is predominantly immersed in the activity, resulting in the automatic psychological adjustment to task-relevant cues; manifested by complete absorption in the movement task, and often includes altered perceptions about time, space, and the quality of the experience.

focusing: Concentrating on a given stimulus even under conditions of distracting stimuli.

FOG: See *fast-twitch oxidative glycolytic fiber*.

foot contact: In gait, the initial point at which any part of the foot contacts the ground.

foot dominance: Consistent preference for use of one foot instead of the other foot.

foot flat: In gait, period when the foot is flat on the ground.

foot preference: Person's choice to use one foot rather than the other for a given task. It may or may not be the dominant foot.

foot strike: Contact of a foot or feet with a surface in a locomotor skill after a period of flight or recovery from a preceding step.

force: An action, push or pull, that causes a change in the state of motion of an object; the product of the mass of an object and its linear acceleration. Force is measured in newtons (N).

force arm: See *moment arm*.

force concept: Concept that emphasizes the performer's understanding of variations of movements that are heavy and firm or soft and light.

force couple: Two non-colinear forces, equal in magnitude and acting in opposite directions, producing rotation about an axis.

$$\text{Couple} = F \times d$$
$$= F \times 2r$$

where F = force
d = distance between the forces
r = 1/2 the distance between the forces

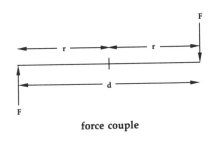

force couple

forced expiratory volume (FEV$_{1.0}$): Dynamic measure of lung function; expressed as a percentage of the vital capacity that can be expired in one second; an indication of the expiratory power and resistance to air movement in the lungs.

forced responding: Type of physical guidance or prompt that provides kinesthetic cues by moving the learner through the correct procedure during response execution.

forced-pace task: Motor skill wherein the environment dictates how and when the performer initiates action.

force platform: A flat, usually rectangular, device designed to measure the three-dimensional components and point of application of a contact force applied to the device's upper surface.

force–velocity relationship: The relationship between tension developed by a muscle or muscle group and the velocity of shortening or lengthening of a muscle; states that as the velocity of movement increases, the total tension produced decreases.

foreperiod: Period of time between a ready signal and presentation of the stimulus in an experimental trial.

forgetting: Failure to retain a skill or information that has been learned. Compare *retention*.

formal operations stage: Piaget's fourth stage of cognitive development, characterized by (a) deduction by hypothesis, (b) formulation of laws, (c) systematic approach to problems, and (d) abstract ideas. See also *concrete operations stage, preoperations stage, sensorimotor stage*.

formative assessment: Evaluation of a child's form or technique in relation to a defined model or standard of performance.

form constancy: Person's ability to recognize a shape or form as the same regardless of its orientation, size, color, or the context.

form drag: Drag force that is dependent primarily on the cross-sectional area of an object and its shape. Also called *profile drag*.

form perception: Ability to recognize shapes, forms, and symbols presented in a variety of formats.

forward chaining: See *shaping*.

fovea: Small central area of the retina in which vision is most distinct.

foveal demanding stimulus: See *central demanding stimulus*.

fractionated reaction time: Reaction time measurement that is divided into component parts based on neurological function. The components include reception time, optomotor integration time, motor outflow time (premotor time), and motor time.

fragmentation: Regarding educational groups, a reference to a student participating in an activity alone and separately when the large group could be participating in the task at the same time.

Frankfort plane: Imaginary flat surface passing through the eye socket at its lowest point and the margin of the ear canal at its highest point; the eye–ear plane.

Frank-Starling mechanism: Force of the ventricular contraction during systole is a direct function of the resting end diastolic fiber length; the greater the ventricular filling, the greater the stretch on the ventricular cardiac fibers, the greater the force of ventricular contraction; partial mechanistic determinant of stroke volume.

free body diagram: Stick-figure drawing of a system, isolated from its surroundings, showing all forces resulting from the interaction of the system and its surroundings.

free energy: Energy that is available (free) to do work; of primary importance in biological reactions such as muscle contractions.

free operant training: Development or maintenance of behaviors through the delivery of a positive reinforcer after a response is emitted.

free recall: In memory research, permitting subjects to remember items or movements learned in a series in any order. See also *serial recall*.

free recall learning: Learning strategy that allows the learner to repeat the movement in the time period after instruction has been terminated.

frequency of training: Number of training sessions on a daily, weekly, or monthly basis; minimum of three training sessions per week are thought to be needed to obtain a training effect.

friction: Force that resists the movement of one surface over another.

frontal plane: The axis that divides the body into anterior and posterior parts.

front facing: The position in throwing when the thrower's shoulders rotate to a position facing (parallel with) the target.

Frostig Movement Skills Test Battery: Norm-referenced assessment, for children from 6 to 12 years of age, to evaluate sensory-motor development. The battery contains 12 tests of fine and gross motor skill to assess coordination, balance, visually guided movement, strength, and flexibility. Reliability, based on the common factor variance from a factor analysis of results from seven age groups, ranges from .44 to .88.

frustration–aggression–displacement hypothesis: The contention that frustration causes aggression. Aggressive behavior will be displaced onto another person or object if the subject cannot respond directly to the source. In a later reformulation, frustration creates a readiness to respond aggressively but can be modified by learning.

fulcrum: Pivot point or center of rotation of a lever.

full-wave rectified electromyogram: Electromyographic signal in which all negative raw signals are made positive.

functional ability: The level of physical fitness or motor performance that is needed to function to achieve practical skills.

functional adaptation: Modification of the demands of a task or the use of assistive devices to allow participation in an activity.

functional aggressive behavior: Aggressive or assertive behavior that facilitates successful performance, such as blocking a shot or rebounding.

functional attribution model: Posits that the motivation to maintain or improve feelings of self-esteem is central to explaining the causes of one's performance outcomes. See also *attribution model, self-serving attributional bias*. Compare *cognitive attribution model*.

functional leg length: See *leg length*.

functional relationship: The cause and effect of a relationship between an independent and dependent variable. A functional relationship is demonstrated if the behavior changes when the contingency is applied, reapplied, or withdrawn.

function generator: See *pattern generator*.

Fundamental Motor Pattern Assessment Instrument: Criterion-referenced assessment of fundamental locomotor and manipulative skills. Five skills can be evaluated into three levels of development. Test–retest reliability is rated at 88.6%, and inter-rater reliability ranges from 80.0% to 95.0% agreement.

gain score: The score by which the post-test score is predicted from a regression of the posttest on the pretest. Used when subjects to be compared are equal or similar at the start of instruction or before some treatment is introduced.

gait: Sequence of body movements in which the body is first supported by one limb (or one set of limbs) on the ground and then by the other.

gait pattern: The spatial-temporal (space-time) relationship exhibited by the legs during locomotion.

galloping: The locomotor pattern wherein one foot takes the lead to step forward and the trailing foot closes with a leaping step; the landing of the leaping step is even with the lead foot; the pattern is repeated with the same foot always leading.

Gamma-Ray Spectrometry: Technique for measuring the naturally occurring K-40 (body potassium) by using a whole-body counter or isotope dilution; measurement of potassium serves as an index of fat-free body mass and can be used in the calculation of percent body fat.

gamma system: One of two pathways by which the central nervous system controls muscle length. Efferent output is via small-diameter axons called ''gammamotoneurons'' to contractile fibers in the muscle spindles.

gender identity: The affiliation with being male or female that influences one's roles, behaviors, and thoughts in society that is consistent with society's expectations of the particular gender. Also called *sex-role expectancy.*

general intellectual functioning: Assessment of intelligence or performance on a standardized IQ test.

generalization: 1. Inferences made to similar larger populations or situations from a smaller unit or sample that was investigated. **2.** [ad] Transfer of functional or relevant behaviors that are never directly trained and are similar to originally trained behaviors.

generalized motor program: Group of muscle commands formed and stored in the central nervous system, containing the information necessary to carry out a class of skilled movements.

general motion: Movements that are combinations of linear and angular motion.

general motor ability (GMA): Hypothesized ability that is global in regard to motor aptitude, such that a person high in general motor ability would perform or acquire any motor task more quickly than a person low in general motor ability.

general to specific: Progression of motor skill development from mass, uncontrolled movements to those that are voluntary and coordinated.

general trait anxiety: See *trait anxiety.*

genetic disposition: Tendency to develop a disease or condition, based on inheritance, if an individual encounters certain environmental conditions. Hence, a genetic disposition for an allergic condition is manifested only with exposure and sensitization to an allergen.

genetics: Biological study of heredity or features transmitted in chromosomes from parent to child.

genotype: The genetic makeup of an individual.

gestation age: The length of time the developing human organism remains in the uterus; usually described in number of weeks, beginning with conception.

giftedness: Cognitive (intellectual) superiority, creativity, and motivation of sufficient magnitude to distinguish the child from her or his peer group.

girth: Circumference of body segment; selected measures include neck, shoulders, biceps, buttocks, thigh, calf, and ankle; may be used to help determine somatotype and to predict percent body fat.

glaucoma: Condition in which there is excessive internal pressure on the eyeball; if untreated, will result in blindness.

glucagon: Hormone secreted by the pancreas that works antagonistically to insulin; primary function is to raise the level of glucose in the blood by stimulating glycogenolysis and glyconeogenesis in the liver; also mobilizes free fatty acids from adipose cells; levels increase with exercise.

gluconeogenesis: The formation of glycogen or glucose in the liver from energy substrates other than carbohydrates (i.e., fats and proteins); process aids in maintaining glucose levels during endurance events when glycogen stores may be depleted.

glucose–alanine cycle: A form of gluconeogenesis; the amino acid alanine is formed from the breakdown of glucose in muscle cells with input from other amino acids and is transported to the liver where it serves to complement as a precursor for the formation of glucose; helps to maintain blood glucose levels in prolonged exercise.

glucose polymer: Chain of glucose molecules; product of corn starch metabolism; used in glucose replacement drinks, as they have been shown to be quickly absorbed into the blood stream; aids in maintaining blood glucose levels during prolonged exercise.

glucostatic theory: The theory that when blood glucose levels fall too low, stimulation of the satiety centers of the brain decreases, leading to feelings of hunger; hypothesis related to a mechanism of appetite control.

glycogen: The storage form for carbohydrates in the body; stored in skeletal muscle and the liver; a highly branched molecule made up of glucose units bonded to one another; depletion of this substrate as a result of prolonged (generally greater than 2 hours), high-intensity exercise is associated with the onset of fatigue.

glycogen depletion: With endurance-type exercise that exceeds 2 hours and is relatively high in intensity, the stores of glycogen in the muscle and liver become decreased as this preferred fuel source is utilized; leads to feelings of "hitting the wall" as the stores are exhausted.

glycogenolysis: The breakdown of glycogen to supply glucose for glycolysis; an enzyme-catalyzed series of reactions breaks the glucose subunits off of the glycogen "tree"; process aids in maintaining blood glucose levels during prolonged exercise.

glycolysis: The energy pathway responsible for the initial catabolism of glucose or glycogen; results in a net production of 2 or 3 ATP, respectively; takes place in the cytoplasm of the cell; can operate without the presence of oxygen; results in either pyruvic acid (aerobic glycolysis) or lactic acid (anaerobic glycolysis); primary metabolic pathway for all-out high-intensity exercise lasting between 30 s and 3 min.

GMA: See *general motor ability.*

goal: Anticipated outcome of an act or acts. See also *competitive goal, outcome goal, performance goal.*

goal aggression: Intentional infliction of injury against another person with the purpose of causing physical harm (injury or pain). Usually accompanied by anger. Also called *hostile aggression, reactive aggression.*

goal ball: Competitive game for the visually impaired using auditory stimuli in an air-filled ball. Performers attempt to catch or intercept the ball before it crosses a goal.

goal-directed behavior: Action initiated by the need to achieve a goal. It is affected

goal ball

by one's evaluation of one's own abilities and an estimate of the most effective behaviors for attaining a goal.

goal proximity: The time period allotted for reaching a goal. Goal proximity is typically labeled as proximal, intermediate, or distal.

goal setting: Perceiving some desirable outcome and then planning a set of actions to achieve this end. The outcome may be long-term (a season or year), intermediate (a month or several weeks), short-term (within a week), or immediate (within 24 hours). Its purposes are to motivate and focus the person's attention and effort. See also *interval goal-setting*.

Golgi tendon organ: Sensory receptors located between the muscle and its tendon that are sensitive to the stretch of the muscle tendon produced by the stretch of its associated muscle.

good behavior game: Behavior management technique that requires participants to use peer pressure to control group behavior in a game-type setting. The rules of the game promote behaviors to be reinforced.

graded exercise stress test (GXT): This test is used either as a diagnostic tool or to evaluate the functional capacity of the cardiovascular system; usually involves continuous incremental exercise performed on a bicycle ergometer or treadmill where the electrocardiogram and blood pressure (occasionally oxygen consumption) are monitored; specific exercise protocol should match intended purpose and estimated ability of patient; may be maximal or submaximal with symptom-limited maximal being the recommended end point; end-point symptoms include, but are not limited to, extreme dyspnea, angina, ischemic electrocardiographic changes, failure of heart rate and blood pressure to rise with increasing workload, and excessive blood pressure response; positive GXT indicates evidence of cardiovascular disease while negative GXT indicates no disease is discernible. See also *false negative exercise test, false positive exercise test, ischemia*.

grand mal seizure: Major motor seizure characterized by loss of consciousness, falling, muscle tensing, rigidity, and involuntary muscular contractions. Also called *tonicoclonic seizure*.

grasp reflex: Reflexive contraction of the flexor muscles of the hand and fingers (grasp) when an object is placed in the hand or on the palm.

gravity: The attraction of two objects with a force proportional to the product of their masses and inversely proportional to the squared distance between them (law of gravitation).

gross motor skill: Motor task either requiring large musculature or moving the body in space.

ground reaction force: The resultant reaction force, equal and opposite to the applied force, of the supporting surface.

group: Collection of individuals who may be together because of a common interest but may not necessarily know each other or have any meaningful social interaction (e.g. spectators at an athletic event). See also *psychological group*.

group alerting: The act by which the teacher is able to keep students on task and attentive.

group climate: See *climate*.

group cohesion: See *cohesion*.

group contingencies: See *class rewards*.

group dynamics: Interaction and roles of group members as determined by directly observing group member interaction or recording each member's responses to questions about their feelings toward other group members.

group integration: 1. The quality of interpersonal relations in the group and the relative homogeneity of ability and security (tenure) among group members. A high degree of group integration (heterogeneity) increases the likelihood of conflict among group members about the outcomes of a decision. Therefore, high group heterogeneity dictates that members be relatively more involved in decision making than highly homogeneous groups. **2.** (member's perception): (a) The perception of the closeness, similarity, and bonding within the group as a whole. (b) The perception of the degree of unification of the group field. **3.** (social-related): Team member's feelings about his or her personal involvement, acceptance, and social interaction with the group. **4.** (task-related): Team member's feelings about the similarity, closeness, and bonding within the team as a whole around the group's task. See also *social cohesion, task cohesion*.

group-oriented contingency strategy: The control of group misbehavior in which a group of individuals competes for reinforcement as a unit. If any group member violates a rule, the entire group suffers the consequences of the infraction; or the group can receive a reward as a unit for positive behavior.

group productivity: A group's best possible performance given all relevant knowledge and skills of individual group members plus the task demands minus losses due to faulty process (e.g., the inability or unwillingness of group members to carry out necessary tasks and utilize group resources that, otherwise, would meet the group's performance potential).

group social orientation: In terms of members' perceptions, a general orientation or motivation toward developing and maintaining social relationships within the group. See also *group task orientation*.

group's social attractiveness to member: A team member's feelings about her or his personal involvement, acceptance, and social interaction with the group.

group's task attractiveness to member: A team member's feelings about his or her personal involvement with the group task, productivity, and goals.

group task orientation: In terms of members' perceptions, a general orientation or motivation towards achieving the group's goals and objectives. See also *group social orientation*.

growth: Quantitative increase in the size or mass of a living being or any of its parts as a result of an increase in already complete units and the transformation of nonliving nutrients into protoplasm.

growth plate: See *epiphyseal growth plate*.

Grusky's theory of formal structure: Predicts that behavior is based on a person's spatial location in a group. The more central the individual's group position, (a) the greater likelihood of performing tasks that are coordinated with other group members, (b) the more frequent the interaction with occupants of other positions, and (c) the higher the relationship between performance on dependent tasks and frequency of interaction.

guided discovery learning: See *discovery learning*.

guided learning: Method of instruction in which the learning experiences are structured and the learner continually prompted. Improvising and adaptation are deemphasized.

guided placing: Direction of a limb to a particular point or object in the environment by use of visual information.

GXT: See *graded exercise stress test*.

gyroscopic stability: Resistance of a rotating object to a change in its plane of rotation.

habilitation: The use of movement as a stimulus for encouraging physical and motor development.

habit strength: 1. Hull's concept that the extent of learning is dependent upon the frequency, amount, and timing of reinforcement. **2.** A change in some internal stage (learning) as a result of skill practice, not necessarily reflected by a change in skill performance.

Haldane procedure: Chemical method used for analyzing the O_2 and CO_2 concentration in air; used as a technique to calibrate electronic O_2 and CO_2 analyzers.

Haldane transformation: Inspired ventilation may be converted to expired ventilation using the following equation:

$$Ve(STPD) = Vi(STPD) \cdot [\%N_2i \,/\, \%N_2e]$$

where $\%N_2i = 79.04$
$\%N_2e = [100 - (\%0_2e + \%CO_2e)]$

Underlying assumption is that nitrogen is metabolically inert; any change in the concentration of nitrogen in the expired air in comparison to the inspired air simply reflects a change in the relative proportion of nitrogen in the air, and the number of nitrogen molecules remains constant.

half-time: Time required for $\dot{V}O_2$ to reach one half the steady-state or baseline $\dot{V}O_2$.

half-wave rectified electromyogram: Electromyographic signal in which the negative raw signals are removed and only the positive remain.

Hamm-Marburg Body Coordination Test for Children: Norm-referenced test, for children 5 to 14 years, assessing total body coordination. Four subtests are given: balancing backward, one-foot hopping over, jumping sideways, and shifting the body. Retest reliability is .80 on separate tasks and .93 for the entire test.

hand dominance: A person's consistent preference to use one hand rather than the other hand.

hand–eye coordination: See *eye–hand coordination*.

handicap: A problem a person encounters because of a hindrance or difficulty imposed by physical, health, learning, or behavioral characteristics that interfere with achievement or acceptance by society. See also *disability*.

hand preference: A person's choice to use one hand rather than the other for a given task. It may or may not be the dominant hand.

hand shaping: Appropriate, anticipatory positioning of the hand and fingers when reaching to grasp an object.

haptic perception: The component of kinesthetic perception that combines information from the cutaneous receptors and the proprioceptors.

hard of hearing: Having a sufficient amount of residual hearing to process linguistic information with or without a hearing aid.

harmonic entrainment: Synchronization of two oscillators with similar frequencies.

harmonic motion: Oscillatory motion that may be described by sinusoidal wave components.

harmonic oscillator: See *linear oscillator*.

Harvard step test: Method for estimation of maximal oxygen uptake using a recovery heart rate; individuals step up and down from a bench that is 20 inches high at a rate of 30 steps/min for 5 min; pulse rate is taken 90 s post exercise and is used to estimate cardiovascular fitness; developed back in the 1950s, it is not used any longer to assess cardiovascular fitness; serves as the basis from which other recovery heart rate tests were developed.

Hawthorne effect: The tendency of participants to perform with more effort when they perceive an event to be new or special.

HDL: See *high density lipoprotein.*

head circumference: Anthropometric measurement of head size, taken as the minimum circumference obtainable one inch above the ears and above the eyebrows. Large deviations from average head circumference for age in infants may indicate a need for medical attention, often because of abnormal brain growth.

health impairments: Variety of conditions common in the mainstreamed physical education setting that decrease the functional capacity of individuals, including respiratory, cardiac, and nutritional disorders.

health psychology: Aspect of the discipline of psychology pertaining to promoting and maintaining health, preventing and treating illness, and identifying causes and diagnostic correlates of health, illness, and related dysfunction.

hearing impaired: Generic term used to describe a hearing disability; includes deaf and hard of hearing.

heart attack: See *myocardial infarction.*

heart failure: See *congestive heart failure.*

heart murmur: Sound detected by a stethoscope of the backward flow of blood through defective heart valves.

heart rate (HR): Frequency of cardiac cycles or ventricular contractions, usually expressed on a per-minute basis; monitored noninvasively by the electrocardiogram or by the carotid or radial pulse rate; used in exercise prescription for defining appropriate intensity. See also *cardiac cycle, pulse rate.*

heart sounds: Vibrations caused by the closing of the cardiac valves; the first heart sound results from the closing of the atrioventricular valves, and the second heart sound results from the closing of the semilunar valves; heard as "lub-dub" with a stethoscope.

heart valves: Four leaf-like flaps of tissue separating chambers of the heart and attached to the heart muscle by strong, fibrous rings; allow for control of blood flow into and out of the atria and ventricles and into the pulmonary and systemic circulation.

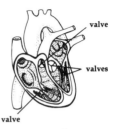

heart valves

heat cramps: Painful but benign heat injury characterized by involuntary contractions or spasm, usually in the legs, arms, or abdomen; results from electrolyte (primary salt) depletion.

heat disorder: Any of a series of conditions in which the thermoregulatory mechanisms cannot compensate for the combined external heat load and metabolically produced heat in an exercising individual, such that core temperature rises and physiological functioning is impaired; these disorders include, in the order of danger, heat cramps, heat exhaustion, and heat stroke.

heat exhaustion: Form of heat stress brought about by a combination of ineffective circulatory adjustments and fluid depletion caused by excessive sweating thus reducing cardiac output; characterized by "goose pimples," reduced sweating, dry mouth, weak and rapid pulse, low blood pressure, thirst, headache, dizziness, general fatigue, weakness, and loss of coordination.

heat of combustion: The heat released consequent to the oxidation of food; expressed in kilocalories.

heat stroke: Thermoregulatory failure that poses a life-threatening medical emergency; characterized by fatigue of the sweating mechanism, hot and dry skin, dangerously elevated core temperature, muscle weakness or spasm, tachycardia, and loss of mental functioning or other central nervous system disturbances.

heel contact: The instant in a locomotor skill when the heel of the foot touches the ground after swing or flight.

height of release: The vertical distance above the landing surface or level from which a projectile is released.

helplessness: See *learned helplessness*.

hematocrit: The ratio of the volume of packed red blood cells to the volume of whole blood; used as a diagnostic tool for assessing anemia; typical values are in the range 40% to 54% for males and 34% to 49% for females.

hemiplegia: Paralysis of the arm and leg on the same side of the body resulting from a cerebral vascular accident (stroke) or neurological dysfunction (cerebral palsy).

hemispheric dominance: The concept that one hemisphere of the brain is more important than the other in controlling particular bodily functions and mental processes. For example, in most people the left hemisphere is more important than the right for language functions.

hemoconcentration: Increased concentration of cells and solids in the blood, usually resulting from loss of fluid to the tissues; transiently occurs with exercise as a result of decrease in plasma volume.

hemodynamics: Physical laws and mechanisms involved in the regulation of circulation.

hemoglobin: The iron-protein molecule in the red blood cell that carries oxygen throughout the body; approximately 1.34 ml of oxygen combines with each gram of hemoglobin.

hemophilia: Hereditary blood disease characterized by a deficiency of the clotting factor in the blood and a lengthened coagulation time.

heredity: The characteristics biologically transmitted from parents to offspring at conception.

heritability: The quality of being inherited.

hertz (Hz): Unit of measurement to determine the frequency of a sound; equal to one cycle per second.

heterohypnosis: State of hypnosis induced externally by another person.

Hick's law: The prediction that reaction time lengthens approximately 150 ms with every doubling of the number of stimulus-response choices in a choice reaction time task.

hierarchical integration: The characteristic of developmental stages indicating that subsequent stages incorporate the previous stage, and new structures are formed by transforming or reorganizing the preceding structures.

hierarchical task analysis: Description of subskills that must be mastered before the terminal objective is achieved. See also *task analysis*.

hierarchy sequence: Continuum of development in which lower order tasks of lesser difficulty are prerequisite to achieving tasks requiring more intricate patterns and environmental variables.

high avoidance in motor skills: 1. Withdrawal reaction in response to perceiving a novel situation as unpleasant or possibly dangerous. **2.** Skilled movements associated with anxiety and hesitancy when the performer is first confronted with attempting them.

high density lipoprotein (HDL): Lipoprotein in blood plasma that is composed of a high proportion (50%) of protein with little triglyceride or cholesterol; HDLs transport cholesterol away from the peripheral tissues to the liver, where it is broken down by bile acids and excreted; a high concentration is associated with decreased probability of developing atherosclerosis; endurance-trained individuals have been shown to have high levels.

high guard: The arm position in locomotor skills wherein the arms are abducted at the shoulders, the elbows flexed, and the hands held at or above shoulder level; often seen in early development of a locomotor skill.

high means interdependence: The tendency of group members to interact in order to achieve success; exhibited in team sports in which teammates are required to depend upon each other to achieve team goals.

high-probability behavior: Response occurring with a high degree of frequency if the learner is given an opportunity to select between alternate behaviors. See also *Premack principle*.

hinge joint: Joint that has only one degree of freedom—that is, allowing only flexion and extension.

hitch: Delay in forward movement of the swing leg during the hop in skipping.

hitting the wall: Slang expression used to describe the phenomenon of depletion of muscle glycogen stores with a concomitant increased reliance on fat as a fuel source; typically occurs in marathoners at about the 19- or 20-mile mark and results in a decrement in performance.

home court advantage: The notion that playing before the home crowd is advantageous to performance because of fan support. Thought to be a function of heightened arousal and assertiveness or instrumental aggression.

homeostasis: The maintenance of relatively stable internal physiological conditions in higher animals under fluctuating environmental conditions; as the stress of exercise causes changes in the internal environment, the subsequent physiological responses attempt to regain the balance within the internal environment.

homeotherm: Organism in which the body temperature remains constant (i.e.,

warm-blooded); for example, as more heat is produced internally following exercise, increased blood flow to the skin and an increase in sweating occur to dissipate heat so that core temperature remains constant.

homework: Assignment for completion outside the formal instructional setting to provide extra time, practice, and opportunity to develop age-appropriate cognitive, fitness, and motor development.

homing: The final portion of a ballistic arm movement wherein visual guidance corrects the arm's trajectory to facilitate hand placement on the target.

homing in: Correcting the arm's trajectory during the last portion of a ballistic arm movement to facilitate placement of the hand on the target.

hopping: The locomotor pattern wherein the body is projected from the floor by one leg and the landing is on the same leg, while either stationary or traversing a distance.

horizontal decalage: The developmental lag between an individual's entrance into a developmental stage and the appearance of a behavior characteristic of that stage. Not all of the characteristic behaviors appear at once.

hostile aggression: See *goal aggression*.

HR: See *heart rate*.

humanism: Psychological theory that envisions humans as being essentially good, striving for self-actualization, and developing their potential.

humanistic leadership style: Approach to group management in which the leader is primarily concerned with the welfare, achievement, and interests of group members.

humerus lag: Characteristic of efficient overhand throwing in which the arm follows the trunk in rotating forward. The humerus does not horizontally flex past the trunk before the latter faces front.

humpback: See *kyphosis*.

hustle: Verbal or nonverbal behavior

used to energize or motivate students to participate.

hydraulic resistance exercise: Partial accommodating resistance-training equipment for isokinetic exercise in which the resistance is provided by oil that flows from one chamber of a cylinder to another through an orifice that restricts the rate at which the oil can flow; can be pushed and pulled at varying rates of speed dependent on the strength of the exerciser; used for improving strength and power; generally exercises on these machines are performed at an all-out rate for a specified period of time. See also *isokinetic*.

hydrocephalus: Condition that develops when excessive cerebrospinal fluid accumulates in the cerebral ventricles and causes enlargement of the skull area, increased cranial pressure, and mental retardation.

hydrodynamic drag: The drag force produced when an object moves through water.

hydrodynamic lift force: The lift force produced when an object moves through water.

hydrodynamics: Branch of fluid dynamics that deals with the effects of water on objects moving through water.

hydrometry: Measurement of total body water by the dilution of a tracer substance such as deuterium oxide; total body water may be used to estimate fat-free body or in a multicomponent model to determine percent body fat.

hydrostatic weighing: Criterion measure for estimating body fat percentage by measuring body density; based on Archimedes' principle; body is weighed in air and then weighed fully submerged in water; underwater weight is corrected for residual volume, gastrointestinal air, and water temperature; percent fat is then calculated using body density in either the Brozek or the Siri equation. Also called *underwater weighing*. See also *body density, body volume, Brozek equation, Siri formula*.

hyperactivity: Higher degree of inappropriate or excessive motor activity than is common for a specific age group. Commonly accompanied by immature emotional behavior and inability to focus attention. Also called *hyperkinesis*. Compare *hypokinetic*.

hypercapnia: The presence of an excess of carbon dioxide in the blood; may occur with intense exercise as increased CO_2 is produced via metabolism and lactate buffering.

hyperelexia: Exaggeration of reflexes, occurring when the spinal cord is severed. The sympathetic nervous system is then no longer under control of the spinal cord.

hyperemia: Increased amount of blood flow; during exercise, the increase in blood flow that occurs in the working muscles.

hyperextension: The continued extension at a joint that is beyond the normal limit of motion for that joint.

hyperextension

hyperglycemia: Condition in which there is too much sugar in the blood, necessitating administration of insulin.

hyperkinesis: See *hyperactivity*.

hyperlipidemia: The presence of excess fat or lipids in the blood, associated with an increased risk of coronary heart disease. See also *cholesterol, high density lipoprotein, low density lipoprotein, very low density lipoprotein*.

hypermobility: Motion at a joint that occurs as a result of excessive ligament, muscle, or capsular laxity.

hyperopia: Correctable condition resulting when the eyeball is too short and the image focuses behind the retina. Also called *farsightedness*. Compare *myopia*.

hyperplasia: Growth in a tissue or organ through an increase in the number of cells.

hyperpnea: Rapid or deep breathing that occurs in anticipation of or during exercise.

hyperresponsivity: An overload or over-reaction to sensory stimuli. Compare *hyporesponsivity*.

hypertension: High blood pressure; when chronic resting values are greater than 140 mm/90 mm Hg or a mean arterial pressure is in excess of 110 mm; in approximately 90% of cases the origin of the disease is not known and is identified as either idiopathic or essential hypertension; approximately 10% of the cases are secondary to kidney disease, endocrine disorders, and pregnancy; essential hypertension is a risk factor for coronary heart disease; regulation of disease is attempted via drug therapy, weight loss, diet changes, and exercise.

hyperthermia: Elevated body temperature; may be caused by prolonged high-intensity exercise, especially when done in high-temperature and/or high-humidity conditions and when fluid is not being replaced when exercise is accompanied by excessive sweating.

hypertonia: Increase in muscle tone resulting in muscular tension.

hypertrophic obesity: Classification of obesity characterized by a normal number of enlarged fat cells.

hypertrophy: Growth in a tissue or an organ through an increase in size of tissue elements, not cell number. See also *cardiac hypertrophy, hypertrophic obesity*.

hyperventilation: Prolonged, rapid, and deep breathing that is not consistent with normal breathing patterns.

hypnosis: Externally induced sleep-like state wherein suggestion from an external source is uncritically accepted. See also *autohypnosis, heterohypnosis*.

hypocapnia: Decreased level of blood CO_2 that delays the humerally mediated drive that stimulates breathing; this delay can be dangerous when brought about by hyperventilation and combined with underwater swimming, since the blood PO_2 levels can decrease below that required to maintain consciousness before PCO_2 levels stimulate ventilation. See also *hyperventilation*.

hypoglycemia: Abnormally low level of blood sugar caused by an increase in metabolism requiring ingestion of quick-acting sugar.

hypokinetic: Lack of motor response, lethargy, or responsiveness. Compare *hyperactivity*.

hypokinetic disease: Illness caused by or associated with a lack of physical exercise, such as cardiovascular disease, obesity, and osteoporosis.

hypometric: Referring to a movement that falls short of a target.

hypoplasia: Defective development of the brain.

hyporesponsivity: Underreaction to sensory stimuli in which the person's response is either absent or of insufficient magnitude or duration. Compare *hyperresponsivity*.

hypothyroidism: See *cretinism*.

hypotonia: Inability to exert muscle force when a muscle is set at short length.

hypoxia: Insufficient amount of oxygen. See also *anoxia*.

Hz: See *hertz*.

I

iceberg profile: Personality and mood profile on six factors measured by the POMS (profile of mood state) that resembles an iceberg. The term *iceberg* was first used by Morgan.

ICP: See *isovolemic contraction period*.

identical-elements theory: The view that the extent of transfer of learning between two tasks or situations is a function of the similarity between the elements or components.

ideomotor principle: The historic notion that any idea that dominates the mind finds its expression in the muscles.

idiopathic: Relates to an unknown cause of disability or dysfunction.

iEMG: See *integrated electromyography*.

IEP: See *individualized education program*.

imagery: Symbolic coding of information in pictorial (visual) forms; used as a mental technique to favorably affect motor performance, although it may also negatively influence performance in response to unpleasant thoughts; entails thinking about performance and the feelings, situations, and information from all senses that surround the activity. Also called *mental imagery, visualization*. See also *external imagery, internal imagery*.

impact: The collision of two bodies; usually classified as elastic, in which the objects rebound away from each other, or inelastic, in which the objects remain together.

impaired: Having identifiable organic or functional disorder that may restrict performance. See also *disability, handicap*.

impedance plethysmography: Technique used to determine and register variations in the size of an organ or limb; also used to detect blood flow through a specific region by determining the resistance to flow in the circulatory system.

impulse: See *angular impulse, linear impulse*.

impulse–momentum relationship: States that the impulse is equal to the change in momentum of an object.

$$\text{impulse} = mv_i + 1 - mv_i - 1$$

where m = mass
v_i = velocity at time i

impulse-timing model: Hypothesized mode of movement control, holding that the nervous system modulates both the duration and the amplitude of the accelerative and decelerative movement forces. Variation of force in movement is achieved by overall scaling of the amplitude of kinetic and neural events, but variation of movement time is attained by change in the temporal (timing or rhythmical) sequence of these events.

impulse-variability model: Theory of control of accurate, rapid movement that relates accuracy to the variability in muscular impulse (the integral of force produced over time). A symmetric-impulse-variability model proposes that the positive and negative portions of the acceleration–time relationship in a movement are mirror images.

impulsive cognitive style: See *impulsive learning style*.

impulsive learning style: Category of conceptual tempo or type of cognitive style wherein a learner responds quickly but commits many errors. Also called *impulsive cognitive style*. Compare *reflective learning style*.

impulsivity: Tendency to respond quickly and inappropriately to a stimulus without considering the alternatives.

incentive: 1. The reason a person strives to achieve a goal. Determined by the consequences of particular actions and manifested by the person's tendency to approach or avoid these specific consequences. 2. [pd] See *reinforcer*.

incentive motivation: 1. The degree of desire that one attaches to possible outcomes or experiences that are perceived as being available in a particular situation or sport in order to persist in the activity. **2.** A person's willingness to select certain courses of action partly based on the value that he or she attaches to possible outcomes of those actions. Thus, if increasing one's muscle mass or strength is perceived as an important goal, then the person will make the necessary investment of time and effort to engage in an ongoing weight-lifting program.

incentive value of success (IS): The perceived value of being successful. Conversely related to the motive to avoid failure, the probability or expectation of failure, and the unattractiveness or incentive value of failure.

incidence: The rate of occurrence individuals who at some time during their development will be identified as having a specific condition; usually reported as the number of cases per thousand.

incidental learning: The acquisition of motor skills or concepts that occurs without the learner having an intention to learn or receiving specific instructions.

incompatible behavior: Action that cannot be performed simultaneously, or that interferes, with other behaviors.

incontinence: Lack of bladder or bowel control.

independence incentives: Need or desire to do things on one's own without the help of others.

independent observation: Process of determining the reliability of observations by recording the percentage of agreements or disagreements by two or more individuals.

independent variable: The factor in an experiment that the experimenter manipulates, by setting two or more levels, to observe the effect on some aspect of the subject's behavior.

index of difficulty: Measurement of movement task difficulty in bits: $\log_2$ (A/.5W), where W is the width of the target

and A is the amplitude of the movement required.

indirect calorimetry: See *calorimetry*.

indirect Fick technique: See *carbon dioxide rebreathing*.

indirect instruction: Child-centered instructional process in which students are the prime decision makers. Compare *direct instruction*.

individual differences: The area of study involving identification and measurement of individual traits or abilities. See also *intraindividual differences*.

individual differences principle: The principle that the ways in which individuals respond to the same training stimulus may be different due to such factors as genetics and initial level of fitness.

individualized education program (IEP): Written plan of instruction including goals, objectives, services, and evaluation procedures for each learner receiving special education services.

individualized instruction: Variation of instruction according to the child's level of ability and development.

indwelling electrode: Electrode, either needle or fine-wire, that is placed into the muscle in order to detect its electrical signal.

inertia: Resistance of an object to a change in its state of motion.

inertial lag: Lag of a distal segment behind the more proximal segments due to the distal segment's inertia.

inertial reference frame: Fixed or non-moving reference frame; a reference frame with zero acceleration.

infant reflexes: Involuntary responses to specific stimuli, present prenatally or in infancy, but that disappear or are inhibited as the infant matures. Also called *neonatal reflexes*.

infarction: Death of tissue due to a prolonged lack of oxygen; term is most commonly used for myocardial infarction or heart attack.

inferior: A description used for a body part

that is below a reference body part. Compare *superior*.

inflection: The change in pitch or loudness of the voice to indicate mood or emphasis.

information aspect: See *cognitive evaluation theory*.

information processing: Manipulation of information in humans or machines through a number of operations leading to a response or output.

information processing theory: The view that humans and machines manipulate information through a number of operations, including sensory input, perception, retrieval and storage of information (memory), and response selection before a response is made.

informing task: Type of task used for building progressions leading to skill achievement by providing new information and directions (to begin and during an activity sequence).

inherent feedback: See *intrinsic feedback*.

inhibition: The overriding of primitive reflexes by higher levels of the central nervous system to permit purposeful, voluntary movement.

innate response system: The natural primitive reflexes present at birth that allow the infant to respond; aids in protection and nourishment.

inotropic response: Altered force of contraction in heart muscle, predominantly in response to drug therapy or autonomic nervous system stimulation or inhibition; a positive response is an increased force of contraction, whereas a negative response is a decreased force of contraction.

in-phase movements: Cyclic movements of two or more limbs that are matched in frequency and arrive at corresponding places along their trajectories at the same time (e.g., the arm action in the breaststroke).

input: The information that enters the body through the sensory apparatus and is processed and deciphered before a motor output. Also called *sensory input*.

input organization: The categorizing of incoming sensory information into meaningful units that can be used in the decision-making process.

inquiry learning: Approach to learning that allows learners the opportunity to think and discover solutions to movement problems. See also *convergent inquiry, divergent inquiry*.

insertion: The point of attachment of a muscle to a relatively more movable or distal bone.

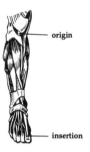

insertion

inspiratory reserve volume: The maximal amount of air that can be inhaled by conscious effort following normal inspiration; decreases during exercise, because the tidal volume increases and comprises a percentage of the inspiratory reserve volume.

instantaneous center of rotation: The immovable point, existing at an instant in time, that has a zero velocity and is created by one segment rotating about an adjacent segment.

instinct theory of aggression: 1. Theory that aggressive behavior builds up in the id and is released through reality or fantasy. 2. Theory that aggressive behavior is innate to the human species and genetically transmitted, and that it must be expressed to preserve the species.

institutionalization: The placement of handicapped individuals in settings isolated from society. Compare *deinstitutionalization*.

instructional approaches: Methods of teaching, viewed on a continuum from direct, teacher-controlled instruction to child-centered approaches in which students aid in arriving at solutions to problems.

instructional objectives: The development and use of tasks to be learned, which include the conditions required for learning and standards required to evaluate the completion of tasks.

instructional time: The period during class specifically structured to provide learners an opportunity to acquire knowledge and skill. They may be receiving verbal or nonverbal information from the teacher and could be active or inactive.

instrumental aggression: Intentional infliction of injury against another person for the purpose of receiving positive reinforcement by attaining some goal (e.g., success). Not accompanied by anger.

insulin: Hormone produced by the pancreas, used in the metabolism of carbohydrates and transportation of glucose to the working muscles.

insulin coma or shock: Condition caused by too much insulin and the resultant reduction of the blood sugar level. See also *hypoglycemia*.

intake-rejection hypothesis: The hypothesis that heart rate (HR) decreases during simple attention-demanding tasks and accelerates during cognitive effort. For example, focusing on an external stimulus such as a starter's gun slows HR, while HR increases when focusing on one's own heart beat. For an alternative explanation, compare *cardiac somatic coupling hypothesis*.

integrated electromyography (iEMG): The area under a full-wave or half-wave rectified electromyogram curve.

integration: 1. [ad] Placement in a school situation in which handicapped and non-handicapped students are educated together. See also *mainstreaming*. 2. [bm] The mathematical process of taking the area under a plotted curve.

intelligence quotient (IQ): The index of intelligence that is determined by standardized intelligence tests.

intensity of training: The percentage of VO_2max or percentage of maximum heart rate that must be maintained during a training session; exercise should be done at a minimum of 60% of heart rate reserve or 65% of maximum heart rate, for an aerobic training effect to occur.

intentional learning: Purposeful acquisition of skills or concepts, usually controlled in experiments by telling the learner that a recall test will be administered after the learning period.

interaction analysis: The study of the frequency and patterns of information feedback that occur between the teacher and student(s); used to evaluate the emotional climate.

interaction and discrimination hypothesis: An explanation for positional segregation in sport; the theory that management, supposedly due to being prejudiced and having negative stereotypes of blacks, tend to exclude blacks from positions requiring interpersonal coordination and decision making.

interactionism: The hypothesis that behavior is the result of an indispensable and continuous interaction between persons' traits or characteristics and the situations or environmental factors that they encounter. Also called *interaction model*.

interaction model: See *interactionism*.

interactive audience: Group of observers that interact emotionally or verbally with the performers. For example, group members may offer verbal encouragement while an individual performs a particular task.

Coaches in sport who offer praise or criticism during skill execution also form an interactive audience.

interdisciplinary team: See *multidisciplinary team*.

interference: Disruption in learning or memory due to conflicting associations between the material to be remembered and an intervening event or experience.

interlimb coordination: Harmonious functioning of two or more of the body's limbs.

intermittent reinforcement: Schedule of reinforcement by which a response is reinforced some but not all times it is performed.

intermodality training: Instruction that involves the preplanned use of more than one of the learner's sensory systems by presentation of instructional tasks using several modalities.

internal attentional style: See *attentional style*.

internal control: The perception that internal, controllable factors determine performance outcomes.

internal feedback: See *intrinsic feedback*.

internal force: Force generated internal to the system (e.g., muscle force) that is not shown on a free-body diagram.

internal imagery: Imagery based on the sensory experiences of the performer. For instance, a performer mentally rehearses a skill by using imagery of how the skill feels while performing it, rather than imagery based on how a spectator would perceive the performance. Also called *first-person imagery, kinesthetic imagery*. Compare *external imagery*.

internal reinforcer: Self-controlled or self-generated reinforcement that manages behavior.

internal rotation: Movement of a body part occurring when the anterior surface of the part is rotated toward the midline of the body. Compare *external rotation*.

internals: Persons who believe that their actions influence performance outcomes and who are highly affected by these outcomes. For example, an internal who experiences success will typically feel more motivated to persist at the task and maintain high performance standards than externals, who may not link their effort with the outcome. Conversely, consistent failure tends to demotivate internals more so than externals. Compare *externals*.

interobserver reliability: Method of testing the dependability of data collection in which two independent observers view, evaluate, and record a subject's behavior with at least 80% agreement.

interpolated task: Task performed during the retention interval between the performance of a primary task and its recall. The interpolated task may be similar to, or different from, the primary task. Researchers study the interfering effect of this inserted task on recalling the primary task.

interresponse interval (IRI): The time span in a series of responses between the end of one response and the initiation of the next response.

interrole conflict: Situation that occurs when an individual is required to perform various roles that require incompatible patterns of behavior, as when, for instance, planning for practice interferes with teaching.

intersegmental coordination: Harmonious movement of parts of a limb to perform a smooth and efficient movement of the whole limb.

intersensory: Use of more than one sensory system to process information, e.g., auditory-visual.

intersensory integration: Ability to match sensory information from multiple sources, e.g., visual, auditory, and tactual, simultaneously.

intertask transfer: The influence of a previously learned skill on the learning of a new, different skill.

interval goal-setting: In sport, a technique for setting objective short-term and long-term performance goals in sport, based on a formula taking into account the individual's recent previous performance.

interval recording: The documentation of a behavior occurring within a specific time interval.

interval reinforcement: Schedule of reinforcement that designates a specific amount of time to elapse before a response is reinforced.

interval training: Training characterized by periods of intense activity interspersed with periods of moderate energy expenditure; by optimally spacing work and rest periods, an individual can accomplish more total work in a workout supposedly with less fatigue than would occur with a continuous training workout; rest/work intervals will vary according to goals and objectives of the training and which energy systems need to be stressed.

intervention: 1. Various cognitive and behavioral strategies for altering existing levels of psychological states, such as anxiety, arousal, and self-confidence. 2. [ad] Summation of all preventive, remedial, or compensatory efforts made to increase the functional capacity of people with disabilities.

intraindividual differences: 1. Variations in the degrees to which persons possess various motor abilities. 2. Extent of variability and consistency in performing a motor task.

intraindividual variation: Within-subject trial-to-trial variability during the learning process, computed as the average variance (i.e., dispersion of scores around the mean) for a group of subjects on a pair of trials. Average group intraindividual variation is calculated on the within-subject intraindividual variation.

intransitivity: The characteristic of developmental stages indicating that the ordering or sequence of the stages cannot be changed.

intrarole conflict: Situation that occurs when an individual must respond to expectations from various incompatible groups or individuals, such as parents who only want

to win and others who instead see sport as an avenue for development or participation.

intrasensory: Use of one sensory system to process information.

intrasensory discrimination: Ability to distinguish stimuli within an individual sensory system.

intratask development: See *developmental sequence*.

intratask transfer: Influence of a previously practiced skill on the learning of (a) a version of the same skill or (b) the skill under different practice conditions.

intratask variation: Teaching procedure that requires the teacher to adjust the difficulty of a task to the learner's skill level.

intrathoracic pressure: Force exerted within the chest cavity during resistance exercise; when there is a tendency to close the glottis, there is an increase in intrathoracic pressure, which may put too much overload on the heart in certain individuals.

intrinsic: Coming from within; for example, one's motivation to complete a task or demonstrate an appropriate behavior could be fun or pleasure, in the absence of external rewards. Compare *extrinsic*.

intrinsic feedback: 1. Information available to a performer, through one or more of the senses, as an inherent consequence of performing a task. 2. Information available to a performer through the proprioceptors, as a consequence of performing a task. Also called *inherent feedback, internal feedback*. Compare *extrinsic feedback*.

intrinsic mastery: 1. Preference for engaging in challenging tasks rather than easy ones. 2. The incentive to work to satisfy one's own interest rather than to please others. 3. Preference for figuring out problems on one's own in contrast to depending on others for assistance. See also *cognitive evaluation theory, intrinsic motivation*. Compare *extrinsic mastery*.

intrinsic motivation: The desire to perform a skill or activity for the enjoyment and satisfaction derived from the activity itself, and without external reward or incentive.

The activity is performed due to feelings of satisfaction, self-competence, and self-determination. See also *cognitive evaluation theory*. Compare *extrinsic motivation*.

intropunitive behavior: Aggression against oneself. Compare *extropunitive behavior*.

introversion: A person's orientation inward; a tendency to be especially concerned with one's own thoughts; to be inwardly reflective rather than overly expressive. Compare *extroversion*.

in utero: 1. Within the uterus. **2.** Referring to the developing human organism in the womb.

invariance: 1. Stability in the kinematic values of a set of movements. **2.** Fixation in some aspects of movement, such as temporal structure or a skill's inherent rhythm, while more superficial aspects, such as movement speed, change.

invariant characteristics: The features of, or a motor program for, movements that remain stable (e.g., temporal structure, sequence of events in an action pattern) while more superficial features (movement speed, trajectory, load) change.

invariant teaching: The use of one instructional approach in all educational settings.

inventory assessment: Checklist of tasks to be accomplished that are usually not related or sequenced.

inversion: Raising the medial border of the foot and/or a rotation inward of body parts. Compare *eversion*.

inverted-U hypothesis: 1. Proposed optimal level of arousal to achieve one's best performance; above or below this level will result in poorer performance. **2.** Proposed curvilinear relationship between level of arousal and quality of motor performance as derived from the shape of the relationship when graphically plotted. Also called *Yerkes-Dodson Law*.

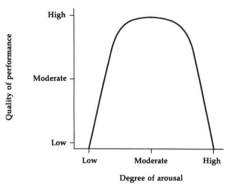

inverted-U hypothesis

inverted-V curve: Seen as an initial sharp increase in heart rate during the preperformance period in reaction to task-relevant thoughts followed by a decrease in HR as the time to initiate a response approaches.

invitation teaching: Teaching procedure that allows students to make their own decisions about adjusting the difficulty of a task.

ipsilateral: On the same side of the body.

IQ: See *intelligence quotient*.

IRI: See *interresponse interval*.

iris: The colored portion of the eye that contracts or expands involuntarily depending on the amount of light.

iron deficiency: Less than normal iron in the red blood cell hemoglobin. A lowered hemoglobin concentration is associated with iron deficiency because hemoglobin is an iron-containing protein; to minimize the risk, the recommended daily allowance for iron in the diet for men and postmenopausal women is 10 mg/day, and for premenopausal women it is 18 mg/day. Female endurance athletes are particularly susceptible to iron deficiency as a result of inadequate caloric consumption and iron intake. Symptoms include fatigue and impaired endurance performance.

IRP: See *isovolemic relaxation period*.

irrelevant appraisal: Type of primary appraisal that implies that an encounter with the environment carries no implication for a person's well-being.

irritability: The capacity of a tissue (e.g., muscle or nerve) to respond to a stimulation.

IS: See *incentive value of success*.

ischemia: Insufficient blood flow to tissue that results in a decreased oxygen supply (hypoxia); increased carbon dioxide and an insufficient supply of nutrients; can be caused by coronary occlusion secondary to atherosclerosis or coronary artery spasms. S-T segment depression and angina are symptoms.

isochrony principle: The relative invariance of movement time for voluntary movement of a body segment, despite the linear extent of movement trajectory, through compensatory change in velocity of the segment. Hence, repetitious movements that traverse different distances compensate by a change in velocity rather than a change in the time to make the movement.

isokinetic: Muscular contraction that occurs at a constant velocity over the full range of motion; tension developed by the muscle while shortening is maximum over the full range of motion; resistance training machines that operate under this principle are

also called *accommodating resistance machines*; exercises that operate under this principle are also called *accommodating resistance exercises*.

isometric: Muscular contraction where the tension developed occurs with no change in the length of the muscle.

isotonic: Muscle contraction, either concentric or eccentric, against a constant resistance through an entire range of motion.

isotonic controller: Response lever that moves when force is applied to it; a joystick.

isovolemic contraction period (ICP): The phase of the cardiac cycle when the amount of blood in the ventricles is not changing, all heart valves are closed, and ventricular muscle has begun to contract to build up pressure in these chambers to force open the semilunar valves; lasts .02 to .05 s. See also *cardiac cycle, semilunar valve*.

isovolemic relaxation period (IRP): Ventricular relaxation with no change in the blood volume in the ventricles; all valves are closed; occurs just prior to diastole; chamber size increases slightly so the pressure becomes less than the pressure in the atria, then the A-V valves can open for diastolic filling of the ventricles; lasts about .02 to .05 s. See also *cardiac cycle*.

jacksonian seizure: Seizure that originates on one side of the body, usually in the arm or leg, and spreads to other parts of the body. Resembles a grand mal seizure without the aura or tonic phase and with no loss of consciousness. Also called *focal seizure.*

jnd: See *just noticeable difference.*

joint: See *articulation.*

joint mechanical power: The product of the joint reaction force vector and the linear velocity vector of the joint. Joint mechanical power is measured in watts (W). See also *power.*

joystick: Apparatus that controls various devices; usually a lever mounted vertically that can be moved in at least two directions, forward/back and side-to-side, and often diagonally.

J point depression: Junction between QRS and S-T segment normally forming part of isoelectric or baseline; when S-T segment has not recovered to the baseline but is upsloping and less than 1.5 to 2.0 mm below baseline at .08 s after J point, J point is said to be depressed; alone, does not constitute diagnostic ischemic response to graded exercise test.

jumping: The locomotor skill in which the performer takes off on one foot or both feet and after a period of flight lands on both feet simultaneously.

just noticeable difference (jnd): Measure that indicates an individual's perceptual sensitivity in identifying the difference between two stimuli in 50% of the trials presented. Also called *difference limen, difference threshold.*

Karvonen formula: (max HR − resting HR) • a value between 65% and 85% of max HR + resting HR; used for prescribing exercise intensity.

kernicterus: The clinical syndrome used to describe the condition and resultant disability due to blood (Rh) incompatability between the mother and the developing fetus.

key observation points: The component parts of a developmental pattern or skill that are observed and identified prior to and during the instructional process. Also called *observation cues.*

keyword: Elaboration strategy that allows the learner to form a mental image or reference point to learn a motor skill.

kilocalorie: The energy needed to raise the temperature of 1 kg of water 1 degree Celsius, specifically from 15 °C to 16 °C; 1 kcal is equal to 4186 J. See also *calorie.*

kilopond (kp): One kilogram (of mass or weight) under the acceleration of gravity; in common usage 1 kp = 1 kg.

kinanthropometry: The area of study concerned with the body's physical measurements as they relate to movement.

kinematics: Area of mechanics concerned with the position, velocity, and acceleration (angular or linear) of a system without reference to the forces causing motion.

kinesiology: The scientific study of human movement.

kinesthesiometer: Apparatus that allows for active or passive movement in positioning of the forearm over a range greater than 90 degrees. The forearm is placed in a tray (trough) with the elbow at the pivot end; indicators mounted below the tray indicate the position of the arm on a scale in degrees or millimeters.

kinesthesis: 1. Information derived from a combination of senses through muscle spindles, Golgi tendon organs, joint receptors, cutaneous receptors, semicircular canals, and hair cells in the utricle and saccule; gives the performer a sense of limb position and body position in space. **2.** Sense of movement.

kinesthetic discrimination: Ability to identify differences in objects such as size, weight, texture, and shape through kinesthetic (tactual) exploration or manipulation.

kinesthetic imagery: See *internal imagery.*

kinesthetic perception: Awareness of limb and body position in space and movement, and aspects of the external environment with which the body comes in contact. See also *kinesthesis.*

kinesthetic recognition: Ability to identify objects and their features through kinesthetic exploration or manipulation.

kinesthetic sensitivity: Ability to perceive in the kinesthetic modality such that one judges the affective qualities (e.g., pleasantness or agreeability) of a stimulus and localizes, identifies, and integrates characteristics of objects or movements. See also *epicritic sensibility, protopathic sensibility.*

kinetic energy: Capacity of an object to do work by virtue of its linear or angular motion. Kinetic energy is measured in joules (J).

$$\text{linear kinetic energy} = 1/2 \ mv^2$$

where m = mass of the object
v = linear velocity of the object's center of gravity

$$\text{rotational kinetic energy} = 1/2 \ I\omega^2$$

where I = moment of inertia of the object about an axis through the segment center of gravity
ω = angular velocity of the segment about an axis through the segment center of gravity

kinetic link principle: Increased distal segment velocity due to appropriate sequencing of proximal joint-limb segments.

kinetics: Area of mechanics concerned with the forces that act on a system.

knee angle: The angle between the thigh and the shank.

knowledge of performance: Information given to the performer regarding the movement pattern or technique used to execute a motor skill; typically provided from an external source after the task is performed.

knowledge of results: Information given to the performer at the conclusion of performance regarding the outcome of a movement response; often verbal in nature.

kp: See *kilopond.*

Krebs cycle: Series of chemical reactions that metabolize carbohydrates, fats, and proteins and liberate energy for the synthesis of ATP from ADP and Pi; takes place in the mitochondria; CO_2 is produced, and H^+ ions and electrons are removed, via oxidation of carbon compounds, and carried by electron carriers (NAD^+ and FAD^+) to the electron transport chain. Also called *citric acid cycle, TCA cycle, tricarboxylic acid cycle*.

KR interval: See *post-knowledge-of-results interval, pre-knowledge-of-results interval*.

Kukla's attribution theory: Based on the concept of perceived difficulty of a task. The theory that a decision about the amount of effort a person is willing to expend precedes the undertaking of a task and that, as the perceived task difficulty increases, so does the amount of expended effort for successful performance.

kwashiorkor: Disease of malnutrition, particularly protein deficiency, characterized by edema, pot belly, change in hair color, anemia, bulky stools, and depigmentation of the skin.

kypholordosis: Condition resulting from exaggerated thoracic and lumbar spinal curves. Also called *round swayback, swayback*.

kyphosis: Excessive forward bending in the anteroposterior curvature of the vertebral column in the thoracic area. Also called *humpback*.

kyphosis

L

labeling: Rehearsal strategy to aid recall of a movement by attaching to it a meaningful verbal label.

labyrinthine righting reflex: Reflexive response that brings the head to its normal position in space by action of the neck muscles when the proprioceptors of the fluid-filled chambers of the inner ear are stimulated.

lactacid oxygen debt: The slow component of excess postexercise oxygen consumption that is used to convert lactic acid to CO_2, water, and glycogen; late phase of the oxygen recovery curve.

lactacid phase: Former name of the slow phase of excess postexercise oxygen consumption.

lactate threshold: The workload or oxygen consumption level where lactate production by the working muscle exceeds the rate of lactate removal by the liver; at approximately 50% to 80% of $\dot{V}O_2$max; a higher lactate threshold has been associated with better endurance performance. Also called *anaerobic threshold, onset of blood lactate accumulation*.

lactate turnover: Rate at which lactate is removed from the blood and either reconverted back to glycogen or oxidized to pyruvate or carbon dioxide and water.

lactic acid: Reduced form of pyruvate (contains additional hydrogen atoms); under resting and low-intensity exercise below the lactate threshold, lactic acid does not accumulate, and the blood concentration remains at approximately 1 mm; during prolonged high-intensity exercise, more pyruvate is reduced (NAD^+ releases its H^+ ion to pyruvate), and the lactic acid concentration increases; increased concentration is associated with the onset of fatigue.

lactic acid system: Energy pathway used in high-intensity work over a short duration (less than 2 min); ATP is produced as a result of glycolytic breakdown of glucose to lactic acid. See also *glycolysis*.

lag: Delay, slowing, or stoppage in the forward movement of a limb, limb component, or implement held by a limb during execution of a ballistic skill. See also *developmental lag*.

laissez-faire leadership style: Refers to a leader's preference to avoid contact with group members; allows the group to make decisions that affect group members. Entails relatively little or no influence over the actions and feelings of group members. *Laissez-faire* literally means "let alone."

laminar flow: The parallel layers of moving air as an object moves through the air.

Landau reflex: Involuntary flexion of the legs in a response to passive head flexion, or extension of the legs with passive head extension, in infants. Also called *pivot prone reaction*.

language disorders: Problems with receptive language (deriving meaning from what is heard) and expressive language (verbally expressing oneself). See also *aphasia*.

lateral: The side of a body part away from the longitudinal midline of the body.

lateral dominance: The consistent preference for use of one eye, ear, hand, or foot instead of the other, although the preference for different anatomical units is not always on the same side.

laterality: The awareness that one's body has two distinct sides that can move independently; a component of body awareness.

later learning: The end of the skill acquisition process, close to the point where a skill is said to be learned.

law of acceleration: One of Newton's laws of motion; states that the rate of change of momentum is proportional to the applied force and takes place in the direction of the applied force.

law of action–reaction: One of Newton's laws of motion; states that for every action there is an equal and opposite reaction.

law of effect: If consequences of responses are positive, then the probability that the same or similar response will recur under the same set of stimulus conditions increases; and if the consequences are negative, probability of response recurrence decreases.

law of inertia: One of Newton's laws of motion; states that a body will continue in its state of motion unless acted on by an external force or torque.

lazy eye: See *amblyopia*.

LDL: See *low density lipoprotein*.

leader: **1.** Person who exerts and commands more influence than the other group members and is in a position of making decisions that influence their actions and feelings. **2.** Person who can effectively organize, control, and direct the work of others. **3.** Act of exhibiting the highest level of skill in the group for the task at hand in a given situation.

leadership: Position and act of influencing individuals and groups toward set goals due to authority within a social relationship or group.

leadership style: The qualities in the relationship between the leader and followers in a particular situation; concerned with the actions of leaders rather than their personal characteristics. See also *leader, leadership*.

lean body mass: Fat-free body plus essential fat stores; equals body mass minus storage fat.

lean-to-fat ration: Index of leanness, calculated as follows: lean body mass/fat mass; an expression of lean body mass relative to the fat mass; average value is approximately 6 for males and 3 for females; may exceed 10 in low-fat, high-lean-mass individuals.

leaping: Locomotor pattern consisting of an elongated running step; can be interspersed in a run or performed continuously in an alternating foot pattern.

learned effectiveness: Describes an individual who (a) maximizes her or his potential by setting realistic goals, (b) improves weaknesses in training/learning, (c) focuses on the present, and (d) has an internal locus of control (i.e., takes responsibility for her or his performance).

learned helplessness: **1.** Condition descriptive of individuals who demonstrate maladaptive achievment patterns such as avoidance of challenging tasks, low task persistence in the face of obstacles, and feelings of low ability, low pride, and low satisfaction under unsuccessful conditions. **2.** Condition in which one feels that one has no control over one's performance outcomes and that failure is inevitable. **3.** Expectancy that one's own reactions and the environmental consequences that result are unrelated. If the person cannot gain control over the situation, the result is often lowered motivation, cognitive deficits, and depression. Also called *helplessness*.

learning: Relatively permanent improvement in behavior as a result of practice or experience. It is inferred from a person's behavior or performance and not observed directly.

learning curve: Plot of performance over the course of practice, from which learning can be inferred if performance improves with practice. See also *negatively accelerated learning curve, negatively decelerated learning curve, positively accelerated learning curve, positively decelerated learning curve*.

learning disability: Disorder in one or more of the basic psychological processes involved in understanding or in using language, spoken or written, which may manifest itself in an imperfect ability to listen, think, speak, read, write, spell, or to do mathematical calculations; includes such conditions as perceptual handicaps, brain injury, minimal brain dysfunction, dyslexia, and developmental aphasia; does not include learning problems that are primarily a result of vision, hearing, or motor handicaps, mental retardation, or environmental, cultural, or economic disadvantage.

learning environment: Variables in the instructional process that interact with the ability to learn, including teacher or student attitude, class size, facilities, equipment, and discipline.

learning goal: See *outcome goal*.

learning score: Measure of the extent of learning, determined by various mathematical procedures. Examples include summing or averaging performance scores on all learning trials, determining the gain or difference score, or recording the best score.

learning stations: The inclusion of several activity areas in the teaching space to provide small-group instruction designed to achieve specific objectives.

learning style: One's preferences for processing externally derived information for storage into, and retrieval from, permanent memory to facilitate skill acquisition and knowledge. See also *cognitive style*.

least restrictive environment: The environment, selected from a continuum of educational placements from mainstreamed to segregated, that presents the best possible learning environment for a handicapped learner, based on his or her educational needs and functional ability.

left atrioventricular valve: See *mitral valve*.

left semilunar valve: See *aortic valve*.

left ventricular end diastolic pressure: The pressure in the left ventricle immediately before ventricular contraction; related to the amount of stretch on the cardiac fibers and the left ventricular end diastolic volume; the higher the pressure, the greater the force of the subsequent ventricular contraction. See also *left ventricular end diastolic volume*.

left ventricular end diastolic volume: The amount of blood in the ventricles at the end of the filling phase of the cardiac cycle; the higher the volume, the greater the ventricular contraction and stroke volume. See also *left ventricular end diastolic pressure*.

legal blindness: Visual condition characterized by sharpness of vision (visual acuity) of 20/200 or less in the better eye after correction or a field of vision of less than 20 degrees.

Legg-Calvé-Perthes disease: See *Perthes disease*.

leg length: Anthropometric measurement of linear size of the leg, measured as (a) the distance from the greater trochanter to the lateral malleolus, (b) the distance from the greater trochanter to the bottom of the foot (floor, if subject stands), or (c) the difference between standing height and sitting height. Also called *functional leg length*.

length–tension relationship: The relationship between the length of the muscle and the tension produced by the muscle; states that higher tensions are developed the closer the length of the muscle is to its resting length.

lens: The clear part of the eye that refines and changes the focus of light rays upon the retina.

lesion: Pathological or traumatic interruption of tissue.

lesson plan: Written instructional program designed to accommodate learner needs, including class size, length of instructional periods, facilities, equipment, characteristics of the learner, skill levels, and interests, as well as environmental factors that will influence learning.

leveling effect: Tendency of more highly skilled individuals to perform beneath their optimum when competing against less skilled persons, and of less skilled persons to perform at their best when competing against highly skilled individuals.

level of aspiration: Degree of goal difficulty one sets for one's own achievement.

level of fixity: Extent to which a motor skill has developed, in the context of its retention after a period of inactivity.

level of involvement: Point at which a disability, with resultant loss of functional ability, occurs.

levels: 1. Movement concept used to divide the body's location in space into high, middle, and low. **2.** The steps in a developmental sequence based on qualitative change in behavior. Sometimes used when the sequential change is not known to meet the criteria of "stages" of behavior, and sometimes also called *component steps*, *stage*, *step*.

lever arm: See *moment arm*.

lever positioning: Task in which the subject grasps a lever and moves it, sight unseen, to produce or replicate a specified arm movement.

lever system: Simple machine, consisting of a fulcrum (axis of rotation) and eccentri-

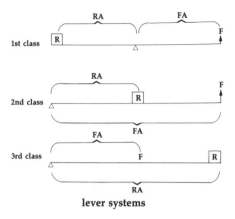

lever systems

cally applied forces, that does mechanical work (usually classified as first-, second-, or third-class).

life-cycle model of group cohesion: Tendency of groups to proceed through a cycle of five states: encountering, the testing of boundaries and creation of roles, creating a normative system, producing or constructing, and separation/dissolution.

life-cycle theory: Leadership approach in which group task success and personal fulfillment are viewed as more dependent on subordinate maturity than on leader behavior.

lift–drag ratio: Ratio of the lift force to the drag force.

lift force: Component of the fluid force acting in a direction perpendicular to the fluid drag force.

limb-girdle muscular dystrophy: Type of muscular dystrophy affecting both genders and occurring in the second decade; earliest symptom is usually difficulty raising arms and awkwardness in climbing stairs; weakness in the shoulder girdle or muscles of the hip and thigh.

limit cycle oscillator: Nonlinear system characterized by sustained cyclic motion that quickly returns to a stable mode (the limit cycle) after perturbation (tends to maintain frequency and amplitude of oscillation) and tends to synchronize with other

such oscillators. This system is proposed to provide a model for collections of muscles.

limited channel capacity: See *limited channel processing.*

limited channel processing: Hypothesis that there is a limit to the amount of stimulus information that can be handled simultaneously in the central nervous system to produce multiple responses. This limitation is likely due to the person's optimal capacity to process information. Exceeding this capacity often results in cognitive interference between tasks that slows response time and increases errors. Also called *limited channel capacity, limited concentration channel.*

limited concentration channel: See *limited channel processing.*

linear displacement: The magnitude and direction between an initial and a final position. Also called *displacement.*

$$x = x \text{ final position} - x \text{ initial position}$$

where x = linear displacement

linear envelope: Method whereby a full wave rectified electromyogram is filtered using a low-pass filter.

linear forces: System of forces that act serially along the same line of action. See also *colinear forces.*

linear impulse: 1. The product of the applied force and the time over which the force is applied. **2.** The integral of force as a function of time. Linear impulse is measured in newtons • seconds (N•s). Also called *impulse.*

$$\text{impulse} = \text{force} \times \text{time}$$
$$\text{impulse} = \int_{ti}^{tf} F dt$$

linear model of cohesion: A model that predicts that group cohesion continually develops as the group moves through progressive development stages.

linear momentum: 1. The quantity of linear motion. **2.** The product of mass and velocity of a body. Linear momentum is measured in kilogram-meters per second $(kg\text{-}m\text{·}s^{-1})$ and is usually designated by the letter p. Also called *momentum*.

$$p = mass \times velocity$$

linear motion: Movement that occurs along a straight or curved path. See also *curvilinear motion, rectilinear motion*.

linear movement apparatus: Apparatus consisting of a slide on a low-friction trackway. A pointer on the slide moves along a scale visible only to the experimenter so that the exact position of the slide or the extent of its movement by a subject can be recorded. The blindfolded subject grasps a handle on the slide to make a linear movement. For some tasks the experimenter can set a stop to the movement at a particular location on the scale. Also called *linear positioning slide*.

linear oscillator: System characterized by cyclic motion in which the force required to move the system a certain distance from its equilibrium point is a constant times that distance. A plot of force versus distance is linear. The linear oscillator often used to model muscle collectives is the mass-spring system. Also called *harmonic oscillator*.

linear positioning slide: See *linear movement apparatus*.

linear thinking: The search for an answer to a problem by utilizing a solitary solution without exploring reasonable alternatives.

line of action: The path along which a force acts.

line of gravity: The line of action from the center of gravity of the system to the center of the earth along which the force of gravity acts. Due to the size of the earth, the line of gravity acts vertically downward and perpendicular to the horizontal.

line of pull: The line of action of the tension developed by a muscle.

link system: Dividing of the body structure into separate units in order to precisely describe the contribution of the various links or body parts in the movement.

lipolysis: The catabolism of fat that liberates energy for the synthesis of ATP from ADP and Pi.

lipreading: See *speech reading*.

little league syndrome: Condition most prevalent in youth sports whereby the young athlete experiences physical discomfort or mental anguish before competing in sport due to unpleasant associations with previous participation.

load: Resistance to a movement.

locomotion: Movement of a body from one locus to another.

locomotion (group): Motivational construct that represents the reason or purpose behind a group's existence; symbolizes group activity in relation to its achievement of task objectives. Usually accompanied by an authority figure to ensure the coordination of group members.

locomotor skills: The group of skills in which the performer translates the body through space from one place to another.

locus of causality: A perception (i.e., attributions) about whether the cause of performance was internal (i.e., based on the performer's ability or effort) or external (e.g., due to luck or task difficulty). Stronger feelings are experienced with internal than external attributions. The feelings, in turn, lead to higher motivation.

locus of control: Classification of attribution about a person's disposition toward making internal or external ascriptions of causality (i.e., the extent of one's beliefs about explaining performance as a function of factors under one's own control).

locus of control theory: Suggests that internals believe that rewards or other reinforcements follow from their behavior or from the explanations they offer in attributing behavioral outcomes. Externals, on the other hand, believe that rewards are determined primarily by luck or fate and do not perceive themselves as having control over their environment. Internals, then, are more reinforced by success than are externals.

longitudinal axis: Axis or line running the length of a body or a segment.

longitudinal design: Research technique in which the same individual is observed performing the same task or observed on the same measurement over a long time period to determine developmental change.

long-term motor memory: 1. Recall, recognition, and retrieval of a movement after a delay of hours, days, or years without rehearsal. **2.** Structure within the information processing areas of the brain in which input is selectively and permanently stored. The input may be forgotten or subsequently retrieved through recall or recognition after a delay of hours, days, or years without rehearsal.

looking-glass self: Persona that reacts to other people's responses to us.

looming: The accelerated expansion of the visual image as an object or portion of the visual field approaches the observer.

lordosis: Excessive forward curvature of the lumber spine in which the pelvis is tilted forward (i.e., the anterior superior iliac spine is positioned forward and downward from its normal position). Also called *swayback*.

lordosis

low birth weight: Birth weight usually below 2,500 g without regard to length of gestation.

low density lipoprotein (LDL): Composed of a moderate proportion of protein with little triglyceride and a high proportion of cholesterol; LDLs transport cholesterol to all nonhepatic cells, where it is taken up by the process of endocytosis; excess cholesterol tends to be deposited on the blood vessel wall; associated with an increased probability of developing atherosclerosis. See also *high density lipoprotein*.

lower body negative pressure: The pressure working against the blood flow from the lower regions of the body; effects of gravity on the rate of return of blood from the lower parts of the body.

low guard: The arm position in locomotor skills wherein the arms hang down at the sides and do not swing in coordination with leg action.

low means interdependence: Behavior exhibited in coactive teams such as golf or gymnastics in which the interaction among group members is not required to meet group goals.

low-pass filter: Type of digital filter designed to remove random or high-frequency noise.

lumbar: The portion of the spinal column that occupies the lower back.

luteal phase: The period of time from ovulation until the commencement of the next menstrual flow; approximately 14 days in length; exercise and training has been associated with menstrual dysfunction related to a shortened luteal phase.

luxation: Dislocation or displacement of a body part.

macrocephaly: Condition in which the head is unusually large. Also called *megacephaly*. Compare *microcephaly*.

magnitude of behavior: The force with which a behavior is demonstrated.

magnus effect: The deviation of a rotating object from a straight-line path due to fluid forces that develop because of the object's rotation. The rotation causes a pressure differential on either side of the object, resulting in the object's traveling along a curved path.

mainstreaming: The placement of handicapped students into regular education programs with appropriate support personnel and services, as needed, to meet program goals.

main task: Prerequisite component to obtain a more difficult and intricate skill.

maintenance goals: Target criterion from a previously learned and practiced skill that the learner is not currently practicing directly but that must be retained in the learner's repertoire.

maladaptive achievement pattern: Pattern of achievement behavior characterized by maladaptive cognitive, motivational, and emotional components: cognitively, the deterioration of effective strategies or the failure to develop new and sophisticated strategies; motivationally, avoidance of challenge and low persistence in the face of obstacles; emotionally, experiencing pride and satisfaction only when ability is exhibited under successful conditions (failure conditions are experienced as indicating low ability and yield minimal pride and satisfaction). Compare *adaptive achievement pattern*.

management skill analysis: The information feedback provided to teachers concerning their effectiveness or performance; may include teacher–student interactions, prompts, behavior corrections, reinforcement, and time spent on teaching or management.

manipulation component of prehension: The terminal portion of an arm movement to grasp an object. Arm velocity slows and the hand opens, then shapes and orients, in anticipation of contact with the target object. See also *homing*.

manipulative skills: Gross skills involving the hands or feet that impart force to objects or receive force from objects, often to gain control of them; one type of fundamental motor skill, the other categories being locomotor and nonlocomotor skills; include throwing, catching, kicking, trapping, volleying, dribbling, striking, and fielding.

mantra: Simple, one-syllable sound used in meditation and as an intervention technique for the purpose of focusing attention internally and reducing stress, while fostering mental concentration, visualization, and relaxation.

manualism: The process used by the deaf for communication through signing.

marasmus: Wasting due to prolonged dietary deficiency of calories and protein.

Margaria Kalamen power test: Anaerobic (ATP-PC system) performance test for the legs; timed sprint up a flight of stairs with a running 6-m start; the time between stairs 3 and 9 is generally determined using a switch mat assembly; power output is calculated as the ratio of work (body weight times distance traveled) divided by performance time.

mark-time pattern: Locomotion wherein the swing leg touches down alongside the support leg, rather than swinging past the support leg to move the body forward. Often seen in young children in early attempts to ascend or descend steps.

MAS (motive to avoid success): See *fear of success*.

mass: 1. The measure of the amount of matter that comprises an object. **2.** A measure of the inertia of a body. Mass is measured in kilograms (kg).

massed practice: Schedule of practice with little or no rest between repetitions, such that practice is relatively continuous. The ratio of rest time to practice time is small.

massification of sport theories: The view that the organization of commercial sport meets the needs of the mass society without reference to the power relations or ideological practices that capitalist team owners must necessarily reproduce throughout society.

mass-spring model: Model that likens limbs reaching a given position, even without feedback and with changing initial conditions, to a spring attached on one end to a support and on the other to a mass. This spring equilibrates at a constant length regardless of how much it is pushed or pulled before release—that is, in its initial condition. Muscle length is associated with a given amount of activity in alphamotoneurons of the agonist and antagonist. The nervous system controls motion to a specific position by adjusting the length–tension relationship of muscles.

mastery: The ability to overcome difficult obstacles and achieve a desirable outcome.

mastery goal: The striving to increase competence and to understand or master a new skill based on effort. See also *outcome goal*.

mastery learning: The amount of learning necessary to achieve the predetermined criteria in an instructional setting. It is a function of the amount of time spent in proportion to the amount of time required for learning.

mastery orientation: Demonstrating the ability to adapt to new or challenging situations to achieve a goal. See also *adaptive achievement pattern*.

mastoiditis: Chronic inflammation of the middle ear that may spread to the air cells of the mastoid process.

match: See *contest*.

maturation: 1. Qualitative advancement in biological makeup. 2. Cellular, organ, or system advancement in biochemical composition. 3. [ad] The natural sequence in the development of self-help, motor, and socialization skills that would occur without instructional intervention.

maximal oxygen consumption: See *maximal oxygen uptake*.

maximal oxygen intake: See *maximal oxygen uptake*.

maximal oxygen uptake ($\dot{V}O_2$max): Highest amount of oxygen the body can consume during work for the aerobic production of ATP; expressed absolutely as L/min or relative to body weight (ml/kg BW/min) or relative to fat-free weight (ml/kg FFB/min); a true maximal value requires the achievement of established criteria during the exercise test, such as an RER > 1.0, a maximal HR $\pm$ 10 bpm, or a plateau in $\dot{V}O_2$ despite an increase in work and volitional fatigue; primary physiological index of cardiorespiratory capacity. Also called *aerobic power, maximal oxygen consumption, maximal oxygen intake*.

maximal treadmill time: Maximum time endured by a patient undergoing graded exercise stress testing on the treadmill; related to maximal aerobic capacity; often used as an index of cardiovascular endurance when oxygen consumption is not directly measured.

maximum voluntary contraction: Maximum tension produced by a muscle group during an all-out isometric contraction.

maximum voluntary ventilation (MVV): Test that measures the dynamic ventilatory capacity; determined by breathing as deeply and as rapidly as possible for 15 s; extrapolated to the minute volume; generally 25% higher than the ventilatory volume observed during maximal exercise, suggesting that in normal, healthy individuals, ventilation is not a limiting factor in maximal exercise.

McGregor's Theory X: Hypothesis wherein subordinates are viewed as lazy and irresponsible, inherently dislike work and will avoid it if possible, have little ambition, and wish to avoid responsibility. Compare *McGregor's Theory Y*.

McGregor's Theory Y: Hypothesis wherein subordinates are viewed as naturally self-motivated and responsible, prefer to exert physical and mental effort, are capable of exercising self-direction, and accept and seek responsibility; they only need encouragement. Compare *McGregor's Theory X*.

mechanical advantage: The ratio of the force arm to the resistance arm in a lever system.

mechanical contraction coupling efficiency: See *theoretical efficiency*.

mechanical energy: The ability to do work. Energy is measured in joules. See also *elastic energy, kinetic energy, potential energy*.

mechanical strain: Deformation of an object as a result of external loading; ratio of the change in length of an object as a result of external loading to the real length of the object prior to loading (unitless).

mechanical stress: The load per unit area on a surface as a result of an externally applied load. Mechanical stress is measured in newtons per meter squared (N/m^2).

mechanics: Branch of science that investigates motion and the action of forces.

mechanoreceptor: Specialized sensors located in the joints, tendons, or muscles that are stimulated by mechanical deformation such as stretching of the receptor membrane causing ion channels to open and sensory stimulus to be sent to higher centers; signals from those centers are thought to be partly responsible for control of ventilation during exercise.

medial: The portion of a body part closer than another portion of a body part to the longitudinal midline of the body.

mediation: [ad] The strategy of attaching a verbal label in order to facilitate recall.

mediation-relaxation procedures: Mental techniques used immediately prior to or during physical performance to reduce arousal and heighten relaxation.

mediolateral axis: Axis or line running from the medial to the lateral side of the body or a joint.

mediolateral ground reaction force: The shear component of the ground reaction force exerted in a direction parallel to the surface and perpendicular to the direction of movement.

mediolateral plane: Plane that divides the body into left and right portions. Also called *coronal plane*.

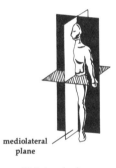

mediolateral plane

mediolateral plane

meditation: Mental strategy used to contemplate concrete sensory images to develop awareness of the present, enhance concentration of attention, and avoid concern for the past and future. Not concerned with reflective thinking or logical reasoning.

megacephaly: See *macrocephaly*.

memory: The process of recalling information that has been learned; includes short-term and long-term storage.

memory drum: The mechanism proposed by Henry wherein specific movements are stored as programs in an unconscious "motor memory," with no sharing of the control of similar movements. That is, two similar movements are controlled independently, without some mechanism such as a program for similar movements where parameters are merely changed to achieve slightly different movements. See also *memory drum theory*.

memory drum theory: Proposal by Henry, regarding control of movement, that specific movements are stored as separate programs in an unconscious "motor memory" while the control of similar movements is not shared. Hence, there is a memory for each movement learned rather than a program for similar movements wherein parameters are entered to achieve a specific movement. See also *memory drum*.

memory trace: 1. Mechanism hypothesized to exist in the central nervous system; said to select and initiate motor responses and to be developed by practice. **2.** Hypothetical change in the central nervous system proposed to account for the persistence of memories.

menarche: Time of the first menstrual period.

meninges: The protective membrane that surrounds the brain and spinal cord.

meningocele: Type of spina bifida characterized by a sac protuding from the vertebral column, containing cerebrospinal fluid but no spinal nerves. Some loss of cognitive functioning may result.

mental age: Reference to the IQ test score that specifies the age level at which the child is functioning.

mental fatigue: Psychological state, often due to mental overload or underload (boredom), that results in reduced mental functioning.

mental imagery: See *imagery*.

mental practice: Internal (covert) rehearsal of symbolic representation and reinforcement of previously learned motor skills and responses; thought to enhance motor performance; similar, but not identical, to imagery. Also called *mental rehearsal, visualization*.

mental preparation: Immediate preperformance cognitive strategy to establish a mental set (i.e., a state of mind).

mental rehearsal: See *mental practice*.

mental retardation: According to the Education of the Handicapped Act (1986), a condition in which the individual has significantly below-average intellectual functioning and deficits in adaptive behavior; occurs during the developmental years.

mental set: Preperformance cognitive state (i.e., psychological readiness) with which one approaches engagement in a particular task. Examples include attentional focus, arousal, and concentration.

mere presence: Component of social facilitation theory describing the facilitative effect of a noninteractive audience or coactors on performing a task. "Mere" presence means that desirable performance can be obtained without competition, imitation of others, reinforcement, or the potential for rewards or punishments.

mesomorph: Body type characterized by a relative prepondance of muscle, bone, and connective tissue that easily facilitates movement and functional ability.

MET: The unit used to represent the metabolic equivalent of work for a particular activity; calculated by dividing the metabolic rate at work by resting metabolic rate; one MET is equivalent to 3.5 ml of oxygen per minute per kilogram of body weight.

metabolism: Chemical changes that utilize energy and result in tissue and compound building (anabolism) or breakdown of substrates and release of energy (catabolism). See also *anabolism, catabolism*.

methods: In teaching, the way instruction is presented to facilitate learning, based on variables including age, skill level, class size, discipline, and the physical environment.

microcephaly: Condition in which head size is abnormally small, more than two standard deviations below the mean. Compare *macrocephaly*.

middle guard: The arm position in locomotor skills wherein the hands are held nearly motionless at waist level.

midsupport: The point approximately halfway through the support phase in the step of a locomotor skill.

mildly mentally retarded: Classification by the American Association on Mental Deficiency used to specify individuals whose IQ score is between 52 and 67, with concurrent deficits in adaptive behavior. See also *educable mentally retarded*.

milieu of teaching: The social, political, and economic factors that directly affect the support, quality, and effectiveness of teacher preparation.

minute volume: See *pulmonary ventilation*.

mirroring: Modeling technique designed to visually prompt a movement. The teacher and student face in the same direction, as in looking in a mirror, and perform the movement together.

mirror tracer: Apparatus consisting of a vertically mounted mirror and shield to prevent the subject's view of the horziontal surface and, instead, to require visual input by means of the mirror. In an experiment, a pattern (usually a star) is placed on the surface, and the subject is asked to trace it, the mirror reversing the movement's dimensions. Also called *stabilimeter*.

misbehavior: Inappropriate responses or conduct by an individual or group.

mitochondria: Cell organelle; contains enzymes that catalyze reactions for the generation of ATP from aerobic metabolism via the Krebs cycle and the electron transport system; commonly referred to as "the powerhouse of the cell"; aerobically trained individuals have larger and more mitochondria in the trained musculature to enhance their capacity for aerobic ATP production.

mitral valve: The dual cuspid valve between the left atrium and left ventricle; comprised of two triangular flaps; regulates the flow of blood into the left ventricle and prevents backflow during ventricular contraction. Also called *bicuspid valve, left atrioventricular valve*.

mixed cerebral palsy: Most common form of cerebral palsy, characterized by no predominant type but a combination of symptoms from various types.

mixed dominance: Consistent preference for use of one eye, hand, or foot over the other when the preference is for different sides and different parts of the body (e.g., left eye, right hand, left foot). Also called *cross dominance*.

mixed longitudinal design: Research technique combining longitudinal and cross-sectional observations. Some subjects are observed over the full length of the study, and others are monitored part of the time or just once.

mixed venous blood: Blood returning from the systemic circulation to the right atrium with a lowered oxygen content.

mixed venous PCO_2: The partial pressure of carbon dioxide in the venous blood; around 46 mm Hg at rest, and may increase to 55-60 mm Hg at maximum levels of exercise; is "mixed" blood because it represents the PCO_2 coming from the whole body.

mixed venous PO_2: The partial pressure of oxygen in the venous blood; around 40 mm Hg; coming from a maximally exercised muscle, it may be as low as 5 to 10 mm Hg.

mnemonic strategy: Scheme for remembering, usually associated with counting or association of material to familiar numbers. In motor behavior, the strategy can be applied to remembering a distance to be moved.

mobility of articulations: Motion at a joint that results from normal ligamentous, muscular, and capsular laxity; allows for motions other than pure rotation, slide, or glide; important for the achievement of full range of motion.

mobility training: Techniques used with the blind to facilitate orientation and safe movement within their environment.

modal: Pertaining to the mode, or score/behavior that occurs most often in a set of observations. In motor development, often refers to the most frequently observed behavior in a developmental sequence.

modal level: The level in a developmental sequence exhibited most often on the trials composing an observation session.

model: Visual or graphic representation of the relationships between identifiable variables (e.g., Xs or Os that represent players' positions and movements). Based on social learning theory in which behavior is best explained as a function of observational learning.

modeled behavior: Imitated action following the observance of a demonstration of that action.

modeling: 1. Technique of demonstrating skills to enhance motor skill acquisition or performance. The learner/observer's performance is fostered through observation of another person demonstrating the to-be-performed skill. **2.** Act of having a performer observe another individual execute the skill. Also called *observational learning*. See also *cognitive modeling, exemplary modeling, participatory modeling*.

model talk: Technique in which the demonstrator (model) conveys information to the observer (performer) about task execution or other information essential for performance success. Information might not be task specific but positive or negative statements designed to enhance efficacy.

moderately mentally retarded: See *trainable mentally retarded*.

modified tension–time index: See *rate pressure product*.

moment arm: The perpendicular distance from the axis of rotation to the line of action of a force. Also called *force arm, lever arm, resistance force arm*.

moment of force: See *torque*.

moment of inertia: 1. The quantity designating the resistance of an object to an angular change in its state of motion. **2.** The quantity representing the distribution of an object's mass about the axis around which it is rotating. **3.** The sum of the products of the point masses and the distances of the point masses from the axis of rotation. Moment of inertia is measured in kilogram-meters squared (kg-m^2) and is usually designated by the letter I. Also called *rotational inertia*.

$$I = \sum_{i=1}^{n} m_i r_i^2$$

where m_i = individual particle mass comprising object

r_i = perpendicular distance of particle mass from axis of rotation

momentum: 1. [bm] See *angular momentum, linear momentum*. **2.** [ss] See *psychological momentum*.

monitoring: Technique in which the teacher scans the room to observe progress of the lesson, behavior, or pace of the lesson.

monoplegia: Condition in which one limb is paralyzed, usually an arm.

monosynaptic response: Reflexive movement mediated by stimulation to a single sensory neuron and innervation of a single spinal motoneuron, hence the crossing of one neural synapse.

Moro reflex: Reflexive response of an infant, elicited by a sudden noise or jolt, a sneeze, or dropping a short distance through the air; consists of spinal extension and horizontal arm abduction then adduction. Also called *startle reflex*.

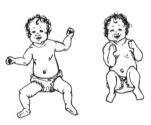

Moro reflex

morphological age: Assessment of biological maturation wherein a measurement of an individual's body height, limb length, breadth, or physique is compared to the average measurement for a given chronological age.

morphologic growth: Growth in terms of body structure, proportions, and physique.

morphology: The science of form and structure.

motion: Progressive change in position of an object with respect to time.

motivation: Drives, needs, or desires that regulate the direction, intensity, and persistence of behavior and are directed toward goals; what energizes, directs, maintains, and sustains behavior.

motivation orientation: The type of motivation that tends to most effectively spur one to engage in an activity, generally incentives either of intrinsic mastery or of extrinsic mastery. See also *extrinsic mastery, intrinsic mastery*.

motive: Latent, relatively stable dispositions a person has toward certain classes or groups of consequences; a personality characteristic involving a persistent or constant desire to either approach or avoid a particular course of action.

motive force: A force that causes movement.

motive to avoid success (MAS): See *fear of success*.

motive torque: Torque that causes rotation.

motoneuron: See *efferent neuron*.

motor ability: See *ability*.

motor capacity: A person's hereditary potential for general motor performance. Thought to be minimally influenced by environmental factors and experience.

motor control: Subdisciplinary area of study concerned with the mechanisms, both voluntary and reflexive, that control human movement. See also *control*.

motor development: Subdisciplinary area of study concerned with change and stability in motor behavior with advancing age, from conception to death.

motor educability: A person's capacity (genetic predisposition) to learn new motor skills. Thought to be minimally influenced by past experience and environmental factors.

motor-engaged time: See *activity time*.

motor fitness: Capacity in performance-related components of physical fitness that require some degree of skill, including coordination, agility, speed, and power.

motor learning: 1. Relatively permanent improvement in skill, resulting from practice and inferred from performance. 2. Subdisciplinary area of study concerned with the acquisition of skills as a result of practice and the manner in which skills are taught (instructional strategies) and executed. See also *learning*.

motor memory: Retention and retrieval of movement from storage in the central nervous system.

motor milestones: Set of fundamental skills acquired during infancy in a relatively fixed order at a rate that varies among individuals; so named because they are often landmarks (key points) in motor development.

motor neuron: See *efferent neuron*.

motor outflow time: Component part of reaction time consisting of the time period between (a) the change in electrical potential in the motor cortex and (b) the beginning of electrical activity in the muscle bringing about motor response.

motor output: The overt motor response that is demonstrated after sensory input and integration of the sensory information.

motor pattern: Combination of limb and trunk movements organized in a particular temporal–spatial (time and space) arrangement.

motor point: Point on a muscle where the

strongest action can be elicited by a given low-intensity electrical stimulus.

motor program: Abstraction of one or more movements that is thought to be previously learned and stored in the central nervous system. In traditional views, the movement is selected and initiated without regard to sensory feedback, with corrections based on sensory feedback only after at least one reaction time has elapsed. Other views incorporate sensory feedback correction of movement execution, but still not movement selection.

motor set: Readiness of the central nervous system to carry out a planned action.

motor short-term memory: See *short-term motor memory*.

motor stage: The second of Adams's two stages of movement learning, in which skill performance is habitual or automatic. See also *verbal-motor stage*.

motor task classification: Placement of motor tasks into categories or along a continuum according to some specified dimension of the task.

motor time: The span of increased electromyographic activity before an observable movement in response to a stimulus.

motor unit: Smallest controllable muscular unit consisting of a single motor-neuron and the muscle fibers it innervates.

motor unit action potential: Waveform detected by electromyography, consisting of the summation of individual muscle-fiber action potentials from a motor unit.

movement awareness: Knowledge of the extent of movement that takes place at one or more body joints, often demonstrated by reproducing some movement as accurately as possible.

movement confidence: The sense of feeling adequate (confident) during a skilled movement based on one's assessment of one's movement sensations; a consequence of personal evaluation process. For example, in basketball one could be confident in one's ability to execute a free throw but not in one's ability to execute a jump shot.

movement generator: Functional stage in an information processing model wherein, once the decision mechanism loads one or more motor programs into the generator, one organizes and initiates the programs, selecting the appropriate musculature to achieve the movement goal.

movement parameters: Values supplied to a generalized motor program to define how a movement should be executed. The movement can vary in duration, speed, force, and other dimensions by supplying various values of the dimension to the same motor program. Also called *parameters*.

movement pattern: Series of anatomical movements that have common elements in their configurations and goals.

movement time: The elapsed time between the first overt movement of a response to completion of that movement.

moving average: Smoothing technique in which groups of successive data points—the previous point(s), the current point, and the succeeding point(s)—are averaged to generate a best estimate of the current point.

multiarticulate muscle: Muscle or group of muscles crossing two or more joints.

multichannel processing hypothesis: Information processing viewpoint in which simultaneous perceptual inputs result in parallel motor outputs.

multicomponent model: Refinement of the two-component model of body composition by taking into account body water and/or bone mineral content of fat-free body when calculating percent body fat from body density; more accurate than two-component model. See also *two component model*.

multidimensional model of leadership: Theory of leadership effectiveness in which the satisfaction and performance of the subordinate are viewed as a function of three interacting components: (a) leader behaviors that conform to the established norms of the group or organization, (b) behaviors that are preferred by subordinates, and (c) behaviors that the leader actually exhibits irrespective of group norms or preferences. Ostensibly, as group members mature, relation-oriented behavior should progressively decrease, and the task-oriented behavior should take the curvilinear form; thus, in sport, a more task-directed approach is increasingly compatible with greater athlete maturity that reaches some optimal level; beyond this point, the task-directed approach is less appropriate for highly mature athletes and a relation-oriented style is preferred. In sport, the athlete's performance and team-member satisfaction are a function of the learner's behaviors, which in turn are modified by existing characteristics of (a) the situation, (b) the learner's personality and needs, and (c) team members.

multidisciplinary team: [ad] A team composed of members from various disciplines developing the educational plan, placement, and appropriate services for handicapped children. Also called *cross-disciplinary team, interdisciplinary team.*

multihandicapped: Inclusion of two or more handicapped conditions at the same time.

multiple sclerosis: Chronic, progressive disease of the central nervous system characterized by the breakdown, hardening, or scarring of the protective myelin sheath of the nervous system. See also *demyelinating disease.*

multisensory approach: Employment of more than one sensory modality in an effort to facilitate learning.

multivariate approach: Measurement technique that deals with multiple measures of some factor (e.g., measuring different personality traits jointly) rather than treating each component of this variable as independent entities.

muscle atrophy: See *atrophy.*

muscle biopsy: Removal and examination of muscle tissue from the body; removal is either by using a needle (needle biopsy)

or by making an incision through the skin and taking a sample of muscle tissue (open biopsy). Used for purposes of classifying an individual's muscle-fiber composition; muscle sample is studied histochemically, biochemically, and morphologically to identify the specific characteristics of the muscle fiber. See also *fast-twitch glycolytic fiber, fast-twitch oxidative glycolytic fiber, slow-twitch oxidative fiber.*

muscle collective: See *coordinative structure.*

muscle fiber: Multinucleate muscle cell containing the contractile elements of the muscle; fast-twitch or slow-twitch.

muscle hypertrophy: Increase in the size of the muscle fibers; results from resistance training; largest changes occur as a consequence of a high-resistance, low-repetition program.

muscle linkage: See *coordinative structure.*

muscle spindle: Sensory organ, located within a muscle, that gives feedback to the central nervous system regarding the change in length of muscle fibers and the rate of change of length.

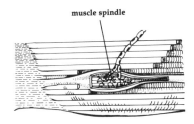

muscle spindle

muscle testing: Subjective, manual assessment of prime movers, used by therapists to evaluate the functional strength and endurance of muscles.

muscle tone: A muscle's state of tension.

muscular atrophy: Degenerative muscular disease of motor neuron cell bodies, characterized by a wasting away of muscular tissue from a lack of innervation to these muscles.

muscular dystrophy: Hereditary muscular disease characterized by progressive weakness due to the degeneration of muscle tissue. See also *Becker's muscular dystrophy, Duchenne muscular dystrophy, facioscapulohumeral muscular dystrophy, limb-girdle muscular dystrophy.*

mutual contingency: In a sport context, the fact that the spectators' demands influence the responses of the sport organization and athletes, and vice versa.

MVV: See *maximum voluntary ventilation.*

myelin: The protective covering along pathways linking neurons in various parts of the brain and spinal cord that acts to insulate the cells and increase the speed of neural transmission.

myelomeningocele: The most severe type of spina bifida, characterized by a sac protruding from the spinal column and containing portions of the spinal cord, meninges, and cerebral spinal fluid; results in a loss of motor functioning, incontinence, and perhaps hydrocephalus.

myocardial contractility: The strength of contraction of the heart; the greater the myocardial contractility, the larger the stroke volume at a given end diastolic volume. See also *contractility.*

myocardial infarction: Destruction of myocardial tissue caused by a lack of oxygen; obstruction of blood flow in the coronary arteries caused by atherosclerotic disease or a blood clot that blocks blood flow for a significant amount of time. Also called *heart attack.*

myocardial oxygen consumption: Oxygen utilized by the heart; in a clinical setting this is estimated by the rate pressure product, which is equal to the systolic blood pressure times at-rest heart rate; the heart removes 75% of the circulating oxygen, whereas the skeletal muscles use 25% of the circulating oxygen; thus, during exercise the heart requires an increase in coronary blood flow to increase the availability of oxygen to the heart muscle. See also *rate pressure product.*

myocardial oxygen demand: Demand for oxygen by the myocardium increases with exercise; demand is met by increasing the blood flow to the myocardium; a threefold increase in blood flow is seen with exercise at maximum levels.

myocardium: See *cardiac muscle.*

myofibril: The contractile apparatus of the muscle fibers that consists of actin and myosin filaments.

myoglobin: The iron protein molecule in skeletal muscle; contains only 25% of the oxygen-carrying capacity of hemoglobin; aids in diffusion of oxygen from cell membrane to mitochondria; also serves as storage site for oxygen, which is important during high-intensity exercise; a higher concentration of myoglobin is present in endurance-trained muscle.

myokinematics: Relationship between the structure and arrangement of muscle fibers and the amount of angular motion associated with a muscle contraction.

myology: The study of muscles.

myoneural junction: Junction between the muscle fiber and its nerve.

myopathy: Progressive weakening and wasting away of muscular tissue in which there is no suspected evidence of neurological disease or impairment.

myopia: Visual impairment resulting from an elongation of the eyeball; light focuses in front of the retina. Also called *nearsightedness.* Compare *hyperopia.*

myosin: The thick protein filament in the myofibril; has crossbridges that attach to active sites on the actin filament; this attachment is necessary for muscle contraction.

myosin ATPase: The myosin enzyme formed when myosin attaches to actin; catalyzes the reaction where ATP is split to ADP and Pi and energy is released for contraction; amount determines the speed of contraction; the more myosin ATPase, the faster the contraction; found in higher concentration in fast-twitch, glycolytic fibers; used as a marker to classify fiber type.

myositis: Inflammation of muscle or muscle tissue.

myotatic reflex: The reflex resulting when the stretch of the muscle spindles in a muscle cause a contraction of the muscle. Also called *stretch reflex*.

narrow attentional style: See *attentional style*.

natal: The period pertaining to the birth of an infant.

natural consequences: In education, reinforcing events that are not contrived, but are part of the instructional setting. For example, merely completing an activity is a reinforcing event.

nearsightedness: See *myopia*.

neck-righting reaction: See *neck-righting reflex*.

neck-righting reflex: One example of a derotative righting reaction in which there is an involuntary rotation of the body in response to turning a supine infant's head sideward. Also called *derotative righting, neck-righting reaction*. See also *body-righting reflex*.

negative energy balance: Caloric intake lower than energy expenditure; stored fat provides some of the energy needed, resulting in a loss of body fat and body weight.

negatively accelerated learning curve: The plot of a performance index over units of practice that depicts initial rapid improvement then decreasing gains as the curve rises on the graph.

negatively decelerated learning curve: The plot of a performance index, usually an indication of error, over units of practice that depicts initial rapid improvement then decreasing gains as the curve moves downward on the graph, typically because the performance index, error, is labeled low to high on the vertical axis. Lower error is better performance.

negative momentum: Reduced feelings of perceived or experienced control, confidence, optimism, or energy.

negative nitrogen balance: Excess loss

of nitrogen due to inadequate protein intake that causes an increase in the utilization of muscle protein; occurs during nutritionally inadequate dieting or starvation, febrile illnesses, malnutrition, and trauma.

negative psychological momentum: After experiencing failure, the increased probability of subsequent failure.

negative reinforcement: 1. Withdrawal of an action, event, or substance that has previously served as a reinforcer, to increase the desired response. **2.** Removal of a stimulus to increase the likelihood of a response.

negative self-monitoring: Thinking about or recording one's failures. Compare *positive self-monitoring*.

negative support: Lack of weight bearing that occurs during flexion of the knees when pressure is removed from the feet.

negative transfer: Interference or inhibition in learning or performing a task due to exposure to another task.

negative work: The work done on a muscle group by an external force as the muscles act eccentrically in opposition to the external force; measured in joules. When the polarity of the net muscle moment and the angular velocity at the joint are different, negative work is done. Compare *positive work*.

neonatal reflexes: See *infant reflexes*.

neonate: Label given to an infant from birth to age one month.

neoplasia: The formation of a tumor; a new or abnormal growth.

nerve compression block: 1. Application of a blood pressure cuff to a limb to prevent feeling in that limb below the cuff, presumably blocking afferent pathways. **2.** Stoppage of afferent neural impulses (which travel from proprioceptors to the brain) through chemical, as opposed to mechanical, means.

nerve plexus: Network or tangle of nerves.

net force: The vector sum of all forces acting at a joint.

neural noise: Random activity in the nervous system that interferes with the individual's perception of external stimuli.

neurological impairment: Damage or deterioration to the central nervous system with resultant loss of functioning of the brain, spinal cord, ganglia, and nerves. Also called *neuromotor disorder*.

neuromotor disorder: See *neurological impairment*.

neuromuscular feedback theory: The contention that a vivid, well-controlled image produces a minute innervation of the identical muscles used during the overt movement. In turn, this covert action provides kinesthetic feedback for future movement correction in the brain (premotor cortex). Also called *psychoneuromuscular feedback theory*.

neuron: Conducting cell of the nervous system consisting of a cell body with a nucleus and cytoplasm, dendrites, and axons. See also *afferent neuron, efferent neuron*.

neuron

neurosis: A disorder of thought processes, in which reality is maintained although sometimes ignored; hysteria, obsessions, or phobias.

neutral hypnosis: Hypnotic state in which physiological responses are identical to those of relaxation. See also *relaxation response*.

neutral stimulus: Event or situation that fails to change the rate of a behavior.

Newton's laws of motion: The relationships between force and motion formulated by Sir Isaac Newton. See also *law of acceleration, law of action-reaction, law of inertia*.

nitrate: Any one of a group of drugs used to treat angina pectoris; e.g., nitroglycerine; may be administered orally; causes rapid vasodilation of the coronary vessels to increase blood flow and oxygen delivery to the heart.

noise: 1. [sp] Random neural variability of stimuli derived externally from the environment or internally in the subject's sense organs. See also *neural noise, visual noise.* **2.** [bm] Error(s) in a signal introduced by the measurement process.

noncategorical programs: Programs that do not differentiate among or assign labels to children with special needs.

noncompetitive coaction effect: Influence on performance of a passive audience or of persons who work alongside one another—who may or may not observe each others' actions—while independently performing the same activity, such as rowing, without rivalrous incentives. Compare *competitive coaction.*

noncontributing teaching behaviors: Teaching behaviors that make no contribution to lesson content.

nondominant response: Actions that have only minimal probability of occurrence due to the lack of previous skill mastery. Compare *dominant response.*

nonessential variable: See *control variable.*

noninteractive audience: Passive observers who do not interact verbally or emotionally with the performer.

nonlinear oscillator: System characterized by cyclic motion in which the force moving the system, when plotted against the distance moved, yields a curvilinear line; often used to model muscle collectives; the limit cycle oscillator (i.e., an oscillator that returns to a stable mode). Biological systems are nonlinear.

nonlocomotor: Refers to skills performed in a stationary position.

nonregulatory stimuli: Aspects of the environment that are unrelated to achiev-ing the goal of a movement task and therefore are best ignored. Compare *regulatory stimuli.*

nonverbal interactions: [pd] Communication between teacher and student that uses gestures or cues to convey information about inappropriate or appropriate behaviors.

noradrenaline: See *norepinephrine.*

norepinephrine: Hormone secreted by the sympathetic nervous system (SNS) and by the adrenal medulla in response to SNS stimulation; as a general vasoconstrictor (except in the vessels leading to the heart and exercising skeletal muscle) it causes an increase in blood pressure and total peripheral resistance and accelerates the rate and depth of breathing; a catecholamine. Also called *noradrenaline.*

normal force: Component of a force that is acting perpendicular to the surface.

normalization: [ad] The provision of opportunities and conditions of everyday life to enable handicapped individuals the same experiences as the nonhandicapped in schooling, residence, work, and physical activity.

normal sinus rhythm: Normal rate and regular rhythm of the heart, originating from the sinoatrial node.

normative rules: Standards that reflect the collective attitudes, preferences, and values of the participants.

norm referenced: Regarding standardized tasks, administered under conditions that are similar to, and comparisons based on variables that are consistent with, the assessed groups.

nutation: The tilting of a spinning body's principle axis of rotation away from its original position.

nystagmus: Rapid involuntary movement of the eyes (side to side, up and down, and in rotary directions) that may cause difficulty in fixating on objects.

obesity: Pathological condition in which the person's body weight is 20% to 25% above their skeletal and physical requirements for a male, and 30% to 35% for a female. See also *overweight*.

objective competitive outcome: The result of winning or losing after engaging in a competitive event. See also *subjective competitive outcome*.

OBLA: See *onset of blood lactate accumulation*.

oblique plane: Any plane, other than the cardinal planes, segmenting the human body.

observation cues: See *key observation points*.

observational learning: See *modeling*.

observation recording: A form of evaluation and data collection; noting and recording specific behaviors that occur in structured or unstructured activities.

ocular: Refers to the mechanisms of the eye.

ocular tracking: Visually tracking a moving object with eye movements that match the performer's central gaze to the object's position. Also called *visual tracking*.

offensive proactive assertive behavior: Acceptable yet forceful sport behavior designed to acquire a valued resource—for instance, a ball carrier in football running for extra yardage.

Ohio State University Scale of Intra-Gross Motor Assessment (SIGMA): A criterion-referenced assessment of fundamental locomotor and manipulative skills in preschool and elementary-aged children. Eleven skills are evaluated into four developmental levels. Interjudge agreement ranges from .50 to 1.00; intrajudge agreement ranges from .67 to 1.00.

olfactory: Refers to the sensory modality associated with smell.

oligomenorrhea: Infrequent menstrual periods; higher incidence among endurance athletes, particularly runners; etiology may be multifactorial.

omission training: Reinforcement an individual receives for not responding in a particular manner.

onset latency: Time period between a stimulus and the beginning of electrical activity in the responding muscles as indicated by electromyograph recordings. In the study of balance, the stimulus is a perturbation (disturbance) of equilibrium. See also *premotor time*.

onset of blood lactate accumulation (OBLA): See *lactate threshold*.

ontogenesis: The progressing life history of an individual.

ontogeney: 1. The normal course of development and acquisition of skills that is expected of the human organism. 2. [ml] Behavioral changes resulting from learning.

open circuit spirometry: Indirect method for measuring energy expenditure, used to determine oxygen consumption both at rest and during exercise; individual breathes ambient air; ventilation, percent expired oxygen, and percent expired carbon dioxide are measured; the amount of oxygen consumed and carbon dioxide produced can then be calculated from established metabolic equations. See also *closed circuit spirometry*.

opening up: Body movements in throwing and striking skills wherein body parts are moving in the opposite directions simultaneously (e.g., contralateral leg forward, arm and shoulder backward) to ultimately produce force in the direction of object projection. (If observed from the side, performer appears to "stretch out.")

open-loop control: Mode of movement control wherein movement parameters sent from a (functional) movement control center are sufficiently complete to execute the movement completely without alteration based on sensory feedback.

open skill: Forced-paced motor task performed in an environment that is unpredictable and is changing spatially and/or temporally.

operant conditioning: Type of learning in which behaviors are altered by the regulation of consequences that follow the behavior. When a response is followed by an act that reinforces it, the likelihood of that response recurring is strengthened.

opposition: Movement pattern wherein the arm and leg on opposite sides of the body swing forward and back in unison, with the remaining arm and leg swinging in the opposite direction.

opthalamia: Severe inflammation of the eye or the conjunctiva.

opthalmology: The science dealing with diseases of the eye.

optic array: The reverberating flux of light waves resulting from the characteristic way each surface in the environment reflects light according to its color, texture, and angle of inclination. This flux of light waves provides to the viewer the stimulus for visual perception.

optic flow: Change in the pattern of optical texture as the viewer moves forward or backward in a stable environment.

optic nerve: The eighth cranial nerve, which transmits neural impulses to the brain for interpretation and sight.

opticon: Device to enable the blind to read; consists of a camera that converts print into the image of letters that are produced through vibration on the finger.

optimal arousal: The level of excitation (arousal) for a particular skill, action situation, and personality that results in maximal performance quality. See also *inverted-U hypothesis.*

optomotor integration time: Component of visual reaction time consisting of the time period between (a) the first change in cortical activity, as measured by electroencephalograph recordings, indicating the sensory stimulus has reached the cerebral

cortex, and (b) a change in electrical potential in the motor cortex.

oralism: Approach to the education of deaf children that stresses speaking and speech sounds as an essential element to integration into the hearing world.

orbital plot: 1. Three-dimensional graphical display. When skill performance is analyzed, the plot is often of the angles of three joints involved in a movement. 2. Three-dimensional angle–angle diagram.

order of control: The relationship between using a control device and the resulting indicator of the response, for example, a cursor on a display screen. The relationship can be between force and position or force and velocity. See also *first-order control system, zero-order control system.*

organic brain dysfunction: Condition in which damage occurs to the central nervous system.

organizational strategy: The main theme(s) used to develop the arrangement of learning experiences to achieve program goals.

organization-structure model: The positive relationship between central spatial location in the group and the likelihood of performing dependent or coordinated tasks. In turn, this increases the rate of interaction with the occupants of other positions.

origin: The attachment site of a tendon of a muscle attached to the relatively more fixed or proximal bone.

origin–pawn theory: Contention that some people (origins) prefer to control their outcomes, whereas others (pawns) feel powerless to control theirs.

orthogonal: The components of a vector that are perpendicular to each other.

orthopedically impaired: Disability caused by disorder or trauma to the musculoskeletal system.

orthoptic vision: Ability to use and coordinate the extraocular muscles of the eyes.

orthostatic intolerance: Inability of the

circulation to adjust to upright posture due to reduced hydrostatic pressure in the circulatory system from loss of vasomotor control, blood volume, and muscle tone; often seen in bedridden individuals; results in decreased cerebral blood flow, leading to dizziness and fainting.

orthostatic tolerance: The flexibility of the circulatory system to adjust to changes in body position; factors involved in maintaining blood pressure and flow include vasomotor tone, changes in blood volume relative to arteriovenous capacity, and muscle tone.

oscillator: An object undergoing cyclic motion, passing continually through a maximum and minimum within the time interval of interest. Oscillators provide a model for the action of muscle groups. See also *limit cycle oscillator, linear oscillator, non-linear oscillator*.

oscillatory movements: Cyclic movements through the same points in a range of motion (trajectory). An example is the legs in running; they repetitiously make the same cycle of touchdown, support, toeoff, swing, touchdown, etc.

oscilloscope: Test instrument that displays on a screen electronic signals in waves and pulses.

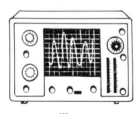

oscilloscope

Osgood-Schlatter disease: Condition affecting the knee, in which osteochondrosis or separation of the tibial tubercle occurs at the epiphyseal junction.

ossification: The formation of bone or a bony substance.

osteoblasts: Cells that function to continually deposit bone; secreted along with collagen molecules to form a polymer of an osteoid; with osteoporosis the activity of these cells is decreased.

osteochondrosis: Disease of one or more of the growth or ossification centers in children.

osteogenesis imperfecta: Hereditary condition in which the bones are formed improperly and are susceptible to break easily as a result of decreased bone density. Also called *brittle bones*.

osteoid: Bone tissue before calcification.

osteomyelitis: Bacterial infection of the bone.

osteoporosis: Porosity and diminution of bone density caused by the reabsorption of calcium and the failure of the osteoblasts to lay down bone matrix.

otitis media: Inflammation or infection of the middle ear that may cause conductive hearing losses.

outcome goal: 1. A performer's objective of striving to either gain favorable judgments or avoid negative judgments of his or her competence in comparison with the performance of another person. **2.** The level of success toward which a competitor strives as determined by the end product of that effort. Also called *learning goal*. See also *interval goal-setting*.

outcome-oriented performer: Person who assesses performance by comparing his or her own ability and actual performance level with others with similar traits and status.

outflow: Efferent neural signals that originate in the brain and move to the muscles to produce movement.

out-of-phase movements: Cyclic movements of two or more limbs with or without the same trajectories but not passing through corresponding points at the same time. For example, in walking, one leg is a half cycle out of phase with the other leg.

output: The observable motor action demonstrated by the learner after sensory input and decision making have occurred.

outtoeing: Characteristic of walking and running wherein the feet are planted with the toes pointed to the front and side, oblique to the line of progression. Sometimes the feet are also swung forward after toe-off at an oblique (outward) angle.

overachieving athlete: Sport competitor who is highly motivated, self-disciplined, and dedicated to virtual performance perfection; may not accept limitations in ability and physical requirements to succeed, so may have unrealistic expectations about future achievements.

overdwelling: Persisting in a chain of actions, verbalization, or instruction that is beyond what is required; for instance, a teacher explaining a movement in far greater detail than is needed for student understanding.

overflow of movement: Lack of voluntary control and extraneous movements, resulting from damage to the cerebellum.

overjustification hypothesis: The contention that if external rewards are offered to persons who engage in an activity for intrinsic reasons (e.g., for enjoyment or fun), the level of intrinsic interest in the activity may decrease; this reward may "overjustify" their participation. An example would be offering trophies, based on performance competence, to athletes who are participating for fun.

overlearning: Practicing a motor task past the point where a designated criterion level has been reached.

overload principle: Training guideline in which muscular and cardiovascular systems are progressively stressed to bring about improvements in strength and endurance.

overshoot: Error in a movement for accuracy wherein the target is passed or exceeded.

overt characteristics: Observable characteristics, as of a behavior, skill, or disability.

overtraining: Constant severe training that does not provide adequate time for recovery; symptoms include an increased frequency of injury, irritability, increased resting heart rate, altered appetite, apathy, and decreased performance. Also called *burnout, staleness.*

overuse syndrome: Injury resulting from continual low-level stress placed on a body part.

overweight: Weighing over 10% more than the weight accepted for one's structural capacities. See also *obesity.*

oxidative deamination: One of two ways amino groups can be removed from amino acids; the NH group is oxidized in the liver and forms uric acid.

oxidative phosphorylation: Process in which $NADH^+$, H^+ and $FADH_2$ are oxidized in the electron transport system and the energy released is used to synthesize ATP from ADP and Pi. See also *electron transport system.*

oxygen consumption ($\dot{V}O_2$): The amount of oxygen taken up and used at the cellular level at rest, during exercise, or in recovery; during incremental exercise $\dot{V}O_2$ increases until it plateaus near maximal effort; normal resting $\dot{V}O_2$ for a young male at rest is approximately 250 ml/min; at maximum exercise this value can go as high as 5,100 ml/min; reflects aerobic energy metabolism. See also *maximal oxygen uptake.*

oxygen debt: See *excess postexercise oxygen consumption.*

oxygen deficit: The difference between the oxygen required during exercise and the oxygen actually consumed during the activity.

oxygen pulse: The amount of oxygen transported by the blood per heart beat; calculated as $\dot{V}O_2$/HR; has been used as an indirect measure of stroke volume.

oxygen uptake kinetics: The rate at which $\dot{V}O_2$ increases to steady-state at the onset of exercise or decreases to resting or baseline $\dot{V}O_2$ at the cessation of exercise; expressed as half-time.

pacing: See *flow*.

pain threshold: The point at which pain is first perceived by the subject.

pain tolerance: The amount of pain (discomfort) a subject is able to withstand prior to terminating the stimulus (the source of pain).

paired associative learning: Elaboration strategy in which the student builds internal associations between two or more items to learn a task.

palmar grasp reflex: Reflexive contraction of the finger flexor muscles in response to a tickling of the palm.

palmar-mandibular reflex: See *Babkin reflex*.

parabolic path: The bowl-shaped path that the center of gravity of a projectile follows if unaffected by air resistance. Also called *trajectory*.

parachute reaction: See *parachute reflex*.

parachute reflex: An infant's extension and abduction of the legs and arms as an involuntary reaction to its body being lowered toward the ground rapidly or tilted forward from an upright to a prone position. Also called *parachute reaction, placing reaction, placing reflex, propping reaction, propping reflex*.

parachuting: Extending the arms to the side and forward in anticipation of losing balance in landing from a jump.

paradigms: Models, patterns, or schema that lead to the development of theoretical constructs; for example, A-B-C paradigm of behavior management theorizes that the B, or behavior, can be modified by changing the A (antecedent event) or C (consequence of that behavior).

parallel activity in play: Sequence of development in which children play in the observable proximity of others without any social interaction.

parallel axis theorem: Theorem stating the relationship between the moment of inertia about an axis through a segment's center of gravity and about any other parallel axis.

$$I_a = I_{cg} + mr^2$$

where I_a = moment of inertia about an axis other than through the joint center
I_{cg} = moment of inertia about an axis through the segment center of gravity
m = mass of the segment
r = distance from the joint center to the segment center of gravity

parallel elastic component: The connective tissue (e.g., fascia, sarcolemma) that surrounds the contractile element of the muscle and exerts a passive elastic force when the muscle is stretched.

parallel forces: System of forces in which the lines of action of the forces are parallel to each other.

parallelogram of vectors: The geometric representation of the composition of vectors such that the resultant of two concurrent vectors is the diagonal of a parallelogram, two of whose sides are the original vector.

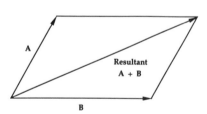

parallelogram of vectors

paralysis: The permanent or temporary loss of voluntary movement and sensation, due to the loss of integrity (intervention) of a motor nerve.

parameters: See *movement parameters*.

paranoia: A combination of fear, distrust, and hostility demonstrated toward others.

paraplegia: Paralysis and resultant loss of functioning in the lower extremities caused by a spinal lesion or neurological dysfunction.

parasympathetic nervous system: Part of the autonomic nervous system that primarily governs the resting functions; its nerve endings secrete primarily acetylcholine; causes excitation in some organs and inhibition in other organs; for example, stimulation causes a decrease in heart rate, stimulation of fuel storage, and enhancement of smooth muscle tone.

paresis: Local or partial paralysis or impaired functioning.

partially sighted: Having a visual impairment characterized by visual acuity between 20/70 and 20/200 in the better eye after correction.

partial pressure: Force exerted by any single gas in a mixture, equal to total pressure times the fraction of the gas; the partial pressure of oxygen at sea level in ambient air = 760 mm Hg • .2093 = 159 mm Hg.

participation motives: The reasons an individual prefers and engages in a particular activity (e.g., the reasons an athlete chooses to participate in a particular sport).

participative leadership style: A style in which the group's leader and its members try to consistently make decisions jointly. The leader assumes the role of just another group member with no more power of persuasion than other group members.

participatory modeling: Technique of demonstrating skills; first a model performs a task as the subject observes, and then the model assists the subject in successfully performing the task. The subject is not allowed to fail.

part teaching method: Instruction that utilizes components of an activity or task to achieve the whole.

part–whole perception: See *whole-and-part perception*.

part–whole practice: Instructional strategy in which learners practice component parts of a task to mastery before the parts are combined and the entire task performed. Also called *whole–part practice*.

part–whole transfer: The carryover benefit to the learning of a skill that comes from breaking down the skill into simpler parts and learning those parts before learning the entire skill. The benefit is assumed to come in speed or efficiency of learning. Also called *whole–part transfer*.

passive insufficiency: The inability of a multiarticulate muscle to be stretched sufficiently to allow a full range of motion simultaneously at all joints it crosses.

passive movement: Movement caused by a force outside the body rather than by concentric or eccentric muscle contractions within the body.

passive recovery: Restoration of resting homeostasis following exercise when the individual is in a nonexercising state; this slows the removal of lactate from the muscles and hence the rate of recovery.

path-goal theory of leadership: The contention that leadership (e.g., by a coach) is a function of the needs and goals of the group members (e.g., athletes). The leader is viewed as a facilitator who helps subordinates reach their goals by providing a path of appropriate behaviors. The strategic function of the leader is to provide the guidance, support, and rewards necessary for the group members' effective and satisfying performance. This will result in increased personal payoffs to subordinates for work-goal attainment, reduced road blocks, and increased personal satisfaction.

pathology: The branch of medicine dealing with the study and treatment of disease.

pathways: 1. Lines of movement through space, such as straight, curved, zigzag. 2. Floor or air patterns of objects, such as arched or curved. 3. A teacher's routes when moving through the class to provide individualized instruction.

pattern analysis: The study of developmental sequences of movement that are designed to reach a prespecified objective.

pattern generator: The oscillator mechanism in the central nervous system that provides muscular synergies to the various motor units involved in a movement. Also called *central pattern generator, function generator*.

patterning: A proposed method of treating children with developmental delays, in which active and passive movements, through crawling-, creeping-, and walking-like patterns, are performed repeatedly.

pattern recognition: The ability to perceive relationships among stimuli; for instance, visually perceiving certain lines as a shape, or auditorily perceiving certain spoken sounds as a word.

peak performance/experience: Nonvoluntary, temporary, and unique state of altered consciousness, occurring during moments of optimal happiness, fulfillment, and immersion in the activity and accompanied by a loss of fear, inhibition, and insecurity.

pedagogy: The systematic study of teaching.

peer isolation: See *contingency observation*.

peer-mediated reinforcement: Reinforcement generated by the peer group as a consequence of social or task-related behaviors.

peer tutoring: Individualized instruction provided by peers, as aides or assistants, to individuals who require special assistance for learning or completing a task (e.g., students instructing other students).

pendular model of cohesion: Model of the development of group cohesion in which developing groups exhibit extreme shifts of interpersonal relationships, as in oscillating from cohesion to differentiation to conflict to resolution (cohesion) to conflict to cohesion, and so on.

pendular motion: Motion of a body or a segment similar to the movement of a pendulum.

people-centered coach: Coach who places primary emphasis on fulfilling the personal needs of his or her athletes. See also *task-oriented coach*.

perceived ability: One's subjective assessment of one's own skills, on which is based one's stable, internal explanation (causal attribution) for one's performance outcomes. Viewed as the essential mediating factor (construct) of achievement behaviors.

perceived ability motivation model: Model based on the view that a person's primary achievement goal is to maximize demonstrating high ability and minimize revealing low ability. Ability is assessed by (a) comparing one's performance with that of others of similar age and/or ability (social comparison processes) and (b) making a comparison between one's performance and personal standards of excellence.

perceived competence: The sense that one has the ability to master a task or some other personal (e.g., body image, self-esteem) or environmental (e.g., relationships with others) feature.

perceived contingency: Subjective assessment of a situation in which success at a future activity is determined to depend upon success in the present activity.

perceived difficulty: Subjective assessment of the effort or exertion that is required to solve a problem or achieve good (desirable) physical performance.

perceived exertion: See *rating of perceived exertion*.

percent fat: The proportion of total body mass that is fat tissue; can be estimated using hydrostatic weighing, skinfolds, or bioelectrical impedance techniques.

perception of causality: See *causal elements*.

perceptual anticipation: The acquiring

or matching of a moving target along a predictable path at a predictable rate, requiring a prediction of target position at the end of the response movement.

perceptual constancy: Ability to recognize objects or distances as stable and consistent even when their dimensions vary at the sensory receptor. For example, perceiving a chair to be stable in size even though viewing it at a distance yields a small image on the retina and viewing it nearby yields a large image on the retina.

perceptual filter: A functional operation during information processing wherein certain input is screened out while other information is identified and passed on for processing (e.g., storage, decision making, rehearsal); in humans, influenced by past experience. Also called *filter mechanism, selective filter.*

perceptual mechanism: The functional stage in information processing that includes the reception, identification, and classification of environmental information.

perceptual-motor skills: 1. Pertains particularly to motor skills in which perception plays a large role, with perceptual discrimination often dictating the appropriate response. **2.** Pertains to the motor skills being acquired by children.

perceptual narrowing: The ability of a person to selectively allocate attention to relevant stimuli. Also called *tunnel vision.*

perceptual style: See *cognitive style.*

perceptual trace: Hypothesized reference mechanism containing memory of past movements, against which sensory feedback from the current movement is compared so that movement quality might be evaluated, adjusted, or terminated.

performance: Observable and temporary behavior in the motor domain, influenced by personal and situational factors.

performance accomplishment: The goal when structuring the environment to create successful experience. The objective is to avoid focusing solely on the outcome of an event without considering the process or level of performance exhibited. A key element for enhancing efficacy as proposed by Bandura's self-efficacy theory.

performance expectancy: The anticipation of succeeding or failing at a task prior to its execution.

performance goal: The desire or objective to experience self-improvement, relative to the level of one's own performance, that is observable, measurable, and to some extent under one's own control.

performance objective: The instructional intent of the learner's behavior; can be changed as a result of the educational experience; must be observable and measurable, have a criterion for performance, and stipulate conditions under which behavior is performed. See also *behavioral objective.*

performance-orientation: Tendency to infer one's ability through self-evaluation processes (i.e., comparing one's performance with personal standards).

performance standards: Expectations about performance; in effective instruction, these are developed by the teacher and communicated clearly to the students.

perinatal: The period of time from shortly before to shortly after birth.

periodic motion: Motion that repeats itself. The amount of time required for each repetition is called the "period."

peripheral feedback: Sensory information that comes to the central nervous system from the sensory receptors during, or as the result of, a response.

peripheral group member: An individual in a group who does not perceive his or her group function as important and, consequently, has a relatively low need for group success and favors less challenging group goals.

peripheral hypothesis: See *chaining.*

peripheral nervous system: The parts

of the nervous system that are outside the brain and spinal cord (central nervous system).

peripheral stimuli: Input located at the outer boundaries of sensory detection (e.g., at the outer boundaries of the field of vision or auditory and tactile perception).

peripheral vision: The sight of objects in the visual field that fall on the outer portions of the retina, away from the place to which the eyes are directed. Because rod receptors predominate in these areas of the retina, peripheral vision is colorless.

peripheral visual field: The outer 98% of the field of vision.

perseveration: The persistent repetition of an activity or behavior.

personal factor: Disposition that originates from within the individual.

personality: 1. The integration of a person's interests, attitudes, capacities, abilities, aptitudes, structures, and modes of behavior. 2. Characteristics that allow for predicting what a person will do in a given situation.

personality structure: The basic psychological and emotional elements or traits of an individual and how they blend together to exhibit that individual's behavioral tendencies in certain situations.

personality traits: Broad underlying dispositions that pervasively influence behavior across many situations and lead to consistent behavioral patterns. Permanent predispositions or tendencies of a person's thoughts and actions that differ among individuals.

personalized learning: System of instruction based on the individual student's level of functioning; student proceeds at her or his own pace to achieve task mastery.

Perthes disease (Legg-Calvé-Perthes disease): Hip disorder in which the head of the femur degenerates.

pertinence model: Model of selective attention proposing that a person focuses on the most important stimuli.

perturbation: 1. Disturbance to a movement that is not anticipated by the performer. 2. Disturbance in balance, induced in experimental settings to measure subsequent postural sway, or the latency and pattern of a movement in response to the disturbance.

petit mal seizure: Nonconvulsive seizure characterized by brief impairment of consciousness followed by immediate recovery, occurring mostly in childhood and adolescence. Also called *absence seizure*.

pH: The negative logarithm of the hydrogen ion concentration; 7.0 is neutral, values less than 7.0 are acidic values, and values greater than 7.0 are basic values; normal arterial blood pH is 7.4; heavy exercise may change pH values.

phase: 1. Step in a developmental sequence based on a qualitative change in behavior. The term is sometimes used when the sequential change is not known to meet the criteria of "stages" of behavior. 2. Portion of the life cycle that is temporary but characterized by typical behavior. 3. In cyclic motion, the factor against which two or more cyclic motions can be compared for identical period or frequency and starting time. See also *in-phase movements, out-of-phase movements*.

phase locking: 1. Pertains to the exact matching of the phases (e.g., starting times) of two or more oscillators, such that one serves as a reference and the others are linked to it. 2. Pertaining to a fixed relationship between the phases of two nonlinear oscillators.

phase plane: Plot of movement velocity against displacement of a limb or body segment.

phasing: The temporal relationship in the sequential pattern of muscle contractions needed to execute a skill.

phenylketonuria (PKU): Metabolic genetic disorder caused by the body's inability to convert an enzyme for digesting protein (phenylalanine to tyrosine); accumulations of phenylalanine affect metabolism and result in abnormal brain development.

Philippson step cycle: The single-limb step cycle in an adult walk, consisting of four phases: (a) the F or flexion phase, from toe-off to beginning of knee extension during the swing; (b) the E1 phase, from this knee extension to heel strike; (c) E2, from heel strike to maximum knee flexion during the stance; and (d) E3, from the latter point to toe-off.

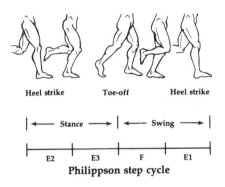

| Heel strike | Toe-off | Heel strike |

|← Stance →|← Swing →|

| E2 | E3 | F | E1 |

Philippson step cycle

phobia: Any persistent abnormal fear of people, situations, or objects.

phocomelia: Deformity in which the limbs of the infant are short or absent; commonly associated with poor maternal care or drugs during pregnancy.

phosphofructokinase: Enzyme in the glycolytic pathway involved in the chemical degradation of glucose to pyruvic acid; regulator of glycolytic rate; athletes involved in anaerobic activities have higher levels of this enzyme, enhancing their capacity for anaerobic ATP production; found predominantly in fast-twitch, glycolytic muscle fibers.

phylogenesis: The progressing life history of a species.

phylogenetic: 1. Refers to the development of a race or species. **2.** Refers to behavioral changes that occur automatically as the individual matures.

physical activity: Movement of the human body that results in the expenditure of energy at a level above the resting metabolic rate.

physical fitness: Physiological state of well-being that provides a degree of protection against hypokinetic disease; a basis for participation in sport; a vigor for the tasks of daily living.

physical impairments: Nonsensory limitations or health impairments affecting body movement, especially the skeletal system, including the spine, bones, muscles, and joints. See also *neurological impairment*.

physical medicine: The branch of medical science that utilizes therapeutic interventions to facilitate the healing process.

physical priming: Physical prompt to support or guide the performer's body parts through the activity to initiate movement or cue a behavior.

physical restriction: Method of physical guidance or prompting in which the learner is blocked from making an incorrect response, such as the use of a spotting belt in gymnastics or flotation device in swimming.

physical self-efficacy: Extent of a person's perception of the effectiveness of her or his physical skills in a specific situation; related to the probability of engaging in challenging physical activities. See also *self-efficacy*.

physical therapist: Medically certified professional responsible for evaluation and restoration of movement and functioning through the utilization of various physical modalities such as heat, cold, light, water, electricity, ultrasound, and exercise; also involved in the fitting and use of assistive devices to facilitate movement.

physical work capacity (PWC): The maximum level of work an individual is able to perform, often at a specified heart rate such as 150 or 170 bpm; used as a measure of aerobic fitness.

physiological arousal: State of heightened activation of the autonomic nervous system on a continuum from deep sleep to high excitement. Usually manifested by changes in heart rate, blood pressure, sweating, and other physiological responses.

physiological dead space: Alveolar dead space or alveoli that cannot function fully due to impaired blood flow in adjacent capillaries, plus anatomical dead space; not a significant factor in normal healthy individuals, but can be in certain pulmonary disease. See also *anatomic dead space*.

pigeon chest: Abnormal prominence of the sternum.

pincer grasp: Hand grasp that opposes the thumb with a finger to obtain a small object.

pitch: Tonal frequency (high or low) of a sound or voice.

pivot prone reaction: See *Landau reflex*.

PKU: See *phenylketonuria*.

placement: [ad] Assignment of instructional setting for handicapped children, generally in the least restrictive environment compatible with the functional ability and needs of the individual.

placing reaction: See *parachute reflex*.

placing reflex: See *parachute reflex*.

plane of motion: The plane in which movement occurs.

plantar: Pertaining to the sole of the foot.

plantar flexion: A movement of the foot, articulating at the ankle, in which the long axis of the foot is brought in line with the long axis of the shank; movement of the foot forward and downward. Compare *dorsiflexion*.

plantar grasp reflex: Reflexive contraction of the plantarflexor muscles of the toes in response to tactile stimulation of the plantar surface (sole) of the foot.

plaque: Protrusion of arterial walls consisting of an inner necrotic core filled with cell debris, cholesterol, and calcium and an outer fibrous cap composed of smooth muscle cells, collagen, elastin, and lipids. See also *atherosclerosis*.

plasma volume: The noncellular portion of the blood; plasma forms a part of the extracellular fluid and communicates directly with the interstitial fluid through pores in the capillaries.

plasticity: 1. [mc] Adaptability and flexibility. **2.** [mc] In physical growth and maturation, the ability of cells or tissue to take on a new function in the event of injury or damage to other cells. **3.** [bm] Ability of a material to be stretched beyond its normal limits and undergo a reorganization of its internal structure, forgoing a return to its original shape.

plateau: Segment in a performance curve that is level, indicating no change in performance.

play: 1. Physical activity that is free (i.e., unstructured), voluntarily begun, voluntarily continued, and voluntarily terminated. **2.** Inconsequential behavior that is internal to itself. It may result in the production of something material (e.g., a sand castle) or symbolic (e.g., poetry). However, such products are not the primary reason for the activity. One plays to experience the act of creativity or transformation. In sport, theoretically, play is a function of experiencing the joy of the human body in motion, although in reality, sport involvement is meant to satisfy a host of other social, psychological, and physical needs.

plexus: Any functional section of the spinal nerves.

PNF: See *proprioceptive neuromuscular facilitation*.

point of application: Point at which a force is applied.

Poiseuille's law: Mathematical description of the relationships between pressure, resistance, and the flow of blood expressed as:

$$Q = \Delta P \cdot \pi R^4 / 8\,NL$$

where Q = blood flow
ΔP = pressure gradient
R = radius of the vessel
L = vessel length
N = blood viscosity; or more simply

volume of blood flow = pressure gradient • vessel radius^4 / vessel length • viscosity

polar coordinate system: System with an origin in which the location of a point in space is determined by the length of a line from the origin to the point and the angle between the line and the right horizontal axis of the reference system. The point is located in the order of the length of the vector and then the angle.

poliomyelitis: Infectious disease that attacks the nervous tissue in the brain or spinal cord, resulting in muscular weakness.

polynomial fit: Mathematical expression consisting of two or more terms.

POMS: See *profile of mood states.*

ponderal index: General indicator of body build or body configuration, usually defined as a ratio of body weight to height.

Ponderal index = $10^2 \times$ (weight/height)1/3

positional segregation: The relationship between race and athletic playing position; a situation in which minority athletes participate in a given sport disproportionately more at some positions than others.

position control system: See *zero-order control system.*

positioning: The placement of a body part in a specified position to facilitate movement or prevent contractures.

positive addiction: Psychological and physiological dependence upon a regular regimen of exercise, characterized by withdrawal symptoms after 24 to 36 hours without exercise.

positive emotional climate: In education, a teaching environment in which teacher–student actions are manifested in a positive manner. See also *classroom climate.*

positive energy balance: Energy intake is greater than energy output, resulting in weight gain.

positive expectancy: 1. A person's belief that he or she will experience future success. **2.** Anticipating a favorable or desirable event or feeling.

positive inhibition: Process whereby success may result in lost momentum and a higher probability of later failure (i.e., the

"fat cat" syndrome). See also *psychological momentum.*

positive interaction: In education, the positive response by a teacher to a student after the learner makes an appropriate behavioral response or skilled performance.

positively accelerated learning curve: The plot of a performance index over units of practice that depicts slow improvements initially followed by rapid improvement, the curve rising on the graph to indicate such improvement.

positively decelerated learning curve: The plot of a performance index over units of practice that depicts slow improvements initially followed by rapid improvement, the curve falling on the graph, typically because the performance index, error, is labeled low to high on the vertical axis. Lower error is better performance.

positively decelerated learning curve

positive psychological momentum: After experiencing success, the increased probability of subsequent success.

positive reinforcement: Presentation of a desirable action, event, or substance when a desired response occurs in order to increase the likelihood of that response occurring again.

positive self-monitoring: Attending to one's successful performances. Compare *negative self-monitoring.*

positive transfer: The facilitation of learning a new skill as a result of practicing, or experience with, another skill.

positive work: The work done by a muscle group as it acts concentrically; when the signs of the net muscle moment and the angular velocity at the joint are the same, positive work is done; measured in joules. Compare *negative work*.

posthypnotic suggestion: See *waking hypnosis*.

post-knowledge-of-results (KR) interval: The period of time, within a series of trials on a motor task, between delivery of knowledge of results regarding one response and performance of the subsequent response.

postlingual deafness: Deafness that occurs after the development of speech and language.

postmature retirement: In athletics, the "hanging on" in sport of skilled but aging athletes who continue to compete and postpone retirement despite an obvious continuous decrement in performance quality and consistency.

postnatal: After birth.

posttest: Test given after a designated amount of practice or an experimental treatment.

postural deviations: The structural or functional deviations from normal postural and body alignment that adversely affect body movement and support.

postural muscle: Muscle or group of muscles controlling the posture of the body.

postural sway: See *body sway*.

potential energy: The ability of a body to do work by virtue of its position relative to a reference; measured in Joules.

$$P.E. = mgh$$

where m = mass of the body
g = acceleration due to gravity
h = height above the reference

potentiometer: Electronic device for measuring or comparing electromotive force, i.e., the amount of energy from an electrical source output per unit of movement.

power: 1. The amount of work done per unit time. 2. The product of force and velocity. 3. The time derivative of work. Power is measured in watts (W).

$$power = \frac{dWork}{dt}$$

$$= F \times \frac{ds}{dt}$$

$$= F \times V$$

where dt = time
F = force
ds = distance
V = velocity

power incentives: Opportunities to influence and control the attitudes, opinions, or interests of others.

practice: The opportunity for students to repeat the task after instruction in order to refine and consolidate its component parts and include the task in their learning repertoire.

practicing sport psychology: Applying cognitive and behavioral techniques to help sport participants become more effective in performing their respective roles.

praise: 1. Motivational or reinforcing remarks (e.g., from a teacher) to increase the frequency or intensity of desirable behavior. 2. Informational feedback (e.g., provided by a teacher) concerning the correctness of the learner's response.

praxis: Planning and execution of purposeful movement; action.

precardial leads: In electrocardiography, the unipolar chest leads V1, V2, V3, V4, V5, and V6 placed at standard locations predominantly on the left side of the chest; each electrode registers electrical potential under it against a central terminal formed by the limb leads.

precision grip: Hand grasp in which the object is held near the ends of the fingers so that it may be shifted or manipulated.

precueing: Technique in which a performer receives information about an upcoming response in advance of the task stimulus, typically to study the effect on speed of the response.

prediction motion: The continuation of tracking motion after disappearance of the target.

preferred leadership: The leadership style preferred by members of a group; for instance, athletes' partiality to a particular approach to, or style of, leadership from their coach.

prehensile: Able to grasp.

prehension: The grasping of an object, usually with the hand.

preinstruction: Advance information that helps students organize and clarify the tasks and goals they hope to achieve.

pre-knowledge-of-results (KR) interval: The time interval after a performer's response on a motor task and before delivery of knowledge of results regarding the outcome of that response.

prelingual deafness: Deafness that occurs before the development of speech and language.

preload: The amount of blood in the left ventricle at the end of ventricular diastole prior to contraction of the ventricles; an important determinant of stroke volume and therefore of cardiac output. See also *end diastolic volume.*

prelongitudinal screening: Research technique in which a cross-sectional study is undertaken before longitudinal research. The purpose is often to observe a behavior to determine whether its developmental change meets the criteria necessary to be labeled "stages of development." The criteria include inclusiveness, stability, and across-trial adjacency; the percentage of individuals showing more advanced behavior would increase with advancing age.

Premack principle: Activity-based behavior management technique in which the performer engages in a high-probability (i.e., comfortable, easy, or frequently occurring) activity that is contingent on first emitting a low-probability target response, such as swimming laps to earn free time on the diving board. The former action reinforces the latter.

premature contraction: Dysrhythmia in which a heart beat occurs sooner than normal; typically initiated from an ectopic focus; may be atrial, junctional, or ventricular in origin; may be benign or suggestive of a problem. Also called *extrasystole.* See also *bigeminy, trigeminy.*

premotor time: The portion of reaction time between onset of a stimulus and the first electrical activity at the neuromuscular junction, as indicated by an electromyograph recording at the motor point.

prenatal: Before birth.

preoperations stage: Piaget's second developmental stage, in which a child begins to think symbolically, role-plays, reasons transductively (assumes cause-and-effect between two simultaneous events), but remains egocentric. This stage usually spans the ages of 2 to 7 years. See also *concrete operations stage, formal operations stage, sensorimotor stage.*

preparatory arousal: Cognitive technique to elevate the level of mental and physiological excitation (i.e., "psyching up") prior to performance, for the purpose of attaining peak performance. Typically used with tasks requiring gross motor coordination, strength, speed, and endurance rather than with tasks requiring fine motor coordination, steadiness, and concentration.

preparatory crouch: The position taken prior to takeoff in a jump wherein the hips, knees, ankles, and trunk are flexed so that they can be more fully extended in the takeoff.

presage variables: The variables a teacher must take into account to teach effectively and increase student achievement; these include a student's experience, age, gender, intelligence, and educational background.

presbyopia: Age-related physiological change in accommodative power of the eye wherein the near point recedes to 22 cm or more.

prescriptive integrity: See *diagnostic integrity*.

preselection: Experimental procedure wherein subjects choose the end point or extent of a movement and make that movement before reproducing it as the experimenter observes their accuracy.

present level of performance: [ad] The apparent level of educational and physical functioning of a handicapped person, determined by an evaluation process.

pressor response: Cardiovascular response to isometric exercise, or the static component of dynamic exercise, involving elevation of heart rate, blood pressure, blood flow, and peripheral vascular resistance.

pressure: 1. [bm] The quantity of force per unit area; that is, the ratio of the force to the area over which the force is applied; measured in newtons per meter squared (N/m^2). 2. [sp] Any factor or combination of factors that increases the importance of performing well on a particular occasion.

pressure epiphysis: In growing children, the growth plate located at the ends of long bones, especially those of weight-bearing nature (hence the name *pressure*).

pressure receptors: Sensory devices that are sensitive to changes in pressure.

pretest: Test given before either the practice of a skill or an experimental treatment.

primacy–recency effect: The principle that initial and ending portions of a series of items or movements are remembered better than those in the middle of the series.

primary amenorrhea: No menstrual cycle has occurred by age 16; generally recommended to see a physician to determine the cause for delayed menarche.

primary appraisal: See *appraisal*.

primary factors: See *first-order traits*.

primary mechanical purpose: The primary goal of a motor skill, expressed in mechanical terms without reference to the energy expended in completing the task.

primary prevention: The prevention of the development and progression of coronary heart disease risk factors by following healthy dietary practices, behavior modification, aerobic exercise, abstinence from smoking, and reduced alcohol consumption; must begin in childhood, as certain risk factors for heart disease begin early in life.

primary reinforcer: Stimulus or event that does not depend on previous learning or association to achieve the probability of a desirable response.

primary task: The constant or ongoing task in a dual-task procedure. See also *secondary task*.

priming: See *prompting*.

primitive reflexes: The class of reflexes that appear prenatally or early postnatally and are often necessary for early survival; typically mediated by the lower brain centers.

principle axis: Axis that passes through the body's center of gravity.

principle of contiguity: See *contiguity*.

principle of contingency: See *contingency*.

principle of the lever: The relationship specified in a lever system in which the product of the force and the force arm equals the product of the resistance force and the resistance force arm.

principles of training: General guidelines that can be used as rules governing training adaptations. Also called *training principles*. See also *detraining, individual differences principle, overload principle, specificity principle*.

proactive assertion: Behavior exemplified by the expenditure of physical effort in an attempt to acquire a goal. These behaviors are implicit in the skill or task at hand, and involve no intent to harm or injure an opponent.

proactive assertive behavior: 1. Sport

behavior that is forceful or active, yet acceptable (i.e., within the rules), task-oriented, and involves no intent to injure. May be performed in an offensive or defensive manner. See also *defensive proactive assertive behavior, offensive proactive assertive behavior.*

proactive inhibition: Interference effect of one task on the later learning or performance of a second task. Also called *proactive interference.* Compare *retroactive inhibition.*

proactive interference: See *proactive inhibition.*

proactive paradigm: Experimental strategy (research design) to study the effects of a prior experience on the learning or memory of a skill.

probe reaction time: The score of a simple reaction-time secondary task in the probe technique. This score presumably reflects the attentional demands of the primary task. If greater attention is demanded by the primary task, the probe reaction time tends to be longer.

probe task: See *secondary task.*

probe technique: Experimental approach in which the subject engages in a primary task when a secondary task is presented. The primary task tends to be discrete (having a specific starting and end point), and the secondary task is usually a reaction time task. The technique indicates the attentional demands of the primary task by virtue of performance level on the secondary task.

problem solving teaching method: Indirect method of instruction in which the teacher designs a problem for which the student finds one or more solutions through exploration and independent strategies.

procedural justice: Concerned with procedures for allocating resources or penalties, such as the coin toss in football or the "ground rule double" in baseball. See also *distributive justice, retributive justice.*

procedural skill: Skill involving a series of discrete responses that must each be made at an appropriate time in an appropriate order.

process disorder: Disruption of learning resulting from a breakdown or lack of functioning in the sensory-input, decision-making, or motor output–feedback system.

process motivation: A person's incentive to continue participating in an activity as a function of intrinsic (internal) pleasure and without external rewards. See also *product motivation.*

process orientation: Tendency to value or emphasize those things that occur in practice or during preparation toward achieving a goal that create the desired outcome or product. See also *product orientation.*

process outcome: See *process product.*

process product: Analysis of the relationships between teacher–student interactions and student achievement. Also called *process outcome.*

process variables: In education, the behaviors of teachers and students in the classroom that can affect student achievement.

product motivation: The incentive to maintain participation in an activity due to the external rewards derived from the experience or from experiencing some desirable outcome. See also *process motivation.*

product orientation: Tendency to stress the final outcome as the most important objective for participating in activities. See also *process orientation.*

product variables: Student achievement or learning outcomes such as learning, skill acquisition, and attitudes.

professional sport team: Groups of athletes who want to make a profit and have acquired the skills and knowledge necessary to sell their labor in an open market as an occupation and livelihood. Refers to both the players as well as the management or owners who organize this activity as a business. The activity of these laborers involves the combination of play and work.

profile drag: See *form drag.*

profile of mood states (POMS): Psychological inventory that measures a person's affective states within the previous 7 days of measurement.

profoundly retarded: A classification of

mental retardation to specify low levels of functioning, usually indicated by IQ scores of 25 or below and deficits in adaptive behavior.

prognosis: The prediction of the course, severity, or extent of a disease or condition.

programmed learning: Program of instructional experiences organized into progressive steps such that skill can be acquired easily and rapidly, often without frequent aid of the instructor. Teaching machines or programmed textbooks are common features of such programs. The learner responds to each stimulus, receives immediate knowledge of results, and works at preferred pace. Exposure to success and accurate responses is far more frequent than to failure or error.

progressive muscular dystrophy: Form of muscular dystrophy in which the disease begins in the muscle, not in the spinal center.

progressive-part method: Teaching approach in which the parts of a complex skill are taught separately but in the same order in which they occur in the skill. As each part is learned, it is combined with the preceding part or sequenced until the skill is eventually practiced in its entirety.

progressive relaxation: Strategy to induce a relaxed state through a process of systematically tensing and voluntarily relaxing the major voluntary muscle groups of the body.

progressive resistance exercise: Originally described by DeLorme in the late 1940s; technique for resistance training to make muscles stronger; training program was three sets of 10 repetitions, where the first set was performed at 50% of the maximum weight that could be lifted 10 times (10 repetitions maximum [RM]), the second set was at 75% of 10 RM, and the third set was at 100% of 10 RM; variations of this progression are used today where the number of sets and repetitions vary according to the objectives of a particular training program. Also called *DeLorme technique*.

projective personality procedures: Psychological inventories in which responses are unstructured, open-ended, and open to interpretation by a trained psychologist.

prompting: The use of physical, verbal, or auditory assistance to cue a specific behavior or task. Also called *priming*.

pronation: The inward rotation of body parts such as the forearm. Compare *supination*.

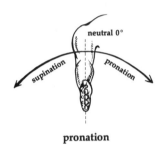

pronation

prone: The assumption of a face-down lying position. Compare *supine*.

propping reaction: See *parachute reflex*.

propping reflex: See *parachute reflex*.

proprioception: Sensory information about (a) position of the body and its parts, (b) extent and force of movement, (c) muscular tension, and (d) physical pressure, all arising from the vestibular apparatus, Golgi tendon organs, muscle spindles, and/or joint receptors.

proprioceptive feedback: Sensory information produced by movement arising from the kinesthetic receptors.

proprioceptive neuromuscular facilitation (PNF): Series of therapeutic techniques designed to enhance the neural or muscular response (relaxation or contraction) of a body part, based on neurophysiological principles.

proprioceptive system: The sensory modality including the muscle spindle receptors, Golgi tendon organs, joint receptors, and vestibular apparatus.

proprioceptors: See *sensory receptors*.

propulsion: The result of a force applied

in the direction opposite to the desired direction of motion.

prosthetic device: Artificial device designed to replace a missing body part.

protective aggression: In sport, initiating assistance to teammates in trouble.

protective extension: Reflex characterized by extension and abduction of the arm, caused by a sudden change in the equilibrium of the body to protect against falling.

protopathic sensibility: Specific form of kinesthetic sensitivity wherein affective qualities are perceived.

protraction: Adduction or forward movement of a body part.

proximal: The portion of a bone, muscle, or segment that is closest to the axial skeleton. Compare *distal*.

proximal goal: Short-term goal.

proximodistal trend: The tendency for developmental advancement in structure or function to proceed in the trunk, then the near limbs, then the far limbs, and finally the hands and the feet.

prp: See *psychological refractory period*.

pseudocontinuous control: Nervous system control of movement that provides "on-line" correction. Visual and sensory feedback update an internal representation of the target for movement.

pseudohypertrophy: Increase in the size of a body part without resultant increase in muscular tissue or strength.

psyching-up strategies: Mental preparation techniques that purportedly increase a person's arousal or motivation. Falls into five categories: attentional focus ("Just concentrate on the task and ignore unimportant cues"), self-efficacy statements ("I can do it"), relaxation ("Relax my muscles and think of something else"), imagery ("I imagine myself executing a perfect skill"), and preparatory arousal ("I'm ready to go for it").

psychobiology: A growing area of science that is concerned with using psychological and physiological measures to provide a better understanding of behavior.

Typically, psychologists examine the interrelationships between physiological and psychological variables by attempting to identify the underlying physiological mechanisms for behavioral outcomes; anxiety, for example, includes a cognitive (emotional) component, but may also be explained or corroborated somatically (physiologically) by changes in physical bodily processes.

psychocybernetic: The theoretical perspective that applies the science of control mechanisms (cybernetics) to human behavior (psychology). See also *cybernetic*.

psychogenic deafness: An inability to perceive sound, having a psychological origin as opposed to an organic basis.

psychological arousal: Heightened state of alertness and readiness on a continuum from deep sleep to extreme excitement. May include positive or negative emotions—joy and anticipation, for instance, or fear and sadness.

psychological group: Collection of individuals who have a set of composite needs that results in group reaction and group interaction.

psychological hardiness: A sense of being in control of one's life. Examples include curiosity, willingness to commit, and perceiving change as a challenge and stimulus for development.

psychological momentum: Subjective probability of winning or losing in a competitive situation as a function of the outcome of preceding events. Also called *momentum*. See also *negative psychological momentum*, *positive psychological momentum*.

psychological presence: The degree to which a performer "feels" or perceives the presence of an audience.

psychological profile: Distinct pattern of responses an individual or group displays that is predicted to further manifest under certain circumstances.

psychological refractory period (prp): The delay in executing a prepared response as another response is carried out.

psychological well-being: Condition,

often associated with engaging in vigorous exercise, in which certain pleasant feelings and attitudes of exhilaration, confidence, and self-esteem are experienced; occurs in the absence of unpleasant emotions. Also called *feel-better phenomenon*.

psychologist: A title legally restricted to individuals who have a formal training in psychology and who are subsequently licensed by the state or province in which they work.

psychomotor domain: The component of behavior concerned with motor (physical) acts and the processes in the central nervous system that control those acts. See also *motor learning*.

psychoneuromuscular feedback theory: See *neuromuscular feedback theory*.

psychophysiology: 1. The application of physiological and biochemical domains (principles) to the understanding of individual behavior. 2. A body of knowledge concerned with the relationship between psychological process and emotional states as a function of physiological measures.

psychosis: Mental disorder exhibited as severely disturbed behavior and lack of contact with reality. See also *autism*.

ptosis: Weakness and prolapse of an organ, such as a dropping eyelid or protrusion of the stomach from weak abdominal muscles.

pulley: First-class lever arrangement in which neither force nor displacement are magnified but only the direction of the pull of the resistive force is changed.

pull-up reaction: An infant's flexion of both arms as an involuntary response to being tipped forward or backward from a supported upright sitting position.

pulmonary valve: The semilunar valve separating the pulmonary artery from the right ventricle; prevents blood from flowing back into the right ventricle. Also called *right semilunar valve*.

pulmonary ventilation: The volume of air that passes in and out of the respiratory system per minute; calculated as frequency of breathing times tidal volume; average adult values of 12 breaths/min times 500 ml/breath = 6 L/min; at maximal levels of exercise, ventilation may exceed 100 L/min. Also called *breathing, external respiration, minute volume*.

pulse pressure: The difference between the systolic and diastolic blood pressure; approximately 40 to 50 mm Hg at rest; increases to 100 to 130 mm Hg during maximal levels of dynamic exercise as a result of large increases in systolic blood pressure with little or no increase in diastolic pressure.

pulse rate: Rhythmical expansion of an artery produced by the ejection of blood by the contracting ventricles; usually monitored at the radial or carotid arteries to quantify the intensity of exercise; used as an indicator of heart rate; at rest, ranges between 60 and 75 bpm; at maximum levels of exercise may exceed 200 bpm. See also *heart rate*.

pulse-step model: Hypothesized mode of movement control in which various levels of final force level or limb position are determined by a step component as the time to reach peak force is held constant.

punishment: Behavior management technique used to decrease, weaken, or eliminate an inappropriate behavior through presentation of an aversive stimulus as a consequence.

Purdue pegboard test: Measure of manual dexterity that involves placing pegs in a predetermined pattern or sequence of holes in a board.

pure dominance: The consistent preference for using an eye, a hand, and a foot that are all on the same side of the body.

pursuit rotor: Tracking apparatus that requires the subject to hold a stylus on or over a moving target rotating in a predetermined pattern, usually a circle, triangle, or square. Also called *rotary pursuit*.

pursuit tracking: Task in which the subject attempts to keep a stylus on, or as close as possible to, a moving target traveling in some predetermined pattern, usually a circle, triangle, or square.

pursuit tracking

PWC: See *physical work capacity*.
Pygmalion effect: See *self-fulfilling prophecy*.
pyruvic acid: End product of glycolysis; if reduced (by the addition of hydrogen atoms) it becomes lactic acid; precursor to acetyl CoA, which enters into the Krebs cycle for further processing and the production of ATP.

Q

Q: See *cardiac output*.
Q-angle: The angle formed between the longitudinal axis of the femur and the line of pull of the patellar tendon.
quadriplegia: The paralysis or involvement of all four extremities resulting from a cervical spinal lesion or neurological dysfunction.
qualitative analysis: Evaluation of a movement in nonnumerical terms relative to some criterion.
qualitative knowledge of results: The form of external, informative feedback that is categorical, relative, or imprecise (nonnumerical).
quantitative analysis: Evaluation of a movement in numerical terms describing the mechanical variables influencing the outcome of the movement.
quantitative knowledge of results: The form of external, informative feedback that conveys the numerical amount or degree of error.
questioning: In education, a teaching method that requests information from a learner for the purpose of evaluating or increasing the learner's perception, awareness, or concept of a specific task. See also *convergent question, divergent question, recall question, value question*.

R: See *respiratory exchange ratio*.

radial acceleration: The acceleration of an object, acting toward the axis of rotation, due to a change in its direction when the object is moving along a curved path. Also called *centripetal acceleration*.

$$a_{radial} = \frac{v^2}{r}$$

where r = distance from axis of rotation to an object following a curved path of motion

v = linear velocity of the object following a curved path of motion

radian: The measure of an angle that describes the ratio of the distance on the circumference of a circle to the radius of the circle (1 radian = 57.3 degrees).

radiation: Emission of energy as waves or particles.

radionuclide angiography: Diagnostic technique used in stress testing of individuals with or without signs of coronary artery disease; enables the visualization of the heart and blood vessels through the use of radioactive substances that are imaged with scintillation camera.

radius of gyration: Measure of the distribution of an object's mass about an axis of rotation. Radius of gyration is usually designated by the letter *k*.

$$k = \sqrt{\frac{I}{m}}$$

where I = moment of inertia
m = mass

radius of rotation: The linear distance from the axis of rotation to a point on the path of rotation.

random noise: The high-frequency error contained in a signal generated by random interference.

range: [bm] The horizontal distance a projectile travels.

range of motion: 1. The angular displacement through which two adjacent segments move. 2. The degree of movement of an articulation before the movement is impinged upon by the surrounding tissues.

rate-limiting: In dynamics, the term used to describe elements or systems that mature slowly, thereby delaying the appearance of a skill during development, even though other elements or systems are advanced.

rate pressure product (RPP): Used to assess left ventricular work during exercise; product of the systolic blood pressure (mm Hg) times the heart rate (bpm); usually divided by 1,000 to express as a two-digit number; highly correlated with myocardial oxygen consumption. Also called *double product, modified tension–time index*.

rating of perceived exertion (RPE): Numerical scale devised by Borg to describe the subjective feeling of effort required at varying levels of exercise intensity; originally designated as a 6–20 scale and recently revised to a 0–10 scale; scales are presented below:

6 – 20 Point Scale

6	
7	very, very light
8	
9	very light
10	
11	fairly light
12	
13	somewhat hard
14	
15	hard
16	
17	very hard
18	
19	very, very hard
20	

0-10 Point Scale

0	nothing at all
0.5	very, very light
1	very light
2	light
3	moderate
4	somewhat heavy
5	heavy
6	
7	very heavy
8	
9	
10	very, very heavy

rating scale: Method of assessing instruction that includes a list of statements or characteristics to be judged by an independent observer. A range of responses, such as poor to excellent, are acceptable.

rationalization: Coping mechanism in which a person resolves an internal conflict by hiding a real motive with the substitution of a more reasonable and socially acceptable motive.

ratio schedule: Pattern of reinforcement in which reinforcers are dispensed based on a specified number of responses performed. An example would be dispensing reinforcement after five correct responses.

raw electromyogram: The untreated electromyographic signal, a measure of a muscle action, characterized by positive and negative values.

reaction board method: Technique to calculate the location of the body's center of gravity in a static situation using the concept of static equilibrium.

reaction force: An equal and opposite force exerted by one body as a result of a force applied by another body.

reaction formation: Development of a personality trait that is the opposite of the original, unconscious, or repressed trait. For example, high self-confidence can mask low self-esteem or insecurity.

reaction time: The interval of time be-tween onset of a stimulus, presented to one or more of the sensory modalities, and initiation of a response to that signal. See also *choice reaction time, simple reaction time.*

reactive aggression: See *goal aggression.*

reactive inhibition: Psychological reluctance to sustain performance, such that this reluctance builds with practice, rendering learning less and less effective.

readiness: Psychophysiological state in which the pertinent systems of an organism are prepared for developmental change, such that the proper experience results in the change.

readying mechanism: Neural component that prepares the person for hostile aggression but is not the cause of it.

rear foot angle: The relative angle be-tween a line bisecting the posterior aspect of the shank and the calcaneus (heel bone).

rear foot angle = angle of shank − angle of calcaneus

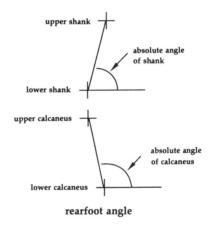

rearfoot angle

recall: Memory of something previously learned.

recall question: Type of question used to elicit memory level answers.

recall schema: The relationship developed with practice between the specification dictating how a motor response is to be executed and the actual movement.

recapitulation theory: The view that an individual prenatal organism passes through stages that recapitulate the evolutionary development of the species to which the individual belongs.

receipt skills: Gross skills in which force is received from some object, as in catching, trapping, and fielding.

reception time: Component part of reaction time consisting of the time period between stimulus onset and the first change in cerebral cortex electrical activity as measured by electroencephalograph recordings.

receptor anticipation: Acquisition or matching of a target moving along a displayed path, requiring the performer to predict the duration of the response movement.

reciprocal inhibition: Phenomenon in which the opposite (antagonist) muscle group relaxes when the agonist group contracts to produce movement at a joint.

reciprocal innervation: Coordination of movement that occurs when the primary movers (agonistic) flex and the muscles that may resist that action (antagonistic) relax.

reciprocal teaching: Method of teaching that uses students to teach other students. Students are paired, with one serving as a teacher for the other member of the pair.

reciprocity: 1. In social learning theory, interaction between individual and environment consisting of internalizing a model's behavior and attempting to match this internalization in progressive approximations. 2. A child's belief that punishment of misbehavior should logically follow from the misbehavior.

recognition: Person's awareness that a present event, object, or person has been previously learned or experienced.

recognition schema: The relationship between the expected sensory consequences of a movement and the actual sensory consequences (response-produced feedback), developed through practice.

recovery oxygen consumption: See *excess postexercise oxygen consumption*.

recreation therapy: Service that utilizes leisure activities to enhance the social and emotional well-being of the disabled.

recruitment: The systematic increase in the number of active motors units in a muscular action.

rectified electromyogram: Electromyographic signal in which all values of the signal are positive. See also *full-wave rectified electromyogram, half-wave rectified electromyogram*.

rectilinear motion: Linear motion that occurs along a straight line.

recumbent length: The anthropometric measure of body length taken while the subject is lying in a standardized body position; typically used to measure the height of children under the age of 2 years.

red blood cell: See *erythrocyte*.

reducer: Individual whose style of perceiving the world tends to minimize the strength of incoming information. Reducers include those with high pain tolerance and the ability to filter out extraneous external stimuli. Compare *augmenter*.

referee: See *arbiter*.

referenced assessment: Evaluation or comparison of the learner's performance based on a difficulty continuum or hierarchy.

refining tasks: Method of teaching designed to improve qualitative aspects of a performance by guiding students to accomplish the tasks more proficiently.

reflective cognitive style: See *reflective learning style*.

reflective learning style: The category of conceptual tempo or type of cognitive style wherein a learner, after searching systematically for the best solution, responds slowly to a stimulus or situation but commits few errors. Also called *reflective cognitive style*. Compare *impulsive learning style*.

reflective teaching: Conscious and considerate introspection of teaching behavior that includes student characteristics, methodology, and learner outcomes.

reflex: Innate involuntary response of the central nervous system that provides nourishment or protection of the infant until higher areas of neurological functioning are developed.

reflex time: The interval between a stimulus and the beginning of a reflexive (nonvoluntary) response.

regeneration: The process of overcoming the effects of fatigue induced by a competitive program and the body's restoration to its full performance potential.

regression: 1. In motor development, the appearance of a movement pattern or technique that has been previously outgrown or suppressed, but evident as a child attempts to learn a new skill; a return to an earlier level of learning. Also called *reversion*. **2.** In conditioning, reappearance of a previously extinguished conditioned response after punishment. **3.** The return to a more immature stage of development or functioning due to a lack of intervention or management of inappropriate behavior.

regular class: The typical educational placement in the school setting.

regulatory stimuli: Aspects of the environment that must be taken into account by a performer if the goal of a movement task is to be realized. Compare *nonregulatory stimuli*.

rehabilitation: The treatment and physical activity provided to restore functional ability after a disability.

rehabilitation psychology: Field of psychology that applies knowledge and behavioral science to meet the unique individual and group needs of the physically impaired (handicapped/disabled).

rehearsal: Overt or covert repetition of a movement, or lengthened experience with certain components of a movement.

reinforcement: 1. Anything, such as the presentation of something positive or the removal of something negative, that increases the chance a response will occur again. **2.** A reward, either tangible or symbolic. **3.** The principle in behavioral psychology that experiencing a certain stimulus following a response enhances the probability of the response reoccuring.

reinforcement schedule: Rules established to reinforce selected response; fixed or variable, intermittent or continuous. Also called *schedule of reinforcement*.

reinforcement value: The degree to which a person prefers the presence of a certain reinforcer if its chances of occurring are equal to that of other reinforcers.

reinforcer: Consequence that either increases or decreases the possibility of a behavior occurring again; can be positive or negative in nature. Also called *incentive, reinforcing stimulus*.

reinforcing stimulus: See *reinforcer*.

related services: Secondary services that may be included in a person's educational plan to enable him or her to benefit from special education services. These may include speech therapy, supplementary therapeutic recreation, physical therapy, and occupational therapy.

relationship concept: Movement concept that involves the action of the body in conjunction with its parts, with other students, and between objects and other students.

relationship motivation leadership style: Refers to a leader's preference to consider group members' needs and assign them high priority.

relative angle: The included angle between two segments; the angle of one segment relative to the adjacent segment.

relative motion: The motion of one object relative to another.

relative oxygen consumption: Units of work, power, or energy that are adjusted for body size, gender, or fitness differences; weight-bearing activities are measured in relative units; examples include watts/kg, ml/kg/min, and METS • weight/min.

relative workload: Exercise intensity expressed relative to an individual's maximum capacity (e.g., percent of $\dot{V}O_2$max).

relaxation: Procedure that uses psychological or physiological means to alleviate anxiety and muscular tension. See also *progressive relaxation*.

relaxation response: Physiological phenomenon that uses mental techniques to create physiological changes opposite to the fight or flight (stress) response of the sympathetic nervous system. Specific changes include decreases in oxygen consumption, heart rate, respiration, and skeletal muscular activity. Skin resistance and alpha brain waves increase. Examples of techniques that result in these somatic changes include autogenic training, progressive relaxation, and transcendental meditation.

reminiscence: The phenomenon of improvement in the performance of a skill after a period of no practice called the ''retention interval.''

repolarization: Return to a negative internal polarity in a muscle or nerve cell following depolarization; accompanied by movement of potassium ions from the inside to the outside of the cell. See also *depolarization, restoration of ionic balance*.

RER: See *respiratory exchange ratio*.

research sport psychologist: Person with a graduate degree in physical education, exercise science, kinesiology, or psychology with an emphasis in sport psychology, who maintains membership in a professional sport psychology and/or psychological organization, and makes scholarly research contributions to the field of psychology with applicability to sport behavior.

residual paralysis: The remaining loss of functioning apparent after therapeutic interventions have been implemented.

residual volume: The volume of air that remains in the lungs after maximal expiration; average 1 to 2 L; not altered by training, but increases with age and is larger in smokers; normally does not exceed 25% of vital

capacity, and if higher may be an indication of a pulmonary disorder.

resistance devices: Any instrument that provides resistance to muscle actions and can be used as a strength training device.

resistance force arm: See *moment arm*.

resistive force: A force that hinders motion.

resolution of vectors: The mathematical process of breaking down a resultant vector into its horizontal (tangential) and vertical (normal) components.

resource room/teacher: Services provided for handicapped students and their teachers within a school, including assessment of special needs, special teaching materials or methods, small group instruction, or consulting with the regular (homeroom) teacher.

respiration: The process of biological oxidation; describes cellular metabolism where oxygen is consumed and carbon dioxide is produced.

respiratory exchange ratio (R or RER): The ratio of the volume of CO_2 produced to the volume of O_2 consumed; measured at the mouth using open circuit indirect calorimetry; used as an estimate of the caloric expenditure per liter of oxygen consumed; can also be used to estimate the proportion of fat and carbohydrate being used; at high exercise intensity levels where there is significant lactate accumulation, this ratio no longer characterizes the substrates being used, as increasing amounts of CO_2 are produced as a result of lactate buffering. See also *respiratory quotient*.

respiratory frequency: Breaths per unit time (usually per minute); in normal young adults, the respiratory frequency is approximately 12 breaths/min at rest and may exceed 40 breaths/min at maximum levels of exercise.

respiratory quotient (RQ): Reflects the amount of CO_2 produced to the amount of O_2 consumed at the tissue level. See also *respiratory exchange ratio*.

response-biasing paradigm: Strategy in short-term motor memory experimentation to study the effects of interpolated experience on recalling a movement, usually in terms of directional shifts in recall error.

response complexity: Difficulty of a motor response in terms of the number of component parts of the task or its information-processing demands.

response contingency: Condition in which occurrence of a response is contingent upon a particular stimulus.

response cost: In behavior management, a consequence used to decrease, weaken, or eliminate a behavior that withdraws a positive reinforcer or a previously earned reinforcement.

response execution: The stage of an information processing model wherein (a) parameters for a movement are chosen in terms of direction, velocity, amplitude, and end position, (b) muscles are organized, and (c) effector mechanisms generate the response.

response induction aid: Physical and psychological device that may reduce the perceived discrepancy between an individual's current versus desired performance.

response preparation: The time-consuming readying of the motor system to perform a movement. Sometimes considered an indicator of alertness. See also *signal preparation*.

response selection: The stage in an information processing model wherein a movement is chosen from a repertoire of possible responses, based on information from previous stages.

response-stimulus relationship: A relationship, central to the view that most behavior is learned, said to exist between a behavior (response) and the factors (stimuli) that precede the behavior.

response time: The total time to complete a response to a stimulus. Consists of reaction time plus movement time.

resting length of muscle: The length of the muscle when it is not stimulated nor stretched.

resting membrane potential (RMP): The electrical charge difference between the negative interior and the positive exterior environment of the cells.

restoration of ionic balance: Active transport of sodium ions out of and potassium ions into a muscle or nerve cell following depolarization and repolarization; returns cell membrane to the resting state both electrically and ionically.

resultant force: The force describing the result of the addition of two or more forces.

resultant vector: The vector describing the result of the addition of two or more vectors.

retaliation hypothesis: The notion that an individual who fears counteraggression from a potential victim will not participate in aggression.

retention: Persistence of a skill that has been learned over a period without practice. Compare *forgetting*.

retention interval: In memory experiments, the time span between performance of a task, or presentation of information to a subject, and a request for the subject to repeat the task or recall that information.

reticular formation: Netlike mass of interwoven neurons, extending from the brain stem up to the thalamus, that moderates arousal, attention, and perception.

retina: The back portion of the eye that contains the nerve fibers, is connected to the optic nerve, and is sensitive to light.

retinitis pigmentosa: Hereditary disease

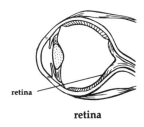

retina

resulting in degeneration and atrophy of the retina.

retraction: Abduction or backward rotation of the shoulder girdle.

retribution: See *retributive justice*.

retributive justice: Refers to the assignment of penalities to rule violators. Also called *retribution*. See also *distributive justice, procedural justice*.

retrieval: The process of searching for, locating, and extracting specific information from memory.

retroactive inhibition: The interference effect of one task on the retention of a previously learned task. Also called *retroactive interference*. Compare *proactive inhibition*.

retroactive interference: See *retroactive inhibition*.

retroactive paradigm: Experimental strategy to study the effects of a subsequent experience on the learning or memory of a skill.

retrolental fibroplasia (RLF): Visual impairment caused by a buildup of scar tissue behind the lens from excessive concentrations of oxygen at birth.

reversal of movement: Change in the direction of fast movement, thought to increase the movement's complexity.

reverse mainstreaming: The practice of placing nonhandicapped children in classes that are predominately composed of handicapped children.

reversibility principle: See *detraining*.

reversion: See *regression*.

rewards: Positive reinforcers.

reward training: The use of positive reinforcers to develop or maintain a behavior or accomplish a task.

rheumatic fever: Disease occurring from streptococcal infections, characterized by inflammation of the joints and fever that may lead to rheumatic heart disease.

rheumatic heart disease: Cardiac condition caused by rheumatic fever that damages the heart, valves, or blood vessels by developing scar tissue.

rhythm: A formed pattern, usually of sounds or movements, with elements that are organized in duration and intensity; a serial recurrence that is balanced and harmonic, and repeated in regular groupings.

rhythmicity: 1. Characteristic occurrence in regular time intervals. **2.** The fundamental characteristic of locomotion pertaining to limb alternation recurring automatically in regular time intervals.

right atrioventricular valve: See *tricuspid valve*.

right hand rule: A technique for determining the direction of an angular vector whereby the fingers of the right hand are curled in the direction of the rotation and the extended thumb points in the direction of the angular vector.

righting reactions: See *righting reflexes*.

righting reflexes: Reflexes that bring the body to its normal position in space, when any force tending to put it into a false position stimulates any one of a variety of sensory receptors in the labyrinth, eyes, muscles, or skin. Also called *righting reactions*.

right–left discrimination: The ability to label the lateral dimensions of the body as "right" or "left."

right semilunar valve: See *pulmonary valve*.

rigidity: Set of characteristics of one classification of cerebral palsy, comprising difficulty with initiating movement, continuous muscle tension, and uncoordinated reciprocal muscle groups.

rigid link system: System in which the segments of the human body are represented by rigid links that have uniform density, constant location of the center of gravity of the segment, and frictionless hinge joints separating the segments.

Ringelmann effect: Loss of individual motivation or motor coordination in group situations. Based on the observation that group performance is superior to individual performance, but not as much so as would be predicted from the additive combination of individual scores. See also *social loafing*.

risk-taking behavior: Engaging in tasks that are challenging, will predictably result in achieving some desirable end if successful, and involve about a 50% probability of failure. Persons high in need for achievement pursue such behavior.

Ritalin: Medication commonly used in the treatment of handicapped children manifesting hyperactive or attention defects.

rivalry: Behavior oriented toward another individual in which a favorable comparison is sought relative to the performance of the other individual and not to a distinct task or goal. See also *competition*.

RLF: See *retrolental fibroplasia*.

RMP: See *resting membrane potential*.

Rockport Fitness Walking Test: A one-walk field test that can be used to estimate $\dot{V}O_2$max; mile walk time is obtained, and the heart rate during the final 15 s of the walk is used, along with age, gender, and body weight, to estimate maximal oxygen uptake using generalized or gender-specific equations to estimate $\dot{V}O_2$max.

role conclusion theory: Theory that the retiring athlete values "going out in style." The benefits of leaving sport with honors, having high recognition and visibility, and being personally satisfied with one's performance would consitute a proper role ending and contribute to subsequent high life satisfaction.

role conflict: Discrepancy between an expected position or role in sport and the actual assigned position or role. Has a negative effect on job satisfaction and increases the tendency to leave an organization or environment.

role model: Person who demonstrates desired behaviors or attitudes in accordance with her or his position that are compatible with what mainstream society expects.

role-modeling hypothesis: A sociological explanation for positional segregation in sport that claims that youths of particular minorities or ethnic groups segregate themselves into specific positions in sport because they wish to emulate highly successful athletes from the same group who perform in a similar setting. For example, sport sociologists theorize that perhaps skilled black athletes tend to compete in noncentral positions on sport teams due to their exposure, as younger competitors, to other black elite athletes who served as their role models.

role overload: Condition in which a person's resources for meeting the demands of their roles are below the demands placed upon them from external sources. Often leads to role stress and role strain. See also *role strain, role stress*.

role performance: The extent to which a member of a task-performing group understands, willingly accepts, and effectively carries out the responsibilities that go with his or her group role.

role strain: Subjective feelings of frustration, tension, or anxiety for role actors. A function of role overload. Extensive role strain is associated with low-quality work, low job satisfaction, quitting, and absenteeism.

role stress: Effect of demands of two positions that require engaging in psychological or physical activity that go beyond (or are perceived by the person to go beyond) the person's resources to cope with performing each role successfully. Often a function of role overload.

rooting reflex: An infant's involuntary turning of the head to the side in reaction to a touch on the cheek on the same side with a smooth object. Also called *searching reflex*.

rotary motion: See *angular motion*.

rotary pursuit: See *pursuit rotor*.

rotational energy: See *kinetic energy*.

rotational inertia: See *moment of inertia*.

round swayback: See *kypholordosis*.

RPE: See *rating of perceived exertion*.

RPP: See *rate pressure product*.

RQ: See *respiratory quotient*.

rules: Guidelines stating expected behaviors. In education, guidelines stating behaviors that are expected of students and that provide the basis for effective classroom management.

runner's high: Euphoric sensation in which the runner feels a heightened sense of well-being, enhanced appreciation of nature, and a loss of self-consciousness; other enhancements can also include elation, gracefulness, exhilaration, or spirituality.

running: The locomotor pattern in which weight is transferred from one leg to the other. There is a period of flight between toe-off of the rear leg and touch down of the forward leg.

running economy: Steady-state oxygen consumption during horizontal treadmill running at various speeds; an economical runner has a lower oxygen consumption at a given speed than an uneconomical runner; has been shown to explain individual differences in endurance running performance when factors such as $\dot{V}O_2$max and lactate threshold do not differ.

S

saccade: Eye movement in which the eye moves quickly from one fixation to another.

sagittal plane: Plane that divides the body into right and left halves.

St. Vitus's dance: See *chorea minor*.

sarcomere: Basic functional contractile unit of striated muscle fibers.

sarcoplasmic reticulum: Network of channels and vesicles in muscle fibers; storage site for calcium; when an action potential reaches the sarcoplasmic reticulum, calcium is released and the complex process of muscle contraction begins.

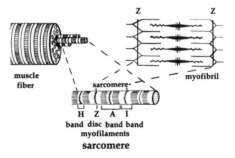

sarcomere

Sargent's Jump and Reach Test: Performance test to measure the vertical jump of an individual from a standing position; considered to be a measure of lower body power.

satiation: Excessive use of a reinforcer,

leading to a loss of effectiveness of the reinforcer.

satisfaction: For a group member, the extent of one's positive feelings about being a member of, and participating with, a particular group.

scalar: Quantity completely described by knowledge of its magnitude but not direction.

scaling: Varying the value of a constant (parameter) to observe systematic changes in a second constant (parameter), thus establishing a relationship between the two.

scanning: Attending rapidly to many aspects of the stimulus field.

SCAT: See *Sport Competition Anxiety Test*.

schedule of reinforcement: See *reinforcement schedule*.

schema: 1. Set of rules, formed by abstracting information from related movement experiences, that includes the underlying movement principle for this class of responses. See also *schema theory*. 2. Unit of thought that grows and differentiates with the experiences of childhood.

schema theory: Schmidt's model of motor control, which proposes (a) two separate memory states, the recall schema and the recognition schema, a schema being a set of rules or relationships established with experience; (b) generalized motor programs containing all details necessary for movement execution, but requiring the response specifications for any movement; (c) a variable role for sensory feedback dependent on the duration of the movement; and (d) four sources of information for establishment of schemata: response specifications, initial conditions, actual outcome, and sensory consequences of the response.

Scholander procedure: Chemically based method of O_2 and CO_2 gas analysis where the change in volume of each gas is determined as a chemical that totally absorbs the gas is introduced into a closed chamber system; highly accurate and time-consuming technique that is used to calibrate electronic analyzers.

school effectiveness: A school's achievement, affected by the administrative practices and resources of the school as well as student aptitude.

scissors gait: Spasticity affecting the flexor muscle groups that force crossing the legs at the midline during walking and producing a scissors-type movement.

scoliosis: Lateral deviation of the spine caused by functional or structural problems resulting in S curve, reverse S, C curve, or reverse C.

screening: In education, a procedure in which groups of students are examined or tested to identify those in need of special assistance.

SDA: See *specific dynamic action*.

searching reflex: See *rooting reflex*.

secondary amenorrhea: Cessation of normal menstrual function for a period of at least 3 to 6 months; associated with such factors as stress, excessive weight loss, and strenuous physical activity, although the exact mechanism is unknown; may also be a result of various pathologies such as pituitary tumors and estrogen deficiency.

secondary appraisal: See *appraisal*.

secondary reinforcer: Event that becomes reinforced by being paired with another event (primary reinforcer) that is already a reinforcing effect.

secondary sex characteristics: Aspects of form or structure appropriate to males or females, often used to assess biological maturity during the adolescent years; specifically, breast development and menarche in girls, penis and testes development in boys, and pubic hair in both sexes.

secondary task: Task periodically administered to a performer during repetitive performance of a primary task in order to investigate the attentional demands of the primary task. Also called *probe task*. See also *primary task*.

second-class lever: Lever in which the line of action of the resistive force acts between the fulcrum and the line of action of the motive force.

second law of thermodynamics: The principle that energy will always proceed in the direction of randomness or disorder (entropy), therefore entropy always increases in any system; when energy is exchanged, some energy will escape as entropy, usually in the form of heat.

second-order traits: See *surface traits*.

secular trend: Change in a landmark of physical growth or development, such as menarche, over successive generations, usually by influence of environmental factors.

segment power: The sum of muscle power and joint power as measured in watts (W).

seizure: Sudden alteration of consciousness and motor reaction, caused by an abnormal discharge of electrical impulses in the brain. Also called *convulsive disorder*.

selection effect: Process whereby certain group members who lack a certain characteristic that is common among other members leave the group over a period of time.

selective attention: Focus on specific stimuli or features, ignoring other (presumably irrelevant) concurrent stimuli.

selective filter: See *perceptual filter*.

self-actualization: 1. The desire for self-fulfillment and self-realization of one's potential; the highest level of Maslow's hierarchy of needs. 2. Self-actualizers are more fully functioning and live a more enriched life while utilizing all of their unique capabilities and potential, free from the inhibitions and emotional turmoil of less self-actualized persons. 3. The tendency to develop one's own talents and capacities.

self-adjusting system: See *self-organizing system*.

self-assessment: For a teacher, the development of an accountability system to maintain one's teaching performance.

self-concept: 1. An individual's self-acceptance, comfort, security, and other thoughts about who she or he is. 2. Set of self-expectations of behaving appropriately in a given situation.

self-confidence: 1. As a state, a transitory and situational belief or degree of certainty at one particular moment about one's ability to be successful (in sport, for example). Sometimes used interchangeably with, but differs from, self-efficacy, which is a situation-specific perception of belief about one's competence level, whereas self-confidence refers to a more generic feeling of self-assuredness and performance capability. 2. As a trait, a predisposition to have a particular belief or degree of certainty about one's ability to be successful in an activity. See also *confidence, self-efficacy*.

self-contained class: Special classroom, usually located within the regular public school building, that includes the equipment and resources to satisfy the educational needs of handicapped learners.

self-control: Control of responses or behaviors that an individual deliberately undertakes to achieve self-selected outcomes.

self-determining: Having one's actions and decisions under one's own control.

self-efficacy: 1. Capability to make a certain response that produces a successful outcome; a situation-specific factor that can influence a person's choice of activities, amount of effort expended, and how long one will persist in the face of obstacles and aversive experiences. 2. Situation-specific form of self-confidence; the belief that one is competent and can do whatever is necessary in a specific situation; may fluctuate from time to time. Also called *efficacy, efficacy expectations*. See also *collective efficacy*.

self-efficacy statement: A positive statement one says to oneself prior to performance.

self-enhancing attributional bias: See *self-serving attributional bias*.

self-esteem: Feelings of competence or self-worth.

self-focusing: The process of selectively

attending to information that originates from within and concerns oneself.

self-fulfilling prophecy: Situation brought about by acting out (or fulfilling) the expectations held by the self and others. Also called *Pygmalion effect*.

self-monitoring: Paying attention to or recording one's actions and/or feelings after experiencing success or failure over a period of time; independent of external input. This technique is most beneficial when tasks are easy and have been mastered. See also *negative self-monitoring, positive self-monitoring*.

self-motivation: Reinforcement of one's behavior through one's own ideas or goals rather than by those of an external source. Based on the contention that reinforcing one's own desirable behavior is more effective if self-induced and internally controlled than if one is dependent on, and sensitive to, external sources and situational influences.

self-organizing system: System that can establish relationships among its elements without a detailed higher order command. In dynamical models of human interlimb coordination, muscle collectives acting as limit cycle oscillators can entrain to act as a single unit by mutual synchronization, not higher order control. Also called *self-adjusting system*. See also *entrainment*.

self-paced task: Motor skill wherein the performer determines when and how to initiate action. Usually performed in a stable (closed) environment.

self-presentation theory: Proposal that individuals present themselves in a manner that generates positive self-images to others. Promotes social desirability by appearing attractive, competent, and honest. The motives for such behavior are to be recognized and accepted by others (audience-pleasing) and to maintain consistency between one's public and desired self (self-construction).

self-protecting attributional bias: Pattern of ascribing the causes of negative events to external factors, such as task difficulty and luck, to maintain self-worth.

self-regulation: 1. The process of maintaining control over one's own behavior (through a sequence of activities) without immediate external control. 2. Goal-directed behaviors in the relative absence of immediate external constraints, often pursuing goals with conflicting short- and long-term consequences. These behaviors include developing plans for pursuing a goal, monitoring one's behavior, comparing the observed behaviors with the goal (self-evaluation), and evaluating the outcome from one's actions (i.e., deciding whether or not to change the plan based on the discrepancy between the goal and the current level of performance).

self-serving attributional bias: 1. Pattern of ascribing the causes of positive events to internal factors (high ability and effort) and negative events to external factors (task difficulty and luck) to maintain personal self-worth. 2. Self-protective strategy whereby people tend to take personal responsibility for success while denying similar responsibility for failure. Also called *egocentric attributional bias, self-enhancing attributional bias*.

SELSPOT: Nonphotographic camera apparatus that can detect the location of one or more light-emitting diodes (LEDs), thus permitting digitization of movements in two or three planes if sufficient cameras are used. Acronym of Swedish term for Opto-Electronic Motion Analysis System manufactured by the Selcom Co.

semicircular canal: The small circular tubes located in the inner ear that are sensi-

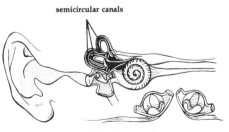

semicircular canals

semicircular canal

tive to change in position of the head and balance.

semilunar valve: See *aortic valve, pulmonary valve.*

semimental functioning: The characteristic seen at a point in cognitive development wherein children can recall events, ponder alternatives, and predict outcomes (contemplate past, present, and future) with mental images and without physical enactment.

senescence: The late years of the life span.

senile macular degeneration: Dated term for aging-related maculopathy, a condition in which the macula of the retina is altered by some of the following: atrophy of neural elements, pigment disruption, drusen formation, and abnormal blood vessel growth and scarring.

senile miosis: Age-related reduction in the resting diameter of the pupil of the eye, resulting in diminished retinal illuminance.

sensation seeking: Being dispositionally attracted to the risk that an activity provides; often evident with new experiences. The need to engage in diverse activities may be due to the sensation-seeker's high susceptibility to boredom. Also called *stimulus seeking.*

sensitive period: Span of time during which a developing organism is particularly susceptible to the influence of an event, stimulus, or mitigating factor. Sometimes used as a more accurate term for *critical learning period* or *critical period.*

sensitivity: Proportion of time abnormal exercise test (positive test) identifies individuals who have cardiovascular disease; is 70% based on angiogram verification of coronary artery disease; measure of validity in identifying disease.

$$\text{sensitivity} = (TP/TP + FN) \cdot 100$$

where TP = true positive
FN = false negative

sensitization: The experiencing of stress in response to repeated exposure to an unpleasant stimulus (stressor); often results from negative experiences such as failure.

sensorimotor integration time: Component part of reaction time consisting of the time period between (a) the first change in cortical activity, as measured by electroencephalograph recordings, indicating the sensory stimulus has reached the cerebral cortex, and (b) a change in electrical potential in the motor cortex.

sensorimotor stage: The first of Piaget's stages of cognitive development, in which bodily movements are the foundation for developing intelligence and the child deals concretely with objects, time, and space. There are six substages of this stage, which spans from birth to 2 years of age. See also *concrete operations stage, formal operations stage, preoperations stage.*

sensorineural deafness: Hearing loss caused by damage to the cells or nerve fibers that receive and transmit auditory stimuli.

sensoriperceptual development: Refinement of the sensory processes and perception based on sensory information such that more and more complex sensory information can be detected and evaluated.

sensory deprivation: Absence of sensory stimuli required for individuals to interact with the environment and provide information to the central nervous system for learning to occur.

sensory input: See *input.*

sensory integration: Ability to match or combine sensory information from multiple sources simultaneously, either within or between modalities. See also *intersensory integration.*

sensory neuron: See *afferent neuron.*

sensory receptors: Specialized nerve cells that detect stimuli. Also called *proprioceptors.*

sensory register: See *sensory store.*

sensory store: The functional location where a physiological representation of information is held for a brief time, usually 2 to 3 s for vision and up to 15 s for other modalities. Also called *sensory register, short-term sensory storage*.

sensory unit: A single nerve cell.

sequencing: See *sequential learning*.

sequential learning: Repetition of movements in the proper order. Also called *sequencing*.

serial recall: In memory research, remembering items or movements learned in a series in the same order in which they were presented.

serial skill: Movement consisting of discrete motor skills performed in a series.

seriation: Sequential ordering of a set of objects or variables by a specified characteristic.

series elastic component: All connective tissue (e.g. tendon, crossbridges, and Z-bands) in series with the contractile tissue in a muscle that provides elasticity to the muscle.

servomechanism: System in which a controller, perhaps a thermostat or a brain center, continuously monitors the system for differences between the present state and the desired one; often used as a model for human movement.

set induction: Introduction to the instructional format, used to briefly explain the purpose of the lesson and create or improve student interest in the activity.

severely mentally retarded: Classification by the American Association on Mental Deficiency used to specify individuals whose IQ score is between 20 and 35, and whose educational program concentrates on basic communication and self-help skills.

sex differences: Differences between males and females with respect to traits, behaviors, feelings, experiences, and responses.

sex role: Set of psychological traits, social expectations, and behaviors generally considered appropriate for the individuals of a given sex.

sex role expectancy: See *gender identity*.

sex-role identity: The identification of behavior that a culture or society labels masculine or feminine.

sex-typed person: One who internalizes society's standards of desirable behavior for men and women.

sex-typing: Labeling an activity as appropriate or inappropriate for individuals of a given sex. For instance, labeling a sport as masculine or feminine.

sexual age: Assessment of biological maturity based on primary and secondary sex characteristics.

shape discrimination: Matching or differentiating between shapes or forms.

shape identification: Naming various shapes and forms.

shaping: Behavior management technique in which reinforcement of small progressive steps or approximations of the targeted behavior lead to its accomplishment (successful completion). Also called *forward chaining*.

sharing time: In education, a narrative event in primary grades that allows students to speak on a topic unrelated to school.

shear force: Force acting parallel to a surface.

short-duration behaviors: Skill or behaviors performed within a minimal time frame or requiring rapid or continuous actions.

short-term memory (STM): The component of memory with a relatively short duration (thought to be less than 60 s) and limited capacity (surmised at seven items or chunks of information, plus or minus two).

short-term motor memory: Retention of the sensory information (feedback) generated by movement over a short time period. Also called *motor short-term memory*.

short-term objectives: Component of the individualized education program that includes observable and measurable behavior that functions as intermediate steps in attaining long term goals and extending the present level of educational performance.

short-term sensory storage: See *sensory store*.

shunt: Device implanted in the body to drain or remove excess cerebrospinal fluid.

SIGMA: See *Ohio State University Scale of Intra-Gross Motor Assessment*.

sigma task: Multicomponent activity in which the subject grasps a handle mounted on a turntable, rotates the handle one revolution, releases it, then makes a linear movement to contact a switch, hence describing the shape of the lowercase Greek letter sigma.

sigmoid curve: The name given the plot of typical whole-body growth measures because of its ''S'' appearance, resulting from rapid gain in infancy and early life, steady gain in middle childhood, rapid gain during adolescence, and slowing in late adolescence until the cessation of growth. Also called *S-shaped curve*.

signal: The desired measured response from a data-detection device.

signal-detection task: Measures the accuracy of visually or auditorily perceiving and reacting to one or more external stimuli, usually against background noise. The subject's task is to discriminate between noise and the presented signal.

signal preparation: Readying of a voluntary motor response to a stimulus, the characteristics of which are often manipulated to study the influence of readying the system on the speed of response. Sometimes considered an indicator of alertness. See also *response preparation*.

signal systems: Situational instructions or cues provided for the lesson behavior. See also *set induction*.

significant others: Individuals viewed by the subject as very important and credible, whose behaviors or opinions are meaningful and relevant, and who affect the subject's perceptions of his or her own appropriate behavior, thoughts, and emotional disposition.

sign language: System of communication in which there are similarities between the gestures and their intended meaning.

silent ischemia: Decreased oxygen supply to an area of the heart, diagnosed by ECG S-T segment changes; no physical signs accompany the abnormal ECG.

simple reaction time: The interval of time between the onset of a single stimulus and initiation of a single response to that signal. See also *reaction time*.

simulation: Technique to maximize skill execution by repeatedly practicing the criterion skills under situations that closely resemble actual performance conditions.

single-knee lock: A characteristic of immature walking in infants, consisting of one knee extension action during the entire support phase following foot strike with a partially flexed knee. In the mature double-knee lock, the knee is extended at foot strike, then flexes as body weight transfers over the foot, then extends again.

single support: The period of time when only one limb is in contact with the ground.

sinoatrial node: Known as the pacemaker of the heart; area of specialized conduction cells located in the posterior wall of the right atrium; action potential that travels through the heart's conduction system originates here; heartbeats originating here establish normal sinus rhythm.

Siri formula: Equation used to estimate percent fat from measurement of body density (Db):

$$\text{Percent fat} = 495/Db - 450$$

sitting height: The anthropometric measure of trunk plus head and neck length, recorded from the sitting surface to the vertex of the skull when the body is in a standardized sitting position (i.e, when the head is in the Frankfort plane).

situational favorableness: Degree to which the group situation will allow the leader to exhibit power, influence, or control taking into account leader–member relationships, task structure, and position power.

situational leadership theory: The belief that as a member's maturity increases, the leader's task-oriented behavior must progressively decrease. Inversely, relation-oriented behavior must increase as maturity increases up to the middle ranges, and then decrease with further increases in maturity. See also *multidimensional model of leadership*.

situational vulnerability hypothesis: The proposal that (a) self-confidence in achievement situations is influenced by situational factors, (b) a lack of clear and immediate performance feedback undermines confidence, and (c) females in achievement situations are more likely to exhibit less self-confidence in performing tasks with a male gender orientation or when they are evaluated or compared to others in social situations.

size constancy: The recognition that objects maintain their size even if their distance from the observer, and hence size of the retinal image, varies.

skeletal age: Assessment of biological age based on the extent of change in the developing skeleton in selected body areas.

skeptical sport personology: The view that trait psychology cannot accurately predict success in sport and should be abandoned. Compare *credulous sport personology*.

skill: 1. Learned movement task. 2. Qualitative indicator of performance denoting proficient execution. 3. Use of the optimal value in the control and coordination of movement such that the movement is proficient and efficient.

skinfold: Double layer of skin and subcutaneous fat; when this thickness is measured by special calipers at standard sites and population-specific formulae are utilized, an indirect estimation of percent body fat may be obtained; selected sites include

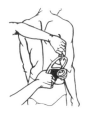

skinfold

triceps, subscapula, iliac, abdomen, chest, biceps, calf, and thigh.

skinfold calipers: Instrument for measuring skinfold thickness in millimeters; a spring keeps a constant tension on the caliper jaws regardless of the width so that an accurate and consistent measure may be taken.

skin friction: See *surface drag*.

skipping: Locomotor pattern in which each leg executes a walking step and a hop before weight is transferred to the other leg. The step is temporally longer than the hop, resulting in an uneven rhythm.

sliding: Locomotor pattern in which one foot steps sideways, then the other foot closes with a leap-step; a type of sideways galloping.

slow learner: Child whose progress is less than expected in relation to the peer group.

slow-twitch oxidative fiber (SO): Small skeletal muscle fiber innervated by alpha-2 motor neuron and characterized by a slow contraction time and high oxidative (aerobic) and low glycolytic (anaerobic) metabolic capacity; recruited primarily for low-intensity endurance-type activities. Also called *Type I fiber*.

small-for-date infant: Neonate born after a full prenatal term who is markedly below the population average birth weight, typically under 2,500 g.

smoothness: Degree to which a lesson is free from stops or breaks in the flow of activities.

SNS: See *sympathetic nervous system*.

SO: See *slow-twitch oxidative fiber*.

social approval: A motivation to perform effectively to gain approval from significant others. Effort is emphasized.

social approval orientation: The tendency to expend optimal effort for task accomplishment due to the need to gain approval from others. For instance, in sport, an athlete's effort may be contingent on the coach's approval.

social climate: See *climate*.

social cohesion: Extent to which members of a group like each other and enjoy each other's company. Compare *task cohesion*.

social comparison processes: Processes of evaluating one's ability against those of another person of similar ability in order to judge accurately the quality of one's own performance.

social control: The means whereby a group or society encourages conformity to norms. In sport, norms are represented by rules.

social facilitation: The benefits or detriments associated with the presence of an audience or coactors that do not interact verbally or emotionally with the performer. See also *Zajonc's model*.

social imperception: Inability to recognize the meaning and significance of the behavior of others; contributes to poor social adjustment; characteristic of learning-disabled children.

social influence: The effects of others' actions or words on one's behavior, feelings, or attitudes.

socialization: Process by which individuals learn socially expected behaviors, skills, attitudes, values, and dispositions that enable them to function within a particular culture.

socialization into sport: 1. Process through which individuals assume roles such as athlete, coach, or spectator; influence of significant others and social agencies on a person's decision to become involved

in sport. **2.** General attitudes, values, skills, and dispositions, such as sportsmanship and character, that may or may not be acquired while playing in specific sport environments such as youth sports.

social learning theory: The contention that behavior is learned in social settings, perhaps through observing others or experiencing aggression.

social loafing: Decreased individual effort or motivation in group settings when individuals are collectively held responsible for a task. Explanations include the diffusion of responsiblity among group members (i.e., when individual efforts are lost in the crowd), the loss of evaluation potential, especially as group size increases, and the lack of monitoring of individual performance. See also *Ringelmann effect*.

social perception: The influence of knowing a person's outward appearance (e.g., physical attractiveness) on judging that individual's personal traits and typical behavioral tendencies.

social physique anxiety: The perceived threat that individuals experience in response to others' evaluations of their physical characteristics.

social-psychological opportunity set: In sport, partly explains the overrepresentation of upper classes and underrepresentation of lower classes in sport, based on a family's social class and particular lifestyle. Based on the assumption that there are different sport-socialization practices among the upper, versus lower, social classes as a result of the different values each class places on sport participation. See also *economic opportunity set in sport*.

social reinforcers: Reinforcers such as praise, attention, smiles, and physical contact, that are generated from interpersonal interactions.

social satisfaction: Involves one's level of satisfaction as a group member in terms of the group's ability to allow the individual to attain the instrumental goals for which he or she originally joined the group.

social support leadership behavior: In sport, coaching behavior characterized by a concern for the welfare of individual athletes, positive group atmosphere, and warm interpersonal relations with members.

social validation: Procedures or standards to ensure that techniques employed by a psychologist are selected and applied in the best interests of the client.

sociogram: Technique for measuring the types of interactions and relationships among group members, based on direct observations or the responses of each group member to questions about her or his feelings toward other group members.

sociometric cohesion: 1. Pertains to the degree to which group members like one another and the amount of positive affect or good emotional feelings associated with team membership. Highly and positively related to the number of friends on the team, the amount of time spent in group-related activities, and the degree of group influence on significant behavior. **2.** Measurement technique that indicates the extent and nature of the interaction of members within a group.

sociometry: Measurement of group cohesion by describing the interactions and feelings among group members through a written profile called a sociogram. Primarily indicates interpersonal attraction among group members.

somatic state anxiety: Individual's perception of threat as exhibited by physiological and bodily responses such as heightened heart rate, shortness of breath, clammy hands, butterflies in the stomach, and tense muscles. Positively related to autonomic arousal. Best reduced by physical strategies, such as exercise, in contrast to cognitive techniques. Compare *cognitive state anxiety*.

somatic stereotype: Set of physical attributes that a person believes others possess, and the inferred relations among these attributes.

somatogram: Graphical representation of an individual's body proportionality and symmetry; developed by A.R. Behnke, it compares different body-segment girths to standard reference values.

somatosensory: 1. Refers to the sensory receptors located throughout the body and yielding body sensations. **2.** Refers to the skin receptors and proprioceptors.

somatotype: 1. Qualitative assessment of body configuration using three general configurations known as mesomorph, ectomorph, and endomorph. **2.** [mc] In physical growth, a physique assessment conducted to study the sex differences and age-related changes in physique during childhood and adolescence.

sound localization: See *auditory localization*.

source traits: See *first-order traits*.

Southern California Sensory Integration Tests: Norm-referenced tests, including the Ayres Space Test, Southern California Motor Accuracy Test, Southern California Kinesthetic and Tactile Perception Test, and the Southern California Visual Perception Test, to detect dysfunctions in sensory integration and determine their nature. There are 17 subtests for children 4 to 8 years old. The Motor Accuracy Test has internal consistency reliabilities ranging between .67 and .94 for various age groups, but the other tests generally have low stability coefficients, below .40.

spaced practice: See *distributed practice*.

spasm: Involuntary muscle contraction that interferes with purposeful movement.

spastic: A classification of cerebral palsy characterized by uncoordinated movements, partially due to an increased stretch reflex and contractures. Most cerebral palsy is classified as spastic.

spasticity: 1. Inability to relax voluntary muscles in an extended (stretched) position.

2. Increased tension in muscles, yielding a drawn-up appearance of limbs and resistance to joint movement and flexibility.

spatial: Set of planes and axes (i.e., a reference system) defined in relation to three-dimensional space.

spatial agnosia: Inability to correctly identify familiar persons or objects by their location in space.

spatial awareness: Appreciation of the arrangement in space of objects, symbols, or the body, and the ability to make judgments about space such as the required amount of space needed for a given object.

spatial orientation: A person's ability to appreciate the orientation or position of objects as they are located in space or in a two-dimensional drawing.

spatial relations: Identification of the associations between two or more objects in the environment as they relate to the body and its movement in space.

special education: According to the Education of the Handicapped Act (1986), specially designed instruction at no cost to the parent to meet the unique needs of a handicapped child, including classroom instruction, instruction in physical education, home instruction, and instruction in hospitals and institutions.

Special Olympics: Organization developed by the Joseph P. Kennedy, Jr., Foundation that provides sports competition and training for the mentally retarded.

special physical education: Generic term used to refer to physical education programs for the handicapped; includes adapted and developmental physical education.

specific dynamic action (SDA): Increased production of heat as a result of the digestion and assimilation of food, especially protein.

specific gravity: Ratio of body weight to the weight of the water displaced by the body (unitless).

specificity: Proportion of time a graded exercise test is negative when individuals without disease are tested; is 90% for males and 70% for females based on angiogram verification of coronary artery disease; measure of validity in identifying lack of disease.

$$\text{specificity} = (TN/FP + TN) \cdot 100$$

where TN = true negative
FP = false positive

specificity principle: 1. Principle that training for specific movements should be done in the exact manner and position in which the movements will be performed. **2.** [ep] Principle that the metabolic and cardiovascular changes that occur consequent to training depend on the type of training overload.

spectators: In sport, an audience or group of individuals observing a competitive sport contest.

speech reading: Use of vision to distinguish speech by watching the lips of the speaker and other visual sources. Also called *lipreading*.

speed: The scalar quantity of the velocity vector. Speed is measured in meters per second (ms^{-1}). See also *velocity*.

speed–accuracy trade-off: Hypothesized relationship between speed and spatial accuracy in a task requiring both components, such that slow speed allows greater spatial accuracy while faster speed is detrimental to spatial accuracy.

speed-control model: Hypothesized mode of movement control in which various levels of isometric force or velocity are achieved by varying force magnitude as the time to reach peak force is held constant.

spina bifida: Congenital malformation of the vertebral column that may include a hernial protrusion. The three main types are meningocele, myelomeningocele, and occulta.

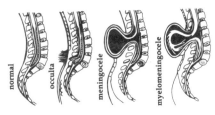

normal   occulta   meningocele   myelomeningocele

spina bifida

spinal animal: Animal whose spinal cord is cut in an experimental procedure to eliminate all control by the brain.

spinal pattern generator: Oscillator mechanism in the interneurons of the spinal cord that provide muscular synergies or collectives to the various motor units involved in certain basic movements, such as the step in locomotor movement.

spline: Polynomial function used to smooth data.

sport: Organized play that is accompanied by physical exertion, guided by a formal structure, organized within the context of formal and explicit rules of behavior and procedures, and observed by spectators.

Sport Competition Anxiety Test (SCAT): Purportedly measures a sport performer's level of trait competitive anxiety.

sport consumption theory: Contends that it is the similarity between the characteristics of sporting events and individuals' everyday lives that explains why middle and upper classes, males, and businesspersons are more likely than other groups to exhibit an ongoing interest in sport.

sport group: Collection of individuals who possess a sense of unity, collective identity, shared purpose or objectives, structured patterns of interaction, structured modes of communication, personal and/or task interdependence, and interpersonal attraction.

sport mastery: 1. Type of achievement behavior in which the goal of the athlete is to focus on performing at optimal efficiency regardless of the outcome. The key issue for the athlete is to demonstrate competence rather than demonstrate higher capacity than others. **2.** Attainment of a specific performance goal or achievement of a predetermined level of competence. Usually based on comparing one's own performance with personal standards. **3.** The goal of a competitor to achieve mastery of a given situation by improving or perfecting a skill. The participant may be attracted to a sport because the challenge of performing well appears enjoyable.

sport pedagogy: The understanding and study of factors associated with sport skill instruction and acquisition.

sport psychologist: Professionally trained person with a graduate degree in psychology or sport psychology who offers clinical, educational, or research services in an attempt to understand and communicate the psychological or psychophysiological factors that underlie physical performance and coaching effectiveness in sport. See also *clinical sport psychologist, educational sport psychologist, research sport psychologist.*

sport psychology: Scientific study of behavior that attempts to apply psychological facts and principles of learning, performance, and associated human behavior in sport or sport-related context. Concerned with observation of events, description of phenomena, explanation of factors that influence events in a systematic manner, prediction of events or outcomes based on systematic and reliable explanations, and control of events or contingencies that result in expected outcomes. See also *academic sport psychology, applied sport psychology, practicing sport psychology.*

sport role-identity: Extent of one's involvement in finding situations for functioning in highly important sport-related roles from which they plan their daily agendas and make decisions, and in which they are emotionally involved.

sportsmanship: Commitment to the primacy of justice and cooperation for males and females in a sport competitive environment.

sport sociologist: Person who studies, and contributes to the understanding of, the roles, conditions, development, and contributions of sport in society.

sport sociology: Study of conditions, behaviors, and the structure of social systems that lead to the development of certain structures and processes within various sport settings.

sport venture-orientation: Tendency to focus on the risk or adventure associated with performing sport skills and to determine success by quality performance in a risky situation.

S-R chaining: See *chaining*.

S-shaped curve: 1. Pertains to the plot of a performance index over units of practice that depicts initially slow improvement, then rapid improvement, followed by decreasing gains. 2. [mc] See *sigmoid curve*.

stabilimeter: See *mirror tracer*.

stability: 1. [ss] Refers to the turnover rate for group membership as well as the length of time members have been together in the group. Positively related to group cohesiveness. 2. [sp] Dimension of attribution theory in which an outcome will either change (e.g., effort) or remain stable (e.g., ability). 3. [mc] Balance or a state of equilibrium. 4. [mc] Pertains to skills executed in a static, balanced position, as opposed to locomotion.

stabilizer muscle: Muscle that is stimulated to act to anchor or stabilize the position of a bone.

stabilometer: Apparatus to test full-body balance. Consists of a horizontal platform that pivots at the middle and upon which a subject stands attempting to keep the platform balanced. Performance quality is measured by time in balance, out of balance, and/or error in which the platform deviates from a prescribed range per trial.

stable equilibrium: State of an object in which the object will return to its original position if displaced from that position.

stacking: Disproportional relegation of athletes to specific sport positions on the basis of ascribed characteristics such as ethnicity or race. Used more specifically to describe the underrepresentation of minority athletes at central positions on the field (e.g., pitcher or catcher in baseball) and overrepresented at noncentral positions (e.g., outfield).

stadiometer: Calibrated device to measure stature. Consists of a base, a rule at a perfect right angle to the base, and an adjustable piece attached to the rule at a perfect right angle. This piece contacts the vertex of the skull and simultaneously indicates the stature measurement on the rule.

stage: 1. A level in a predictable sequence of change, such that each step in the sequence is qualitatively different, intransitive, universal for individuals, and hierarchical. There is a period of flux as an individual moves to a new stage, with new behaviors appearing gradually until they consolidate in a period of stability. 2. Atheoretically, a level of difficulty, phase, step, point, type, pattern, time, or mood, usually in regard to a developmental behavior or shift in a learning process.

staleness: See *overtraining*.

stall: Condition of a projectile in which the angle of attack becomes too steep, creating a highly turbulent airflow past the projectile and a subsequent decline in the lift-to-drag ratio.

stance: Period of time when a limb is supporting the body during contact with the ground.

standard temperature and pressure dry (STPD): Method for standardizing gas volumes to standard temperature, humidity, and barometric pressure conditions; these standard conditions are temperature = 273 °K, or 0 °C, pressure = 760 mm Hg, and no humidity (dry air); gas volumes used to calculate oxygen consumption and carbon dioxide production are expressed in STPD.

startle reflex: See *Moro reflex.*

state aggression: Transitory emotional condition characterized by consciously perceived feelings of belligerence that may result in combative actions.

state anxiety: 1. An immediate emotional experience that is characterized by apprehension, fear, and tension, and sometimes accompanied by physiological arousal. **2.** State of arousal engendered by a stressful or threatening situation. Also called *A-state.*

state of flow: Holistic psychological state or sensation accompanied by extreme pleasure and satisfaction when experiencing activities for which the primary reward is in the experience itself rather than in the outcome. Differs slightly from a peak experience in that flow is more voluntary in nature. Also called *flow.*

static analysis: Mechanical analysis in which the sum of the external forces and torques equals zero.

static balance: See *static equilibrium.*

static equilibrium: State of a body undergoing zero acceleration; the ability to maintain equilibrium in a stationary position. Also called *static balance.*

static friction: Force generated between two surfaces tending to move along each other when no motion is occurring.

statics: Branch of mechanics associated with systems undergoing zero acceleration.

static visual acuity: Sharpness in the sight of stationary objects or displays.

stature: Anthropometric measure of standing height, from the floor to the vertex of the skull, taken in an erect posture without shoes.

status rewards: Recognition for desirable behavior and fulfilling role expectancies in sport through verbal praise from significant others that enhances the player's status and serves to maintain aggressive behavior. Often used in a sport context in terms of aggressive actions. Nicknames such as "The Assassin" or "Enforcer" are examples.

steadiness tester: Apparatus designed to test ability to hold a stylus in place or move it along an increasingly narrowing space without touching the sides of the apparatus.

steady-state exercise: Constant submaximal exercise below the lactate threshold where the oxygen consumption is meeting the requirements for ATP synthesis.

step: 1. [mc] Qualitative change in the movement or behavior comprising a developmental sequence, often used if the change does not meet the criteria for a "stage." **2.** [bm] Period of time from a designated event on one foot during the support period of locomotion to the same event on the other foot.

step cycle: Step of a locomotor pattern from a designated point to return to that point after movement through a complete pattern. See also *Philippson step cycle.*

step length: Horizontal distance covered along the line of progression during one step.

stepping reflex: See *walking reflex.*

step sequences: Series of task approximations that are involved in the shaping process to achieve a terminal objective.

stereotypic: Repetitive and nonfunctional actions that interfere with purposeful movement, often found in blind or severely retarded individuals.

steroids: Group of organic compounds with a discrete chemical composition. See also *anabolic steroid.*

stick figure: Representation of a movement in which the segment endpoints are joined by a line.

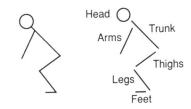

whole body stick figure   segmental components

stick figure

stiffness: Quality of a spring-like element that expresses ease of movement. In mass-spring models of human limb movement, varying stiffness of the spring model corresponds to varying duration of limb movement.

stimulated recall: Study of teachers' thoughts, judgments, and decisions while interacting with learners. Typically involves video- or audiotaping a lesson.

stimulus control: Presence of a particular stimulus that elicits a particular response. The response will be performed when the particular stimulus is evident but not in its absence.

stimulus cueing: Strategy that facilitates goal attainment (e.g., exercising) by identifying and using objects, ideas, or other behaviors associated with the desired goal (e.g., placing one's running shoes in an easily observable place) to create an environment, or a behavioral ritual that will serve as a reminder to perform a preplanned action (e.g., stretching).

stimulus generalization: The phenomenon of increased response strength to a new stimulus due to conditioning to a previous but similar stimulus, with the magnitude of response strength related to the degree of stimulus similarity.

stimulus-generalization   principle: Transferring a response to a new and similar stimulus.

stimulus–response chaining: See *chaining*.

stimulus–response compatibility: See *compatibility*.

stimulus–response mapping: Spatial relationship between a set of stimuli and a set of response buttons or targets. See also *compatibility*.

stimulus seeking: See *sensation seeking*.

S-T index: Ratio of the height of the T wave to the S wave; reduction in the index suggests S-T elevation and an increase suggests S-T depression.

S-T integral: Distance between the S and T waves on ECG.

STM: See *short-term memory*.

storage: The placement of information into long-term memory.

STPD: See *standard temperature and pressure dry*.

strabismus: Condition in which one eye cannot achieve binocular vision, resulting from an imbalance of the eye muscle. Also called *crossed eyes*.

strain energy: Ability of a body to do work by virtue of its deformation (either stretched or compressed) and return to its original shape. Strain energy is measured in joules.

$$S.E. = 1/2 \, kx^2$$

where k = spring constant of the material
x = distance which object is deformed

strain gage: Instrument in which the mechanical strain of a material is calibrated to be proportional to the change in the electrical current passing through it, thereby measuring the force applied to the material.

strength: Ability of a muscle or muscle group to exert force against a resistance; usually measured as one maximal effort.

strength fitness: Capacity to perform repeated maximal contractions of a muscle group or groups.

stress: 1. Any situation that has the potential for eliciting increased anxiety and arousal. **2.** Unpleasant emotional reaction associated with arousal of the autonomic nervous system as a result of situational demands perceived as threatening. Involves the perception of an imbalance between environmental demand and the person's capabilty to respond accordingly. Usually occurs under conditions in which failure to meet the demand is perceived as having important consequences, which in turn elicits heightened state anxiety. **3.** Any behavior response of an organism to environmental stimulation. May be associated with feelings that are negative (distress) or positive (eustress).

stress appraisal: Type of primary appraisal that reflects harm or loss, threat, and challenge.

stress incentives: In sport, the excitement, tension, pressure, and action that sport can provide a participant.

stress inoculation training: Coping skills/stress management program for dealing with noxious input and for building an immunity to stress. Entails guiding the subject through progressively more stressful experiences. Includes muscle relaxation and self-instructional training, which entails teaching clients to give themselves adaptive instructions in dealing with stressors.

stress management training: Program for reducing stress and anxiety, involving the acquisition and rehearsal of cognitive and relaxation skills. Cognitive skills include cognitive restructuring and/or self-instructional training to develop better mental control of attention and behavior. Relaxation skills involve somatic (progressive relaxation) and cognitive (meditation) relaxation.

stressor: Stimulus that a person finds noxious or unpleasant.

stretch reflex: See *myotatic reflex.*

stride: Period of time from a designated event of one foot during the support period of locomotion to the subsequent occurrence of the event of the same foot.

stride length: Horizontal distance covered along the line of progression during one stride.

stroboscopy: Technique of multi-imaging a movement on a single photograph using a still camera and a strobe light that illuminates the subject for a very brief period of time.

stroke volume: Amount of blood pumped from a ventricle per cardiac cycle; increases with an increase in exercise intensity up to approximately 50% to 60% of an

individual's $\dot{V}O_2$max, and then levels off; maximum stroke volume increases with training and is a factor related to the increase in maximum oxygen transport that accompanies the training response.

structural deviation: Deviation of posture caused by changes in the bone structure.

structural wholeness: The characteristic of developmental stages indicating an organic interconnection among a stage's processes such that related tasks are approached in the same way.

S-T segment depression: S-T segment is at least 1 or 2 mm below baseline at .08 s after J point in a horizontal, downsloping, or upsloping direction; primary indicator of ischemia during graded exercise test; other causes include drugs, electrolyte disturbances, and ventricular hypertrophy.

S-T segment elevation: Elevation of the S-T segment from its normal position; primary cause is acute myocardial infarction, but may also indicate vasospasm, acute generalized pericarditis, ventricular aneurysm, or a normal variant in young individuals called "early repolarization."

S-T slope: Direction of the S-T segment in relation to the horizontal axis formed by the isoelectric baseline; normal S-T slope is about 30 degrees; deviations may be downsloping, horizontal, or with varying degrees of upsloping; important in diagnosing S-T segment depression. See also *S-T segment depression.*

student achievement: The learning or performance outcomes of the student in the education process.

student attitude: The perceptions of students concerning teachers and physical activity that affect the process of learning and motivation.

subischial length: An estimate of lower extremity length derived by subtracting sitting height from standing height.

subjective competitive outcome: Individual's perception of success as a result of engaging in competition. See also *objective competitive outcome*.

subjective meaning: A person's own personal interpretation of achievement in any context in an attempt to understand the motivation and subsequent achievement behavior of the individual.

sublimation: Coping mechanism in which one activity is substituted for another that is more accessible and attainable.

subluxation: The partial dislocation of a joint.

subroutine: Group of neural motor commands for executing a component of a movement that, combined with other subroutines and commands, comprises a motor program.

substrate: Substance acted upon; in energy metabolism, the carbohydrate, fat, or protein fuel that is catabolized to produce adenosine triphosphate.

subtalar joint: The joint between the talus and the calcaneus allowing inversion-eversion movements of the foot.

subtalar joint pronation: The three-dimensional movement of the foot comprising calcaneal eversion, forefoot abduction, and dorsiflexion. Compare *subtalar joint supination*.

subtalar joint supination: The three-dimensional movement of the foot comprising calcaneal inversion, forefoot adduction, and plantar flexion. Compare *subtalar joint pronation*.

subthreshold: Level of stimulation or information below that needed to identify the stimulus.

success incentives: In sport, external rewards that sport can provide the participant, such as trophies, praise, or recognition.

success phobia: See *fear of success*.

succinate dehydrogenase: Iron-containing flavoprotein enzyme that catalyzes the dehydrogenation of succinic acid to fumaric acid in the Krebs cycle; important rate-limiting enzyme; aerobically trained indi-

viduals have been shown to have higher concentrations of this enzyme; found in slow-twitch and fast-twitch oxidative fibers.

sucking reflex: Infant's sucking motion as an involuntary response to a touch above or below the lips.

superior: The description of a body part above a reference body part. Compare *inferior*.

supination: 1. Rotation of the palm upward. **2.** Adduction and inversion of the foot. Compare *pronation*.

supine: Lying on the back. Compare *prone*.

support leg: The leg in a locomotor skill that is in contact with the ground, therefore holding the weight of the body, while the other leg is recovering to take the next step; the leg from touchdown to takeoff.

support phase: The portion of locomotor travel between periods of flight when at least one leg contacts the ground, holding the body weight.

surface drag: Drag caused by the passage of a fluid over the surface of an object; drag caused by the friction between the surface and the moving air. Also called *skin friction*.

surface electrode: Detecting device placed on the surface of the skin to monitor the electrical signals of the muscle during electromyography; the recording of muscle actions.

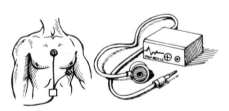

surface electrode

surface traits: Based on the 16 Personality Factor (16PF) profile that indicates eight secondary personality dispositions, which are learned (e.g., self-concept), as opposed to the 16 primary traits, which are fundamental structures of personality. Also called *second-order traits.* Compare *first-order traits.*

swayback: See *kypholordosis, lordosis.*

swimming reflex: Movements of an infant's arms and legs in a crawl stroke–like pattern elicited reactively by holding the infant prone over or in water.

swing leg: 1. The leg in a locomotor skill that is recovering, usually from an extension to propel the body, to a position where body weight can again be supported, that is, the leg from takeoff to touchdown. **2.** In hopping, the nonsupport, nonhopping leg.

swing phase: The portion of a step when a leg is recovering from an extension to propel the body to a position where it can again support body weight; the time from takeoff to touchdown of a limb.

switched-limb paradigm: Experimental procedure in which subjects learn a movement with one limb, then reproduce it with both limbs so that accuracy of reproduction between limbs can be compared.

Sydenham's chorea: See *chorea minor.*

symmetrical tonic neck reflex: 1. An infant's extension of both arms and flexion of both legs as an involuntary reaction to its head and neck being extended while it is supported in a sitting position. **2.** An infant's flexion of both arms and extension of both legs as an involuntary reaction to its head and neck being flexed while it is supported in a sitting position. Also called *tonic neck reflex.* Compare *asymmetrical tonic neck reflex.*

symmetric impulse-variability model: See *impulse-variability model.*

sympathetic nervous system (SNS): The part of the autonomic nervous system that increases activity in response to stress

and primarily governs exercise functions; nerve endings primarily secrete norepinephrine; causes excitation in some organs and inhibition in other organs; for example, stimulation causes an increase in heart rate and contractility, fuel mobilization, vasodilation in the blood vessels of the working musculature, and vasoconstriction in nonworking areas.

synchronization: The state in which the interval and phase of coupled oscillators are exactly matched.

synchrony: Occurrence of oscillatory movements having the same period and phase.

syndrome: Combination of physical traits or malformations that are inherited in the same manner and have a similar prognosis.

synergist muscle: Muscle that actively provides an additive contribution to the agonist muscle during a muscle action.

synergy: See *coordinative structure.*

systematic desensitization: Treatment designed to gradually reduce anxiety using relaxation. Treatment is based on the situations that elicit anxiety and the client's ability to relax and imagine scenes with appropriate levels of emotion.

systematic noise: The error contained in a signal generated by a systematic interference.

systematic observation and analysis: Process of collecting objective information on the instructional process and analyzing that information in a meaningful way.

systole: Contraction phase of the cardiac cycle, during which blood is ejected from the ventricles. See also *cardiac cycle, diastole.*

systolic blood pressure: See *blood pressure.*

tachycardia: Resting heart rate of more than 100 bpm.

tactile: A reference to the sensory modality of touch or feel, including texture, shape, or pressure.

tactile agnosia: See *finger agnosia*.

tactile discrimination: Ability to differentiate one touch point on the skin from one or more others touched sequentially or simultaneously, usually in close proximity, without using vision.

tactile localization: Ability to identify, often by pointing, the place where one has been touched, sight unseen.

tactile perception: Perceptual system that yields information about stimuli in contact with the skin, arising mostly from cutaneous receptors.

tactile recognition: Ability to identify objects and their features through touch and manipulation.

takeoff: The moment in a locomotor skill when the support limb(s) leave the ground to project the body into flight.

takeoff leg: Last leg to leave the ground in a locomotor skill, projecting the body into flight.

tangential acceleration: 1. Instantaneous linear acceleration vector, tangent to a curved path, of an object moving along the curved path. **2.** Product of the angular acceleration vector and the radius of the curve; measured in meters per second squared ($m \cdot s^{-2}$).

tangential velocity: 1. Instantaneous linear velocity of an object moving on and tangent to a curved path. **2.** Product of the angular velocity vector and the radius of the curve; measured in meters per second ($m \cdot s^{-1}$).

tangible reward: External reward that can be observed and has functional value, such as monetary gain, a trophy, recognition from significant others, or social approval.

tapping board: Apparatus with two target plates at the ends of an 18-in board, which must be alternately tapped by a subject with a hand-held stylus.

target behavior: The behavior to be initially assessed, then altered or changed, during the treatment program.

target heart rate: Heart rate that must be achieved during exercise to obtain a cardiovascular training effect; for practical purposes, a range is generally used; American College of Sports Medicine Guidelines recommend 65% to 85% of maximum heart rate; can also be calculated using the Karvonen formula.

task analysis: Method of dividing skills into subskills or subcomponent tasks that are more suitable for the learner to achieve in a series of sequenced steps aimed at meeting the terminal objective. Also called *activity analysis*.

task cards: Series of developmentally sequenced challenging skills used for individualizing instruction that children can practice at their own pace. They may be used in classroom situations, circuits, or for homework assignments.

task cohesion: Extent to which group members work together and function productively to achieve a specific and clearly defined goal. Compare *social cohesion*.

task complexity: Difficulty of a task in terms of either the number of parts composing the task or the information processing demands of the task. See also *task organization*.

task ego-involvement: Degree of importance a subject attaches to successfully completing a task.

task motivation: Style of leadership in which completing one or more tasks successfully is a priority, even at the expense of meeting the performer's individual (personal) needs.

task organization: Difficulty of a task in terms of the interrelationship of its component parts, with relative independence being low organization and relative dependence being high organization. See also *task complexity*.

task-oriented coach: Coach who tends to focus most heavily on winning competitions and whose actions are directed to meet this objective, as opposed to a coach who emphasizes meeting the personal needs of players.

task-reward system: Contingency system in which reinforcement is delivered immediately after performing a task.

tau: See *time-to-contact*.

taxonomy: The science or classification of educational objectives.

TCA cycle: See *Krebs cycle*.

teacher attitude: The combination of the teacher's self-image and feelings concerning teaching, physical education, and students that creates and influences the learning environment.

teacher reaction analysis: The effort designed to redirect teacher reactions to students into positive categories.

teacher–student interaction: Behavior teachers undertake in the instruction setting to praise or correct behavior, provide feedback, and criticize or accept student feelings or suggestions.

team: Social unit with a task that requires a set of performers to accomplish. No individual member can successfully complete the task alone.

team cohesion: A team's "sticking together" and remaining united in pursuing its goals.

teleoreceptors: The sensory receptors that detect stimuli at a distance from the body, such as the eyes or ears. Also called *telereceptors*.

telereceptors: See *teleoreceptors*.

temporal analysis: Movement analysis concerned only with the timing of events in the movement.

temporal awareness: Appreciation of an internal time structure, allowing synchronization of movements in a rhythmical manner and proper sequence.

temporal coupling: Time-related yoking between two or more muscle collectives, such that action of one joint is a referent for action at other joints. This coupling can be quantified by absolute or relative timing.

temporal perception organization: The organization of sensory input and resultant motor output that occur at the right time required to execute the skill.

tensile force: Force that produces tension on a body or an object.

tension: 1. [sp] Feelings of tightness in certain muscle groups as a result of excessive worry and frustration. **2.** [bm] The result of colinear forces acting in opposite directions in an attempt to pull apart.

teratogen: Drug or agent that causes abnormal development in a fetus upon exposure.

terminal behavior: The final behavior achieved at the end of successive approximations or components of that behavior. See also *shaping*.

terminal feedback: Information gathered by the person following performance and typically used to aid skilled movements. Differs from concurrent feedback, which is enacted during skill execution.

terminal goal: See *terminal objective of behavior*.

terminal objective of behavior: The synthesis of all behaviors or subobjectives to be obtained after a designated period in the instructional process. Also called *terminal goal*.

terminal velocity: The constant velocity of a falling object as a result of the equality of the air resistance forces on the object and the object's weight.

Test of Gross Motor Development: Criterion-referenced assessment for children 3 to 10 years of age that includes 12 locomotor and object-control skills. Split-half reliability is .85 for locomotor skills and .78 for object-control skills.

tetanus: Condition in which individual muscle contractions fuse together; the muscle contraction is not followed by a relaxation period, due to stimuli being too closely spaced.

thalamus: The portion of the midbrain concerned with relaying information from the sensory system for vision, hearing, touch, and joint and muscle receptors to the cerebral cortex. Also involved in arousal of the individual for activity.

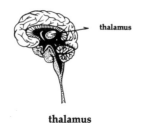

thalamus

thalamus

theoretical efficiency: Thermodynamic approach to efficiency calculations that considers muscle metabolism and the forces and energy required to perform the movements of work. Also called *mechanical contraction coupling efficiency*.

therapy: Interventions used in treatment or rehabilitation of a disease or injury.

thermodynamics: Physical science dealing with energy exchange. See also *first law of thermodynamics, second law of thermodynamics*.

thermogenesis: Production of heat in the body; classified as shivering or nonshivering thermogenesis; nonshivering thermogenesis may be linked to brown fat and the uncoupling of oxidative phosphorylation (i.e., when heat, and not ATP, is produced).

thermoregulation: The body's ability to maintain internal temperature in a dynamic equilibrium by means of numerous interrelated mechanisms; as core temperature rises as a result of excess heat produced following exercise, sweating increases to cool the body via evaporation, and the blood flow to the skin increases to increase excess heat loss.

third-class lever: Lever in which the line of action of the motive force is located between the fulcrum and the line of action of the resistive force.

third-person imagery: See *external imagery*.

thoracic: The area of the vertebral column pertaining to the chest region.

thought stopping: Mental technique in which a person self-verbalizes the term "stop" and then attends to relevant stimuli to cease thinking unpleasant thoughts or focusing on unimportant cues.

threshold value: Minimal level of stimulation or information required to identify a stimulus.

thrust: In education, a disruption to the flow or momentum of the lesson, in which the teacher interrupts an ongoing activity.

tibial rotation: Rotation of the tibia about its long axis.

tidal volume: Amount of air inspired or expired per breath; at rest in a healthy adult, tidal volume is approximately 500 ml and with maximum levels of exercise may increase 3 to 4 times.

tilting reaction: See *equilibrium reaction*.

time on target: Accuracy score indicating the accumulated portion of the total possible time a subject keeps a device or movement on a moving (usually rotating) target.

time out: In child education, a behavior/learner management technique that involves removing the opportunity for the child to be reinforced by placement in a neutral environment for a specific time period. Results in the decrease or elimination of the inappropriate behavior.

time out hypothesis: Suggests that exercise per se does not produce positive emotions but, rather, that it is a time out, or respite, from our daily stress that initiates these changes.

time sharing: Simultaneous performance of two attention-demanding tasks.

time-to-collision: See *time-to-contact*.

time-to-contact: Time interval between (a) some point and the arrival of a moving observer at a fixed point, or (b) a fixed observer with a moving point/object; determined by the inverse of the dilation rate of the object's image on the observer's retina. Also called *tau, time-to-collision*.

timing: Proper moment to dispense reinforcement to ensure its effectiveness.

toe-off: The instant in time during the support period of locomotion when the toe of the foot leaves the ground; the beginning of the swing period for that limb.

token economy: System used to reinforce appropriate behaviors by delivering stars, points, or pennies (tokens) when specified behaviors are emitted. The tokens can be redeemed from a menu of backup reinforcers such as additional activity time or being the group leader. Also called *token reinforcement*.

token reinforcement: See *token economy*.

tonic neck reflex: See *asymmetrical tonic neck reflex, symmetrical tonic neck reflex*.

tonicoclonic seizure: See *grand mal seizure*.

topography: Study of properties of measurement scales that remain invariant despite transformations of scale; applied to kinematics, the study of properties that remain invariant despite transformations of scale such as speeding up or slowing down.

topological analysis: System of assessing the properties of a measurement scale that remain invariant despite transformations of scale. Often applied to movement in order to study the kinematic properties of a movement that remain invariant despite transformations of scale such as speeding up or slowing down.

torque: 1. Rotational or twisting action produced by a force that acts eccentric to the axis of rotation. **2.** The product of force and the perpendicular distance from the line of action to the axis of rotation. **3.** The product of the moment of inertia and the angular acceleration. Torque is measured in Newton-meters (N-m). Also called *moment of force*.

$$\text{torque} = \text{force} \times \text{distance}$$

where distance = perpendicular distance from the axis of rotation to the line of action of the force

$$\text{torque} = I\alpha$$

where I = moment of inertia
α = angular acceleration

total communication: Approach to educating deaf students that combines oral speech, sign language, speech reading, and finger spelling.

total lung volume: Maximum amount of air in the lungs; includes the sum of residual volume and vital capacity.

total peripheral resistance: Sum of the forces opposing the flow of blood in the systemic circulatory system.

touchdown: Instant in time during the support period of locomotion when any portion of the foot first makes contact with the ground; the beginning of the support period.

trace decay: The theoretical cause of forgetting as explained by the passage of time.

tracking task: 1. Task in which a subject with a stylus, control stick, or sight, is to stay as close as possible to a moving target, often on a pursuit rotor apparatus (pursuit tracking). **2.** Task in which a subject is to maintain a constant speed or pressure in varying conditions (compensatory tracking).

traction epiphysis: The part of a bone where a muscle tendon attaches.

traction response: An infant's involuntary flexion of all arm joints when its arm is pulled.

trailing: Mobility technique for the visually impaired, featuring lightly tracing the back of the fingers over a smooth surface.

trailing leg: In locomotor skills such as galloping and sliding, the leg that closes the step initiated by the opposite, leading leg.

trainable mentally retarded: The classification by the American Association on Mental Deficiency of mental retardation at the moderate level or IQ between 36 and 51. The educational emphasis is on self-help and vocational skills. Also called *moderately mentally retarded*.

training: Any program of exercise designed to improve the skills and increase the energy capacities of an individual for a particular activity; adaptations that occur are specific to the systems overloaded. See also *duration of training, frequency of training, intensity of training*.

training principles: See *principles of training*.

trait: [sp] Relatively stable personality predisposition.

trait aggression: Relatively stable personality predisposition to respond in certain situations with acts of aggression.

trait anxiety: Relatively permanent personality predisposition to perceive certain environmental situations as threatening or stressful, and the tendency to respond to these situations with increased state anxiety. Also called *A-trait, general trait anxiety*. See also *competitive trait anxiety*.

trait perspective: Personality paradigm indicating that traits, as relatively enduring and generalizable personality characteristics, predict an individual's behavior in a variety of situations.

trait theory: Theory that views human behavior as primarily determined by stable and permanent personality characteristics.

trajectory: See *parabolic path*.

transamination: Process of deamination in which the removed amino group is accepted by another substance.

transarticular force: Component of the muscle force acting toward the joint along the long axis of the bone.

transcendental meditation: Series of procedures, such as concentration on breathing, visualization, relaxation of muscles, and repetition of a mantra, to gain the desired effect of maximal relaxation.

transentropy: Measure of the amount of information in a signal transmission process containing noise. In motor control, a transentropy can serve as a measure of the variability in human body motion.

transfer of learning: 1. Influence of earlier practice of a skill on the learning of a new skill. 2. The carryover effect of learning in one context to another context. Also called *transfer of training*. See also *bilateral transfer*.

transfer of training: See *transfer of learning*.

transfer test: Situation in which one uses a previously practiced skill in a new situation or context.

transition: In education, a managerial period between activities in which students move to new stations, change activities, or shift to courts.

transit reaction: See *coincidence-anticipation*.

transportation phase: Initial portion, ballistic in nature, of an arm movement toward a target.

transverse plane: Plane that divides the body into top and bottom portions.

trauma: Wound or injury to the system.

tremor: Involuntary quivering or shaking movement of a limb or the whole body.

tricarboxylic acid cycle (TCA cycle): See *Krebs cycle*.

tricuspid valve: Three-cuspid valve separating the right atrium from the right ventricle; regulates the flow of blood into the right ventricle and prevents blood from flowing back into the atrium during ventricular contraction. Also called *right atrioventricular valve*.

trigeminy: Occurrence of a dysrhythmic cardiac cycle every third beat.

triglycerides: Storage form of fat in the

body; each molecule is comprised of three fatty acid molecules and one glycerol molecule.

triplegia: Rare condition in which paralysis occurs in any three limbs (e.g., two arms and one leg).

trisomy 21: See *Down syndrome*.

trophotrophic rebiasing model: Explanation of the effects of muscle feedback (electromyography [EMG] biofeedback) on the person's arousal system. Reduced EMG activity reduces signals sent to the central nervous system, which, by activating the parasympathetic nervous system, reduces the reactions of the somatic and autonomic nervous systems. The result is a more relaxed state.

tropomyosin: Contractile protein wound into the grooves of the actin filament blocking the active sites in the resting state, which prevents crossbridge formation between actin and myosin.

troponin: Contractile protein bound with actin that, when activated by calcium released from the sarcoplasmic reticulum, moves tropomyosin away from the active sites on the actin and myosin is then able to cross-bridge with actin.

tuning: Preparation of the motor neurons in a functional group of muscles and joints acting to produce an action according to a plan (a coordinative structure) in adapting it to the environmental context.

tunnel vision: 1. Restriction in the field of vision or peripheral angle of less than 20 degrees. **2.** See *perceptual narrowing*.

turbulent flow: Erratic intermixing flow of moving fluid about an object caused by the separation of the fluid from the surface of the object.

twelve-minute run/walk test: Endurance performance test developed by Cooper in which the maximum distance covered in 12 min is determined; the greater the distance covered, the more aerobically fit an individual.

two-component model: Division of the human body into fat and fat-free compartments; assumption underlying Brozek and Siri equations for calculation of percent body fat from body density.

2,3-diphosphoglycerate (2,3-DPG): Red blood cell glycolytic intermediate, not produced in skeletal muscle glycolysis; causes a decrease in the oxygen–hemoglobin affinity, thereby enhancing the unloading of oxygen at the tissue. Has been shown to increase with exercise as well as with chronic exposure to high altitude.

2,3-DPG: See *2,3-diphosphoglycerate*.

tympanic membrane (eardrum): Anatomical boundary between the outer and middle ear. Sound impulses from the outer ear resonate on the tympanic membrane and are sent to the inner ear and temporal lobe of the brain.

type A behavior: Actions associated with type A personality (behavioral characteristics) such as time urgency, high need to achieve, impatience, hostility, anger, exhibition of superiority to others, and the inability to relax. Researchers disagree whether type A is, in fact, a personality trait (a predisposition) or a set of behaviors that are not necessarily inherited or permanent. See also *type B behavior*.

type A personality: Predisposition to exhibit behaviors aimed at maintaining environmental control, usually emerging when the susceptible person confronts a challenging situation.

type B behavior: Actions associated with type B personality, such as relaxation without guilt, an absence of time urgency, no free-floating hostility and anger, and having fun. See also *type A behavior*.

type B personality: Predisposition to exhibit behaviors opposite to Type A personality traits. Such persons exhibit no excessive competitive drive, feel less tense and stressed, and have less cardiovascular disease than type As.

Type I fiber: See *slow-twitch oxidative fiber*.

Type IIA fiber: See *fast-twitch oxidative glycolytic fiber*.

Type IIB fiber: See *fast-twitch glycolytic fiber*.

ultrasound: Mechanical radiant energy with a frequency of approximately 20,000 cycles/s; the differential reflection of the waves caused by different tissue densities (i.e., muscle and fat) enables this technique to be used in the estimation of percent body fat.

umpire: See *arbiter*.

underachieving athlete: Competitor who fails to reach his or her "potential" because of ineffective or limited motivational tendencies.

undershoot: An error in a movement for accuracy wherein movement is stopped short of, or under, the target.

underwater weighing: See *hydrostatic weighing*.

uniarticulate muscle: Muscle or muscle group that crosses only one joint.

uniaxial loading: The application of a force along only one axis.

unilateral: Movement or dysfunction on one side of the body.

unipolar leads: In electrocardiography, the augmented limb leads AVR, AVL, AVF, and precardial leads V1-V6; each electrode measures the electrical voltage between the indicated lead, which has a positive charge, and a central terminal formed from the remaining limb leads, whose voltage sums to zero. See also *precardial leads*.

universal behaviors: Particular set of behaviors exhibited by all successful leaders, such as exhibiting friendship, trust, respect, and warmth.

universal sequence: The characteristic of developmental stages indicating that individuals advance through the stages in the same order.

universal traits: Set of personality traits believed to be common to all successful leaders, such as enthusiasm, intelligence, and energy.

unstable equilibrium: State of an object such that, if the object is displaced, it will not return to its original location.

U wave: Wave seen on the ECG tracing, occurring immediately after the T wave with no apparent cause; origin of this wave is not clear; abnormalities of this wave are seen in ischemia and electrolyte disturbances.

valgus: The position in which a segment angle is bowed laterally.

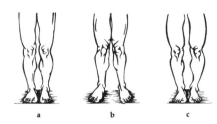

a   b   c

alignment of the lower extremities:
a) normal, b) varus, and c) valgus

valsalva manuever: Expiration against a closed glottis; results in an increased blood and intrathoracic pressure, and hence the work that must be done by the heart; individuals performing exercises with a static component, (e.g., weight lifting, shoveling snow) should make a conscious effort to maintain regular breathing patterns and *not* perform this maneuver; particularly dangerous for individuals with cardiovascular disorders.

value question: Type of question used to elicit a specific attitude, moral or ethical choice, or opinion.

variable error: Measurement indicating the consistency of an individual's responses; calculated by taking the standard deviation of an individual's algebraic errors on a series of trials.

variable-interval schedule: Pattern of reinforcement in which the first occurrence of a target response after a specific time interval is reinforced. The time interval may vary with each reinforced response.

variable ratio schedule: Pattern of reinforcement in which the number of responses required to influence behavior will vary each time reinforcement is delivered.

variable resistance exercise: Training device that alters the amount of resistance within the range of motion of a single repetition.

varus: The position in which a segment angle is bowed medially.

vasoconstriction: Decrease in the diameter of a blood vessel (usually an arteriole), resulting in decreased blood flow to the area; during exercise this occurs to the smooth muscle of the arterioles serving the visceral organs.

vasodilation: Increase in the diameter of a blood vessel, resulting in an increased blood flow to the area; during exercise this occurs to the smooth muscle of the arterioles serving the working muscles to increase oxygen delivery.

vector: Quantity describing magnitude and direction.

vector composition: Addition of two or more vectors ending in a single vector describing all of the vectors added (resultant vector). See also *parallelogram of vectors*.

vein: Vessel that functions as conduit for the transport of blood from the tissues back to the heart; thin-walled with one-way valves and under low pressure. The venous system has the ability to contract or expand and in so doing acts as a capacitance system or storage site; the contraction of surrounding muscles behaves as a "venous pump" to push blood through the system.

velocity: 1. The vector describing the change in position divided by the change in time. 2. The time rate of change of position. 3. The derivative of position as a function of time. Velocity is measured in meters/second ($m \cdot s^{-1}$). See also *speed*.

$$velocity = \frac{change\ in\ position}{change\ in\ time}$$
$$= \frac{s_i - s_i - 1}{t_i - t_i - 1}$$
$$= \frac{ds}{dt}$$

where s_i = position at time i
t_i = time
ds = instantaneous change in position
dt = instantaneous change in time

velocity control system: See *first-order control system.*

velocity curve: Plot of the rate of change; a representation of the first derivative of the function represented by the distance curve. See also *acceleration curve.*

velocity of release: Velocity of a projectile at the instant of its release from its source of movement.

ventilatory equivalent: Volume of air breathed relative to the oxygen consumed; about 20 to 25 L per liter of oxygen consumption at rest; increases to 30 to 40 L per liter of oxygen consumption at exercise intensities above the ventilatory threshold.

ventilatory threshold: Workload or oxygen consumption where the rate of increase in ventilation per unit increase in oxygen consumption increases such that continued linearity is lost, and the new slope of the line describing the relationship between ventilation and work or oxygen consumption gets steeper; may occur twice during incremental work from rest to max; due to an increase in CO_2 production that stimulates ventilation.

verbal desists: See *desists.*

verbal-motor stage: The first of Adams's two-stage model of motor learning, characterized by conscious verbal control, large and frequent errors, a weak perceptual trace, and extreme reliance on external knowledge of results. Practice lessens errors, strengthens the perceptual trace, and makes knowledge of results superfluous, bringing the learner to the second (motor) stage. See also *motor stage.*

verbal persuasion: Act of reassuring and encouraging a person that he or she is capable of performing the desired outcome. A component of Bandura's self-efficacy theory in reference to a person's convictions that she or he can successfully produce a desired outcome. Verbal persuasion enhances self-efficacy, which in turn promotes performance quality.

vertical ground reaction force: The component of the ground reaction force acting perpendicular to the surface of the ground.

very low density lipoprotein (VLDL): Compound fat containing high amounts of triglycerides and moderate levels of phospholipids and cholesterol; primary function is to transport triglycerides synthesized in the liver to the adipose tissue; VLDL residuals may become LDL.

vestibular mechanism: Mechanism located in the inner ear consisting of three soft, semicircular canals filled with fluid that is sensitive to changes in head position, acceleration, and balance.

vestibular system: Semicircular canals and otolith organs in the inner ear; stimulation arouses an aspect of proprioception, giving information about head position in space and sudden changes in direction of body movement.

vicarious learning: Process whereby a person learns a motor skill by observing a model performing the same skill. It is predicted to be facilitated by a close similarity between the learner and the model in regard to characteristics, social status, observation of receiving a valuable reward (or, inversely, intense punishment), and similarity of the environment or social setting.

vicarious punishment: Penalty inflicted on one person that causes another person not to perform a behavior because of having seen punishment administered.

vicarious reinforcement: The increase in performance of individuals whose behaviors are not directly reinforced but are reinforced from observing other students receive a reinforcement.

vigilance: Maintenance of attention over a long period of time for detection of an infrequent signal.

violence: In sport, the act of commiting an act that results in physical damage to a person or property as a function of (a) the act's legitimacy (Was it necessary to meet a contest-related goal?), (b) degree of injury (Was a person injured due to the act?), and (c) intent of the participant (Was it the actor's desire to inflict harm to another person or property?).

visceral afferent feedback hypothesis: Postulates that excitatory activity in the autonomic nervous system can inhibit activity in the central nervous system.

viscosity: Pertaining to the property of an object or body segment wherein its own movement causes forces to arise that oppose that movement. See also *Poiseuille's law.*

viscous load: Attachment to a body segment that initiates forces that oppose the segment's movement once under way.

visual acuity: 1. Sharpness of vision. 2. Ability of the visual system to resolve detail.

visual agnosia: Inability to correctly identify familiar persons or objects by sight.

visual discrimination: Ability to distinguish characteristics of visual stimuli such as organization, orientation, or sequence with varying degrees of precision.

visual efficiency scale: Assessment developed by Barraga (1970) to evaluate visual functioning instead of acuity, including light–dark discrimination, intensity, size, position in space, and spatial perspective.

visual imagery: See *external imagery.*

visual impairment: Generic term used to describe a visual disorder, including blindness and partial sightedness.

visual integration: Ability to match a specific visual stimulus to a specific motor response.

visualization: See *imagery, mental practice.*

visual–kinesthetic integration: Matching of a visual event with its corresponding kinesthetic stimulation.

visually directed reaching: Voluntary arm movement toward objects in the visual field.

visually guided reaching: Voluntary arm movement toward an object in the visual field, in which the hand is adjusted in anticipation of the target; reaching to pick up a pencil, for example.

visual memory: Ability to recall characteristics of visual stimuli.

Visual-Motor Behavior Rehearsal (VMBR): Cognitive-behavioral program that includes mental imagery and relaxation techniques to help athletes cope with stress or improve performance. Consists of an initial relaxation phase followed by visualizing performance during a specific stressful situation, and then performing the skill during a simulated stressful situation.

visual noise: Slight random variations of faint visual signals against an illuminated background causing visual impairment.

visual occlusion: Prevention of visual input during task performance in order to study performance based on the input of other sensory systems.

visual placing: In infants and other animals, an automatic reaction of upper limb extension when the infant or animal is held above a surface then lowered toward it.

visual release action: Ability to complete a grasp even though glancing away.

visual scan pattern: An individual's preferred path of eye movements to inspect or recognize an object.

visual–tactile integration: Matching of a visual event with its corresponding tactile stimulation.

visual tracking: See *ocular tracking.*

vital capacity: Maximal volume of air forcefully expired after a maximal inspiration.

vitreous humor: Transparent, jelly-like substance that occupies the interior of the eyeball between the retina and lens of the eye.

VLDL: See *very low density lipoprotein.*

VMBR: See *Visual-Motor Behavior Rehearsal.*

volume: 1. The three-dimensional space occupied by an object. 2. The product of an object's length, height, and width. Volume is measured in meters cubed (m^3).

$$volume = height \times length \times width$$

$\dot{V}O_2$: See *oxygen consumption.*

$\dot{V}O_2$max: See *maximal oxygen uptake.*

waiting time: In education, a period during formal instruction when no teaching or activity is occurring.

waking hypnosis: State of alertness or arousal while the person is under a hypnotic state and is carrying out suggestions of the hypnotist while in a trance. Also called *posthypnotic suggestion*.

walking: Locomotor pattern of alternate limb-stepping. In humans, at least one foot is in contact with the support surface at all times, and the trunk is upright.

walking reflex: An infant's involuntary response of moving the legs in a walking-like pattern when held upright and then placed feet down on a flat surface. Also called *stepping reflex*.

warm-up: Low-intensity activity that generally consists of light stretching and other exercises designed to increase body temperature; done to elevate the physiological state in preparation for intense activity; may help reduce the incidence of musculoskeletal injury.

WATSMART: Nonphotographic camera apparatus that can detect the location of one or more light emitting diodes, thus permitting digitization of movements in two planes if a sufficient number of cameras are used; acronym of Waterloo Spatial Motion Analysis and Retrieval System.

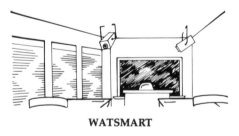

WATSMART

watt: Absolute unit of power equal to the work done at the rate of one absolute joule per second.

wave drag: Resistive force caused by a body moving along or near the surface of the water; results in elevating some water in front of the leading edges of the object.

Weber's law: The principle that the just noticeable difference (jnd) between two stimulus magnitudes is a constant portion of the total magnitude, i.e., is proportional to the magnitude of the standard stimulus.

weight: 1. The attractive force the earth exerts on a body on or near its surface. **2.** The product of the mass of an object and the acceleration due to gravity ($9.81 \text{ m} \cdot \text{s}^{-2}$). Weight is measured in newtons (N).

weight acceptance: The period of time during the support period of locomotion from touchdown to maximum knee flexion of the supporting limb.

weight density: Weight per unit volume; measured in newtons per liter (N/L).

wheel and axle machine: Simple machine consisting of a wheel attached to an axle about which it rotates.

white noise: Sound track consisting of several random sound waves simultaneously presented. Used in experiments to mask sounds associated with the subject's task.

whole-and-part perception: Ability to discriminate parts of a picture or object from the whole, yet integrate the parts into the whole, while perceiving them simultaneously. Also called *part–whole perception, whole–part perception*.

whole–part perception: See *whole-and-part perception*.

whole–part practice: See *part–whole practice*.

whole–part transfer: See *part–whole transfer*.

Wingate anaerobic power test: Exercise performance test designed to assess an individual's ability to perform anaerobic work; performed on a leg or arm cycle ergometer with the resistance set at 75 g per kilogram of body weight; test is 30 s in duration, with the number of revolutions completed in that time period assessed.

winging: Arm action sometimes seen in

inefficient jumping and leaping. Consists of shoulder retraction and backward arm extension, often with elbows bent, while the body is being projected forward.

work: The scalar product of force and the linear distance the object moved; measured in newton-meters (N-m), kilograms, or joules.

$$\text{work} = \text{force} \times (s - s_o)$$

where s = current position
s_o = last position

work–energy relationship: The physical relationship that states that the amount of work done is equal to the change in energy.

$$\text{Work} = \Delta KE + \Delta RE + \Delta PE$$

where ΔKE = change in kinetic energy
ΔRE = change in rotational energy
ΔPE = change in potential energy

working memory: The component of memory holding new information and/or information retrieved from long-term memory. Synonymous with the sensory store and short-term memory in a three-stage memory model.

Yerkes-Dodson law: See *inverted-U hypothesis*.

yoking: The research design technique of pairing experimental subjects on the basis of conditions generated by one of the pair.

youth sport: Program of athletic competition for persons under age 17.

Zajonc's model: Model of social facilitation theory stating that drive increases and dominant responses are emitted when a skill is performed in the presence of observers as spectators or coactors (i.e., persons who perform the same activity simultaneously).

zero-order control system: The relationship between movement of a control device and movement of an indicator (such as on a display screen), where controller force is mapped one-to-one to indicator position. Also called *position control system*. See also *first-order control system*.

About the Authors

Mark Anshel is a senior lecturer in the Department of Human Movement Science at the University of Wollongong in Australia. Author of *Sport Psychology: From Theory to Practice*, Dr. Anshel is a member of the North American Society for the Psychology of Sport and Physical Activity (NASPSPA) and the Association for the Advancement of Applied Sport Psychology (AAASP).

Patty Freedson is an associate professor in the Department of Exercise Science at the University of Massachusetts at Amherst. A specialist in exercise physiology, Dr. Freedson is a member of the American Alliance for Health, Physical Education, Recreation and Dance (AAHPERD) and a fellow in the American College of Sports Medicine (ACSM).

Kathleen Haywood is a physical education professor at the University of Missouri-St. Louis. Author of the popular text *Life Span Motor Development*, she is a member of NASPSPA as well as a member of AAHPERD and former chair of its Motor Development Academy.

Michael Horvat is an associate professor of physical education at the University of Georgia-Athens. A recognized authority on adapted physical education, Dr. Horvat is a member of AAHPERD and the National Consortium on Physical Education and Recreation for the Handicapped.

Joseph Hamill is the director of the biomechanics laboratory at the University of Massachusetts at Amherst. Dr. Hamill is a member of ACSM and the International Society for Biomechanics, as well as a frequently published author on the subject of biomechanics.

Sharon Ann Plowman is the director of the Human Performance Laboratory at Northern Illinois University, where she received the Excellence in Teaching award in 1975. Dr. Plowman is a member of AAHPERD and ACSM.